BLACK MALE DEVIANCE

BLACK MALE DEVIANCE

Anthony J. Lemelle, Jr.

PRAEGER

Westport, Connecticut
London

Library of Congress Cataloging-in-Publication Data

Lemelle, Anthony J.
    Black male deviance / by Anthony J. Lemelle, Jr.
      p. cm.
    Includes bibliographical references and index.
    ISBN 0–275–95004–2 (alk. paper)
    1. Afro-American men. 2. Deviant behavior. I. Title.
E185.86.L39   1995
305.38′896073—dc20   94–25040

British Library Cataloguing in Publication Data is available.

Library of Congress Catalog Card Number: 94–25040
ISBN: 0–275–95004–2

First published in 1995

Praeger Publishers, 88 Post Road West, Westport, CT 06881
An imprint of Greenwood Publishing Group, Inc.

Printed in the United States of America

The paper used in this book complies with the
Permanent Paper Standard issued by the National
Information Standards Organization (Z39.48–1984).

10 9 8 7 6 5 4 3 2

Contents

Preface

The United States has been plagued by several crises since World War II. One of the most serious of these crises centers on the fact that most black men have not accepted the value systems of middle-class, white-male culture, in spite of boldly creative efforts by social agents to inculcate them with the middle-class, white value systems. Some alleged facts are now fairly well known in the national popular mind. Black men refuse to rear their children but continue to produce them. They refuse to use the socially sanctioned process of education to increase their mobility, preferring instead criminal action and deviant productivity. They have also adopted the perverse material values of the dominant culture and combined them with an equally strong commitment to an independent black culture, that is, bourgeois negritude.

Few studies of black men have highlighted the essential conflict between black and white values, despite the fact that this conflict has had historical significance. Instead, the authors of most other studies of black men have, in some cases overtly and in other cases unwittingly, couched their arguments in terms of the total cultural suppression of African-American values and traditions. The underlying reason for these scholars' arguments is largely the middle-class belief in the idea of universal human values. The suppression takes the generic form of viewing black male consciousness with disgust, disparagement, and contempt. This contempt takes two divergent and dominant cultural avenues: (1) the relegation of an independent black culture to emotional representation, as opposed to reason; and (2) a technology of institutional domination, particularly in schools and prisons. In other words, black males are defined by the middle-class as social deviants.

Black male deviance, like independent black culture, is institutionalized by a black middle class, led primarily by black college- and university-trained professional managers. This symbolic leadership is managed by the mass media, primarily through athletics and entertainment. The generic view of the world from this perspective is a classical black middle-class world view, a superficial orientation toward social relations which argues that what is, appears in experience, and is thus viewed as reality. This view of reality is only one world view among many and therefore must be submitted to critical scrutiny.[1]

In the study of black males, this world view operates to sanction the "scientific" categories in most of the studies. In this way, crime becomes crime because policing agents define it as crime; illegitimacy becomes illegitimacy because the welfare agents define it as illegitimacy; poor academic achievement becomes poor academic achievement because the educational agents use that particular definition.[2] The powerful ruling class and its agents in the society define what is deviant while simultaneously defining what is to be considered science. They manage the micro physics of domination through the production and reproduction of knowledge to serve their interests.[3]

Several studies on black males have recently been produced, but none has looked specifically at the creation of black male deviance. Most scholars assume black male deviancy as an unstated given about black males. One of the finest studies of black males is Jewelle Taylor Gibbs's anthology *Young, Black and Male in America: An Endangered Species*.[4] It is a textbook case of bourgeois arguments that rest on the premise that young black males have been left behind in the evolution of social progress and must be given special and affirmative attention if they are to be reformed and acculturated.

Another study, edited by Benjamin P. Bowser, is *Black Male Adolescents: Parenting and Education in Community Context*.[5] It contributes to a critical assessment of black male experience and social organization. Additionally, the study attempts to stress African-American culture and Afrocentric methods of study.

Haki Madhubuti's *Black Men: Obsolete, Single, Dangerous* is a contribution that seeks to understand the black policeman on the streets of Chicago.[6] Unfortunately, Madhubuti ultimately engages in a rearticulation of black middle-class values, namely, the aspiration to essential Anglo conformity. Nonetheless, he is to be credited with the personal intellectual achievement of recognizing the relationship between other forms of dominance, like sexism and racism.

Robert Staples's classic, *Black Masculinity: The Black Male's Role in American Society*, is perhaps the best critical and sociological approach to the subject of black men.[7] Staples employs the theories of Karl Marx and Frantz Fanon in his analysis of the black male's social role, which allows him to contribute a structural explanation of black male culture. However, Staples fails to penetrate the essential aspect of black males' historical development, and at points his polemics have been cited as both sexist and heterosexist.

Jawanza Kunjufu's *Countering the Conspiracy to Destroy Black Boys*, Nathan and Julia Hare's *The Endangered Black Family*, Lawrence E. Gray's *Black Men*, and Richard Majors and Janet Mancini Billson's *Cool Pose* all share a psychological approach to the subject.[8] What is interesting in the psychological approaches is the extent to which they support the middle-class values of self-determination and individual responsibility. These studies finally accept the order of things and, as a result, they fail to consider the social organization of inequality.

There are also two studies important for understanding men and masculinity in the United States. Michael S. Kimmel's *Changing Men* and Clyde W. Franklin's *Men and Society* contribute an understanding of the pressures on men in contemporary society and the functions of masculinity in the society.[9]

The studies of black males lack insight into how black men are depicted in the society. Such an illumination will reveal the historically low social position of black males in the United States and how black laboring human beings created a culture under the constraints of their social positions. Human beings are required to work in order to produce and reproduce their existence. This anthropological fact is very often forgotten in the social sciences when methods are used that conceptualize labor to conform to labor market statistics. My perspective provides two advantages: it highlights the individual's relationship to production and thereby reveals a group's class interest, and it provides an explanation of social change.

The history of labor is a record of various organizational forms. What is important for the study of black male deviance is the organization of labor under capitalism. It is routine for capitalists to take the use of workers' labor, pay wages to workers, and spend money to monopolize the other means of production, including raw materials and machines. Capitalists want it to appear that the wages paid for the work are equitable; they also want it to appear, in reference to the value of the end product the labor produces, that the product has nothing to do with human labor. This means that the capitalists' profits appear to have nothing to do with the exploitation of the workers' labor power because the workers earn a wage that appears equivalent to the cost represented by the work.[10]

While it might be easy for the dominant social group in the United States to accept this interpretation of capitalist profit, it is far harder for the African-American male to possess such consciousness. The process of the change of institutional slavery (its production, reproduction, modification, and legacy) produced an alternative view of social relationships between dominated and dominating groups. The task of this book is to examine the process of change in an effort to contribute to an understanding of the African-American male.[11]

This task assumes an examination of U.S. social and cultural history viewed from the perspective of class struggle. Economic conditions at different periods of history are important for this investigation because they provide the basis for working through a cogent explanation of the juridical, political, and educational institutions, as well as the philosophical, social scientific, and religious ideas of the culture. My method is to explain African-American male "knowing" by his "being" instead of the a priori method of explaining his "being" by his "knowing." This means that I am interested in the patterned social experiences that result in African-American men forming a specific collective world view.

To understand the economic foundations of African-American male experience, it is necessary to unmask the secret of capitalism: its essential character is surplus-value, which is the appropriation of unpaid labor; thus, even if capitalists buy the labor power of workers at its full value as a commodity, they still extract more value from it than they paid for it.[12] For African Americans, this means that the common desire for accommodation and integration in the U.S. social system is ultimately a request to be exploited by white men of power. It is only through the downfall of the structural organization of labor that the society will overcome the obstacles of exploitation.

Is it a general tendency among African-American males to be aware of the contradiction between stated middle-class social goals of black professionals/managers and the exploitation secret of capitalism? How can we know whether black males are generally aware of the exploitation, since it has already been suggested that the exploitation is a secret?

Answering these inseparable questions requires the recognition that most social science methods rely heavily on statistical techniques, and, as a consequence, the methods exempt from investigation most of the reality they attempt to explain. Humans began to use mathematics because they had the need to measure land, things on their ships, the time of the day, and other aspects of various technologies. In the process of the production and reproduction of mathematics, its laws became abstracted from the real world, leaving the illusion that mathematics consists of concrete laws given by gods, to which the world must conform.[13]

Therefore, statistical methods must, like all mathematics, rely on a logic that may be reduced to the axiom that the whole is greater than the sum of its parts. While this is an important postulate for statistical reasoning, it tells us nothing of real social relations. It by no means gives us any clue of the reality that comes from the free imagination of human minds.[14]

The domain of symbolic practice is the site I have selected for the study of African-American male deviance. This study is a contribution to an understanding of the social relations emerging from the free imagination of the mind. It is in the representations of imagination that we may determine whether black males know both the secret of capitalism and some of the effects of that knowledge.

On the other side of the African-American male symbolic structure and function is the dominant middle-class approach to deviance, which represents the interests of the class of exploiters of the labor power of black males. This ideology must be produced and reproduced to serve juridical, political, and educational functions in the society.[15] The subject of the middle-class approach is an object to be rehabilitated while living a life inside the middle-class system of social constraints. The actual social constraints involved in the process of becoming a black male are part of the production of the culture of constraints. How are black males produced as deviant, given different social circumstances? What are the instruments of such production? What stored-up past labor provides the facility for its production?

There were three historical phases in the history of the United States that mark different production periods. Organized plantation slavery is the first phase.

This phase was followed by the industrial revolution, which gave rise to the modern technological society (scientific management). The third phase took place during the post-World War II era, giving rise to popular hedonism, represented at its highest stage by Reaganomics and Bush elitism. Each of these three phases has different social and cultural elements. Nonetheless, I realize it is necessary to determine common cultural themes in all three production periods. Determining the common cultural themes allows us to comprehend the general ways that black males accommodate white supremacist logics. Since these logics must be reproduced daily for the system to maintain itself, it is important to understand how black males handle confrontation with the supremacist logics in the many facets of their daily life. Combining the production phases, common cultural themes, and the accommodation of white supremacist logics constitutes a perspective on black males in the American way of life.[16]

The claim that there is a secret to capitalism suggests that there is something hidden in the organization of the society. It means there is a distinction between the manifest aspects of the organization and the hidden, deeper logic that needs to be examined and exposed. Two methodological principles guide this examination. First, the analysis of the social relations producing African-American males is not analyzed in isolation, but is considered from the standpoint of a reciprocal relationship, the elements of which form a system. Second, the system is analyzed in terms of its internal logic before analyzing its genesis and evolution. These methodological principles are different from those guiding methods that are a superficial glossing of the real functioning of culture and institutions when examining social groups. Additionally, in this book these principles provide a framework for the use of the concept of structure.[17]

By "structure" I mean, to borrow Marx's definition, parts of reality that are not directly observable or uncovered, levels of reality that occur outside humankind's visible relations and whose functioning composes the deeper logic of the social system. To paraphrase Marx, if the appearance and the essence of a thing were equivalent, then all science would be unnecessary. It is a fact that the social and cultural elements of the production of black men are hidden. This fact gives insights into my understanding of them. The production of black men is bound up with the total structure of the society. As many studies that propose an independent black culture assume, I argue that the intrinsic characteristics of the U.S. society are of paramount importance, rather than the exchange of cultural artifacts between the black and white cultures.[18]

Chapter 1 is an analysis of the free imagination of the African-American male from Richard Wright's perspective. *Native Son* represents a classic statement of black maleness in African-American literature. The purpose of this chapter is to provide an Afrocentric, postmodern reading of the internal logic in the production of African-American males. This reading is different from those theories of deviance that build in the ignorance and passivity of African-American men. The natural-seeming economic universe of such theories has a concealed logic. The African-American male fantasy gives us some insight into the integrated social system and its internal logic.

Chapter 2 examines the internal logic of domination of African-American males and the concomitant white supremacist logics. In this chapter, I question the adherence to the dominant logic and present another worldview. A logical historical development of black male deviance is offered. The genesis and evolution of the production phases, the common cultural themes, and the accommodation of white supremacist logics are also presented.

Chapter 3 examines African-American ritual organization. Institutional constraints that reveal the underlying structure contributing to the consciousness of black males are also examined. I believe that the collective consciousness of black males is to be understood as "produced deviance" and as the refusal on the part of black males to reject contestation.

Chapter 4 assesses the history of domination of the black male through the use of a colonial interpretation. In this chapter the relationship between the need for deviance and the capitalist agenda is explored. The black community is considered in light of capitalist interests.

Chapter 5 approaches the history of black male deviance in its ideological form by examining the major theories of deviance and their relationship to African Americans. A theoretical perspective is presented that attempts to make a tentative contribution to the political economy of deviance.

Chapter 6 examines the theoretical connection between social experience and forms of consciousness. It attempts to present a sociology of the mental in respect to the imaginations of African-American males.

Finally, Chapter 7 provides the conclusion and implications for a specifically left-wing social policy approach toward black males.

Acknowledgments

Many people have provided me with assistance and encouragement with this book. My move to the Department of Sociology and Anthropology at Purdue University enabled me to direct my attention to its completion. Over the years I have come in contact with a number of scholars who were helpful in developing the book. Some read parts of the working manuscript; others read it in its entirety. I am, therefore, thankful to Benjamin Bowser, Vicky Demos, Reece McGee, Erskine Peters, and Robert Perrucci.

I am also grateful to my students Peter Okeafor and Christy Simpson for assisting with the research on hip hop culture. I am indebted to the thoughtful advice of my graduate student Bonnie S. Wright.

Professor Vernon J. Williams, Jr., provided the initial copyediting of the manuscript. Without his keen eye for writing style and his broad historical insights, the book would have suffered greatly.

BLACK MALE DEVIANCE

CHAPTER 1

A Reconsideration of Bigger Thomas: Afrocentric and Postmodern Black Male Deviance

Black men in the United States have become a critical problem for late capitalism. With the advance of technology has come a changing and more specialized labor force. Machines increasingly run machines, and high-technology jobs require more and more education. The social sciences literature on black males has lagged behind the social, political, and economic developments. Even more evident than this lag has been the modernist research approach, which orients the questions asked and the solutions generated on the race question. The modernist approach presumes a bourgeois interest grounded in the principle of systematic reason and the idea of a foundational humanism. The black male problem has become so monumental and threatening to the institutional and cultural order in the United States that the positivistic, humanistic, pragmatic, and even phenomenological approaches to the problem of black male "deviance" have proved inadequate. Each of these trends has specific problems that have been revealed in the body of literature on social deviance and social control.[1]

In my view, the adventures and collapse of Richard Wright's protagonist, Bigger Thomas, in his novel *Native Son* reveal salient aspects of the sociology of black male deviance. However, rather than reading Bigger as a modernist character, I intend to present an Afrocentric and postmodern reading of Wright, including several salient themes guiding the postmodern intervention. These themes are found in poststructuralist and superstructuralist literary criticism, and simultaneously have profound implications for sociological theory. The themes I refer to derive from tradition and have emerged as perspectives of profound significance. Furthermore, these perspectives are not confined to one discipline but recognize contributions from various disciplines in many nations. For example, these new perspectives demonstrate that in Hegel's concept of unity and the state we find a bridge between theoretical-scientific concepts and philosophical-metaphysical concepts; thus, our theoretical position is linked to a broadly based philosophical viewpoint.[2]

This study argues that science and philosophy are interrelated and cannot be separated in real life. The idea that no division should separate spiritual, scientific, and philosophical realities is the linchpin of Afrocentric thought. Antonio Gramsci developed themes of civil society and the artificial isolation of the economic base in societies from culture and politics. He advanced the concept of cultural hegemony, a tool we may apply in this theoretical work with the aim of achieving hegemony for the oppressed in civil society. By "cultural hegemony" I mean a pluralism of emancipatory discourses in which the power of social movements challenges the established way of life and thought that is considered to be the reality of the society. The hegemonic perspective becomes the basis of evaluating taste, custom, morality, and religious and political principles; it extends into setting the rules for social relations, particularly the intellectual and moral aspects of those relations.[3]

The theme of language is a part of the problematic concerning the downtrodden. Ferdinand de Saussure's idea that the language system precedes any actual utterances (which he labeled *langue*) is a postmodern theme contributing to an understanding of the symbolic construction of community.[4] *Langue* suggests that African Americans make words to express the organization of their existence. The language of African-American imagination provides information about group experience, cognition, and management of reality.

Bigger Thomas's character is a good candidate for an Afrocentric and postmodern reading, not only because of the African-American male question but also because in Bigger we have a character who suggests that language, culture, politics, and economy are interrelated. Furthermore, Bigger suggests that there are interrelationships of functions that reproduce hegemonic power.

The novel is divided into three parts: fear, flight, and fate. Bigger Thomas is the central, tragic hero who comes to manhood in a society that has excluded him. He is a part of no society. With his mother, brother, and sister he lives in a home that is no home. Bigger develops an alienated conscience, without hope, love, or religion, in spite of the reality of these qualities in his society; he becomes no one. In short, Bigger is the Other. I am using the term "Other" in the sense of describing a being on the edge of the authoritative history, the debris and manure of history. Otherness is difference that has been relegated, in the white mind, to the dark regions of the mind. It describes those "barbarians" who are forced to serve spirits who are not unlike the white God. On the other hand, "sameness" is the myth derived from the liberal belief in a universal individuality which holds that "we are all the same." Holding this view provides comfort for racists who reason that racism does not exist.

The novel's plot develops around Bigger's being offered and accepting a job that is "no job" to speak of. While at work he is *forced* to go beyond the job description, carrying his employer's intoxicated daughter to her bedroom, where he inadvertently murders her, an act that truly is no murder. He shares the details of the experience with his girlfriend, who later threatens to expose him; he then murders her. Finally, he is tried in the press and court, found guilty, and sentenced in a courtroom fiasco that develops as no justice.

The novel *Native Son* pursues the social and social-psychological development of Bigger Thomas. Wright omits a comprehensive account of Bigger's childhood. He is introduced to the reader at twenty years of age while he is living in a lower-class, Northern, single-parent, black, female-headed household. The novel takes place during a period of bust and crisis for the economic arrangements of international capitalism. *Native Son* conducts an expedition into Chicago's South Side, where the relationships of capitalism, racism, and sexism determine the fate of the black and white characters and communities alike.

The novel begins in the 1930s, with Bigger and his family in the one-room apartment owned by Mr. Dalton. Bigger wakes up to the sound of an alarm clock and finds that he must track and kill a large rat. Shortly after, he turns on the light in the room at his mother's command. His mother and her three children must share squalid accommodations that do not allow for basic human privacy. The novel proceeds as if the worst has already happened; the living accommodations are presented as if Bigger is already in a prison cell and facing a death sentence: "Light flooded the room and revealed a black boy standing in a narrow space between two iron beds."

Bigger is presented by Wright as the personification of Job and his trials. Although the Lord restores Job, no one, not even the Lord, delivers Bigger. Bigger becomes a social self in a society that ignores his humanity. It is the action of the community on Bigger that becomes the theme of the novel's action, while concurrently Bigger's urgent fear, flight, and fate represent his necessity. Bigger is constantly engaged in fantasy in an attempt to deny that something awful is about to happen to him. He fantasizes with his closest friend, Gus, that they are white and selling shares of U.S. Steel, and later that he is the secretary of state, commanding the political economy. Bigger's greatest fantasy results in his flight.

The situation leading up to Bigger's flight is his entry into the white world when he accepts a job as a live-in driver for Mr. Dalton. The Daltons have sufficient food, clothing, and space for privacy. Bigger really has no choice regarding the job; yet, he feels his family has tricked him into accepting the position. The job is a mediocre occupation. After driving Mr. Dalton's daughter, Mary, and her boyfriend, Jan, back to the Daltons' home, he helps Mary upstairs to her bedroom because she is too drunk to walk. As he enters the bedroom and places her on the bed, Mrs. Dalton calls to her daughter from the doorway. Bigger is terrified. As a black, how could he explain being in a white woman's bedroom? All of the fear he has internalized from the white power caste results in a desperate situation. He has to keep Mary quiet! He places a pillow over her face and holds it firmly while she smothers to death.

The fear of being discovered, the black-white sexual prohibition, the stigma of losing a job, the hate felt for the white world, the fear of white authority—all result in a desperate situation in which he will have to dispose of the body in order to protect himself. As the body burns in the furnace, he reflects on why it was necessary to decapitate Mary so that the body would fit into the furnace. The murder and the burning of the body make Bigger feel powerful; they give him a purpose for being. He has never felt this sense of power before. Mary's death gives Bigger his new life.

Bigger attempts to deflect suspicion to Mary's boyfriend, Jan, when he is interviewed by the police, but to no avail. The days following the trouble increasingly appear more onerous, for Bigger has to kill his African-American girlfriend to protect himself from the possibility of her revealing his secret. And, finally, Bigger becomes the prime suspect in the murder: Mary's bones are discovered by reporters. Now all he can do is run and hide. Bigger's flight is only thirty-five city blocks, from 18th Street to 53rd Street on Chicago's South Side. In short order the authorities hunt and capture him.

During the trial Bigger is not perceived as an individual by the normative standards of the United States. The white structure can recognize Bigger only as a sociological fact and relate to him in a regulated pattern. Bigger becomes the representation of all black men in U.S. society, whose only comforts in life are intoxication, sex, and religion, and who can never become autonomous adults. Therefore, even Max, the Communist lawyer assigned to Bigger, is unable to represent him. Max is terrorized because, after presenting the underlying causes of Bigger's crime, he realizes that Bigger is a revolutionary—something of which Max has only theoretical knowledge. Max is overwhelmed with terror when Bigger reveals, after his death sentence, that he never desired to kill, but that what he killed for represented the truth of himself.

Bigger Thomas is an enduring and accurate character, reflecting the development of black males in U.S. society. The character is Wright's observational composite of five patterned types of black men: (1) the "black brute" is the Bigger who brutalizes his good friend Gus in Doc's poolroom; (2) the "constant complainer" is the Bigger who fantasizes that he is white and complains about his lack of power; (3) the "subverter" is the Bigger who sneaks into the movie theater, disregarding the price of admission and destroying ascetic-puritanical values by masturbating in the theater; (4) the "dreamer" is the Bigger who thinks he can convince the authorities that Jan murdered Mary; and (5) the "resister" is the Bigger who defies the authority of Buckley, the state prosecutor, and who attempts to evade the police chase.

None of the other characters in the novel is presented with an authentic connection to Bigger. They are all depicted as sacred images of a deceitful social order. Only Mary Dalton's former lover, the Communist Jan Erlone, arrives at some consciousness that he, too, is an oppressor and that there is little reason for Bigger to bond with him. Jan is the only character other than Bigger who begins to see.

Wright's characters are representative of entire social institutions. The family is represented by the triad of Mrs. Thomas, Vera, and Buddy. It is interesting to note that Job had three friends who counseled him and Bigger has three family members. Just as Job's friends were in error regarding his plight, so Bigger's family members are in error with respect to his plight. They each see Bigger as a nigger. Bigger's brother, Buddy, agrees to play the nigger role; Vera is so afraid she can only reaffirm Bigger's nigger status; and Mrs. Thomas simply wants Bigger to be a nigger "Christian."

The institutionalized class order is represented by the Dalton family. Mr. Dalton is a simplistic character who is the epitome of the white, benevolent capitalist. He offers gifts of baseballs, bats, and pool tables to the blacks in the ghetto. At the same time he owns slum housing. Equally simplistic is his wife, who is physically blind. She tries to do her part for poor blacks by giving them games. Of all of the characters in the Dalton family, Mary is the most complex. She is the embodiment of the cult of true white womanhood. She plays with Bigger like a toy, exploring his personal life and representing feminine beauty that Bigger must not openly approach.

In a similar manner, all of the characters developed around Bigger represent social institutions. The most vicious of the institutions is the criminal justice system, represented by Buckley, the state prosecutor. Buckley is merciless in his legal pursuit of Bigger, and his role is to bash the Biggers in the United States.

In this chapter I intend to examine Bigger Thomas as a symbol of African-American deviance in an effort to make a contribution to the theoretical sociology of deviance. There are essentially three authors important to the task at hand: Michel Foucault, Rene Girard, and Antonio Gramsci. From these theorists, four thematic questions are generated: Socially speaking, who is Bigger? What social technologies form Bigger? How are we to interpret Bigger's violence? And, finally, what significance does the "terror" of this reading have for a sociology of change?[5]

WHO IS BIGGER?

Bigger Thomas is a symbol of black male deviance and criminality. This sociological observation is clear. After all, Bigger has allegedly committed two murders, those of Mary Dalton and Bessie Mears, both of whom drink and influence Bigger to stay drunk. However, this interpretation of Bigger's biography lacks an essential ingredient—it omits the fact that although Bigger is a symbol of black male deviance, he is the only character at the novel's end whom readers may conclude to be truly human.[6] Of more significance is the political symbol Bigger represents. In fact, many will be interested in psychoanalyzing Bigger, but this task is impossible because Wright did not depict Bigger's childhood. Bigger's childhood is a secret memory.[7]

A cogent argument may be advanced that Bigger is innocent of both murders if the circumstances of his acts are fairly considered. In the case of Mary Dalton, when Bigger places the pillow over her face, he is trying to keep her from answering her mother's call. Bigger does not want to break the heavily sanctioned, social/moral norm that a black man must not be alone with a white woman in her bedroom. Bigger never intends to kill Mary Dalton. His intention is to follow the social mores. In the case of Bessie Mears, Bigger is attempting to protect himself from Bessie's betrayal. He knows that he can never get a fair trial in America, and Bessie tells Bigger that she is going to turn him over to the authorities. His intention is to protect himself. For these reasons, I will argue that Bigger is innocent.

Bigger is not alone, because he is a social self. A social self is distinct from a psychological or biological personality. The social self becomes in language as it acts on the world and is acted on by the world; it is both partially created by society and partially a creator of society. The self develops during the socialization process, through social interaction. It develops from the way a person perceives himself or herself, as the result of the person's experiences with other people, the way they act toward the person, and the impression the person gets of their view of himself or herself. By internalizing the definitions others have of him and his place in society, Bigger comes to have a conception of who he is and what he is like. The self begins its lifelong socialization in the family.

How does Bigger know himself? He knows that his mother has no respect for him and his purposes. Unlike Jesus' mother, Mary, at no time does Mrs. Thomas display regard for Bigger's earthly purpose. For this reason, Bigger is incapable of becoming a Christian—primarily because the practices of Mrs. Thomas's "Christianity" are traditional and fall short of Bigger's reality. Bigger is a man in search of reality, and therefore a very dangerous man. Mrs. Thomas is the character who is responsible for the primary socialization of Bigger. To her, he is "a no good nigger." A nigger is a ritual role constructed generally in the Western world and specifically in the U.S. experience. The text "no good nigger" is a mythic construction. Here the term "mythic" is used in the sense of a composition of remote goals, ambivalent moral moods, and expectations of the divine good.[8] The nigger Bigger represents a value system and a world view. Even more, I am suggesting a functional role for the myth, stressing the indispensable function of the myth as it is taken literally in a society to enhance, express, and codify belief and enforce morality.[9] By the time we meet Bigger in Chicago, he is twenty years old. We know that he has been to juvenile hall several times for doing "jobs." By this time, Bigger knows his social script, which is the role of the bad nigger, and Mrs. Thomas assures us that she is the "master" who will administer the nigger ethic. Niggers are lazy, and Mrs. Thomas affirms this social construction: "You going to have to learn to get up earlier than this, Bigger, to hold a job" (p. 14)[10]; "You going to take the job, ain't you Bigger?"; "Bigger sitting here like he ain't glad to get a job" (p. 15). Mrs. Thomas enunciates the message that Bigger is not a man, for a man in traditional U.S. history is a laborer and provider: "We wouldn't have to live in this garbage dump if you had any manhood" (p. 12).

Bigger's self is also being constructed by his sister, Vera, who reinforces Mrs. Thomas's sentiments about him: "Bigger ain't decent enough to think of nothing like that" (her reference is to not having to live like pigs) (p. 15). And later, when she meets Bigger on the morning of the day he is to see Mr. Dalton regarding the job: "Bigger, please....You're getting a good job now. Why don't you stay away from [your friends, those other niggers]?" (p. 18). In short, Bigger is being blamed for circumstances he did not create or wish for, and being blamed by his own family.

However, Bigger is aware of the political implications of his primary socialization. He is a political character who is more than an "expression of individualistic revolt, taking the forms of violent assault or personal attack."[11] If we apply the test of Western culture insofar as the "technologies of the self," to use Foucault's conception, are concerned, Bigger is not "individualistic" but rather a classical stoic. In fact, the genealogy of the morpheme "Tom," from Harriet Beecher Stowe's Uncle Tom to Wright's Bigger Thomas, represents a signal that there has been a radical break in the vocabulary of U.S. race relations.[12] For Wright, the new discursive practice was a realization that he, like H. L. Mencken, could engage in a new form of violence. He realized that Mencken "was fighting, fighting with words. He was using words as a weapon, using them as one would use a club. Could words be weapons?"[13]

An informed political citizen, Bigger realizes that "they were thinking of the job...it made him angry; he felt they had tricked him into a cheap surrender" (p. 15). The above quotation gives us insight into Bigger's understanding of the political economy: he does not respect the menial jobs distributed by the elite white, male power structure. He is no fool, he realizes necessity: "Yes, he could take the job at Dalton's and be miserable, or he could refuse it and starve" (p. 16). Wright persistently tells us that Bigger is a political stoic. As soon as Bigger sees the men working on a signboard, he recognizes the face: "That's Buckley!" Buckley is running for state's attorney again, and Bigger immediately supplies a political interpretation of the situation: "I bet that sonofabitch rakes off a million bucks in graft a year" (p. 16). Bigger has a profound understanding of what Manning Marable,[14] in the tradition of the celebrated African-American social scientist W. E. B. DuBois, views as the fraudulent criminal justice system and its function of holding the equally fraudulent political economy in check: "IF YOU BREAK THE LAW, YOU CAN'T WIN! He snuffed his cigarette and laughed silently. 'You crook,' he mumbled, shaking his head, 'You let whoever pays you off win!'" (p. 17). Of more importance, Bigger understands the practice of exploitation under capitalism. Bigger perhaps is incapable of distinguishing the industrial management of Robert Owen from the labor theory of value in David Ricardo and Karl Marx, but at the level of practice he is fully aware that something is awry. Wright makes his readers aware of the fact that Bigger fails to comprehend the differences of opinion about the political economy.

Bigger's discomfort with Dalton's job offer stems from the extreme degree of exploitation in the political economy. His understanding of extreme exploitation is clear in the scene where he and his close friend, Gus, are thrust into the role of street-corner men: "They leaned their backs against the red brick wall" (p. 20). Bigger indicates that he could fly while barely seeing the plane overhead. But he realizes that if he had the opportunity to fly, he would consider dropping a bomb on the power structure. He is clearly engaging in fantasy: commercial pilots do not have bombs in their aircraft. In the next section, Bigger tells Gus he wants to fantasize, "Let's play 'white.'" Here we see that Bigger is aware of race as an important political-economic issue. He is aware of the militarism necessary for political, economic, and social domination. He is aware of its correspondence to tyranny and fascism: "'Yessuh!' Gus said again, saluting and clicking his heels" (p. 20).

Bigger is also aware of the economic and corporate relationship of the military-industrial complex. In the next passage the game resumes with Gus pretending to hold a telephone receiver: "This is Mr. J. P. Morgan...I want you to sell twenty thousand shares of U.S. Steel in the market this morning." In the final scenario, Bigger becomes the secretary of state. He says, "We've got to do something with these black folks" "Oh, if it's about the niggers, I'll be right there, Mr. President," Gus says (p. 22).

Bigger's politics are clear; at some level he must realize that the real work is being done by the oppressed, while the nonproductive jobs that require little physical labor are going to the Daltons of the world. His perception of Dalton is that Dalton is lazy, while he is not. We know that Bigger is a revolutionary. When playing Mr. President he says, "Well you see, the niggers is raising sand all over the country" (p. 22).

Another important aspect of Bigger's biography relates to his living conditions, the metaphor Wright created in reference to his living space. Bigger is in prison from the very beginning of the novel. In a later scene, when Bigger tells Gus that he feels that something awful is going to happen to him, he fails to remember that something awful has already happened to him. In the initial scene of the story, Wright says that "light flooded the room." Symbolic of the characters coming into consciousness, the light "revealed a black boy standing in a narrow space between two iron beds," a symbol of a prison cell. His mother then becomes the prison guard in this arrangement: "From the bed to his right the woman spoke again" (p. 7).

Another clue that Wright uses to develop the theme that Bigger is in prison is given when the family breakfast is prepared. The most rigid period in the management of prisoners is during meals. During Bigger's meal he is not allowed to eat without the constant annoyance of other inmates and the guard. In fact, Herman Melville used the same metaphor in his novel *Moby Dick,* where Ahab becomes the prison guard on the *Pequod.* The *Pequod* symbolically represents both a prison and a coffin. Similarly, Bigger's one-room apartment represents a prison and a coffin. Ahab eats in the cabin with his family of officers as Mrs. Thomas eats with her family. As Ahab's meal has become more than a meal—it is the means by which he maintains discipline over his men—so Mrs. Thomas's meal has become her means of maintaining discipline: "You shut your mouth, Buddy, or get up from the table....I'm not going to take any stinking sass from you" (p. 15). Mrs. Thomas, like Ahab, is the embodiment of totalitarianism.[15]

Bigger has nothing to lose. While his brother, Buddy, has some empathy for him, Buddy has decided to repress his dislike of the "way up South" social relations and strive for a middle way of respectability. Mrs. Thomas and Vera have decided to accept the roles created for them and deal with the resulting conflicts through religion. In any case, all of the members of Bigger's family are accomplices of the hegemonic culture in oppressing the black race. Bigger's purpose is to rediscover that he is in prison, and only the open coffin waits for him; he must meet the white Thanatos, the white death wish, as the path of return to his fate.

SOCIAL TECHNOLOGY FORMING BIGGER

Bigger Thomas is a poor candidate for psychoanalysis in the sense that he is not clinically neurotic. Wright did not present Bigger in a way that would enable the method of psychoanalysis to be used to examine him.[16] Likewise, I am interested in a social explanation of why Bigger becomes a criminal. Wright wrote a classical tragedy, and Bigger is a classic Stoic. It is profitable for us to examine the technology of the self that constructs Bigger. At the heart of this technology is Bigger's relationship to religion.

Wright's epigraph at the beginning of the novel is taken from the book of Job in the Bible: "Even today is my complaint rebellious, My stroke is heavier than my groaning." This apprises the readers that, as the noted African-American novelist Ralph Ellison[17] has indicated, we are to confront a blues lyric: the word "Job" has Hebrew origins and means persecuted, calamitous, afflicted, adversity, and adverse desires. However, that term also connotes the meanings of coming back, restored to one's senses, penitent, and converted.[18] Bigger is Job in the sense that he must move from self-righteousness to a true inner change of heart and an entrance into genuine moral righteousness. What is that moral righteousness?

The moral righteousness Bigger has to realize is that suffering is reality. Job has the blues, as do Noah, Moses, Joseph, Daniel, and Jonah. But Job is different. (Actually, the story of Job has been traced to Arabic and may have Babylonian origins.) Job is an innocent victim, and it is God's complicity with Satan that is the terrain where Job is to be tested. The second difference between Job and other Old Testament figures is that no one, not even an angel of the Lord, comes to his rescue. Even his three counselors (friends) come only to accuse and ridicule him. The third difference between Job and other figures is that he is the only character in the Bible willing to accuse God of his evil complicity. So Job accuses (*"J'accuse"*) God: "For the arrows of the Almighty are within me, the poison whereof drinketh up my spirit: the terrors of God do set themselves in array against me....It is good unto thee that thou shouldest oppress, that thou shouldest despise the work of thine hands, and shine upon the counsel of the wicked."[19]

Now, it is clear that Bigger, like Job, is innocent. Bigger, like Job, comes to despise his life. Job tells us, over and again, "May the day of my birth perish, and the night it was said, 'A boy is born!' That day—may it turn to darkness; and may God above not care about it; may no light shine upon it....Why is light given to those in misery, and life to the bitter of soul, to those who long for death that does not come?" In an exchange between Mrs. Thomas and Bigger the same theme is suggested: "Bigger, sometimes I wonder why I birthed you." And Bigger responds, "Maybe you oughtn't've. Maybe you ought to left me where I was." In fact, Bigger's whole experience is to learn that he does not believe anymore, that he has wished for death from the moment the light came on and his suffering began. Bigger's violence is the violence of the community against him and is projected against Mary and Bessie.

The context of the sociology of Bigger is not simply that he is black and oppressed, or that he appears violent to conservatives, liberals, and radicals alike. The context of his oppression lies in what Foucault has referred to as "technologies," which represent a matrix of practical reason. There are four such technologies: (1) technologies of production, which function to produce, reconstruct, or exploit objects; (2) technologies of sign systems, which function to use signs and convert them into meaningful symbols; (3) technologies of power, which function to objectify individuals and force them to behave as they are instructed; (4) technologies of the self, which allow individuals to effect, by themselves or with the help of others, operations on their own bodies, souls, and minds in a manner that may metamorphose themselves in order to attain a certain state of pleasure, wisdom, perfection, or immortality.[20]

In the classical sense, Bigger's practice of the self has two components. The first is the classical notion of taking care of oneself. The Greeks used the term *epimelesthai sautou* to designate this edict. The second is the edict to know yourself, *gnothi souton,* which represents the second piece of technological advice for living in the Greek cities. These two practices constituted the main principles of cities, the main rules for social and personal conduct in the game of life and how it is played.[21] Bigger is the contemporary example of both classical rules. It must be remembered that Bigger is not a loose cannon with no social connections. He is consumed with his social relations. In fact, his greatest problem in life is the alienation and estrangement created by the social order. This explains the scene in which there is a reconciliation between him and his friends. When he gives them gifts from the money that belonged to the deceased Mary, Gus tells Bigger, "You sure is one more crazy nigger." The text does not read "You sure is crazy" (p. 107), as it read a few paragraphs prior to the final personification of Bigger. Bigger is just another nigger, just one signification of the many. The second example of Bigger's social connectedness is indicated in the text where Wright tells us that "there are rare moments when a feeling and longing for solidarity with other black people would take hold of him" (p. 109). Clearly, Bigger is not an isolated character; rather, he is a stoic one.

Plato, in his treatise *On the Contemplative Life,* relates the technology of the self that Bigger executes perfectly. The practice is of looking and listening to the self for the truth within. This explains why Bigger feels that he can see when the other characters are "blind." Bigger emerges as the most perceptive of all the characters. He knows from the very beginning that he is going to do something, and he knows at an early moment that he is facing the open grave; that "they" are going to kill him.

Bigger never accepts the Christian practice of looking for bad intentions; after all, he is innocent. However, Bigger "thinks too much" (p. 24) in his examination of the self. Again, we find in classical texts the instructions for the technology in the Stoic philosopher Lucius Annaeus Seneca's *De Ira* (Book 3), where faults are just good intentions left undone.[22] This work conveys the impression that one should do something the way it should be done, and ignore what has happened in the past. Bigger is an administrator of justice of the self and not a commander of men; he is similar to Billy Budd and not to Captain Ahab. Bigger is aware of Ahab in the metaphorical sense, but he "never gets a chance" to command because every attempt to do so is frustrated.[23]

For Seneca, like Bigger, the concern is not with discovering the truth in the subject but with remembering truth. Bigger must recover the truth that has been forgotten. For Seneca, like Bigger, the subject does not forget himself, his nature, origin, or supernatural affinity, but he forgets the rules of conduct—what he ought to have done. Bigger's recollection of the errors of the day creates a distinction between what should have been done and what was to be done. Finally, the subject is not the serviceable ground for the process of interpreting a self mystery, but is the point where rules of conduct come together in memory.

In classical Stoic tradition, Bigger is engaged in the constant examination of himself and his conscience. He reviews what he has done and what he should have done, and compares the two. For Plato, the truth is in the individual. For the Stoics, the truth is not in the self but in the teaching of the teachers. One remembers what is heard and converts the statements into rules of conduct. The subjectivization of truth is the aim of these techniques. Christian asceticism constantly refers to the renunciation of the self and of reality, since the self is in the way of getting to a higher consciousness. The Stoic is not concerned with the renunciation of the self but with the progressive consideration of the self.[24]

Bigger, from the first pages of *Native Son,* is preparing for the criminal justice situation he is to confront. He is armed with his memory for reflecting on and reducing future misfortunes. He imagines the future as it is likely to turn out, and in the process he imagines the worst possible outcome. Second, Wright always presents the image of the worst, as if it has already happened: on the first page, Bigger is already in jail. Finally, Wright suggests that Bigger's experiences are not for the purpose of articulating sufferings but are intended to convince Bigger that they are not real ills in him. In these terms, Bigger is a classical Stoic and, we might add, a Stoic without a personal teacher. Bigger is a teacher himself—in the sense that Gramsci uses the term: the state has become the teacher of the teacher.[25] The state assures the production and reproduction of Bigger as criminal while it simultaneously instructs him that he is innocent.

BIGGER THE VIOLENT

The outstanding feature of the literary criticism on Bigger Thomas is the general agreement that he is a violent character, that he lacks art, and that he is a protest character. This consensus among scholars is unintelligible in the light of what we know of violence. Violence is not merely physical, nor is violence only individual and an act against "the law."[26] Violence is a violation of another individual that establishes "immorality" in a community.[27] Violence is a disturbance of duty in the sense of giving another person his or her due; in so doing, Bigger's crime is not a violation.[28] Bigger is a victim of constant violation; he is the Other whose function is to be violated.

The theories of violence in the social sciences form a large collection of studies. They range from individual explanations to metaphysical explanations. The anthropological work of Rene Girard supports the hypothesis that Bigger is the Other. The central concept in Girard is the mimesis that he locates at the "universal proclivity." We copy each other in our actions and gestures, including the actions that are made appropriate objects. Naturally, when one actor imitates other actors, there is not an exact replica but rather a "family of resemblance" where (1) every member shares many defining features with most other members of the group; and (2) no feature is common to every member. The process of imitation is constructed as a spontaneous process in which the actor need not know that the act is an imitation or how to imitate. Imitation is a special case of mimesis.[29]

The representations that mimesis generates of an object are very often false. An actor who is unaware of the process that guides the desires for objects is transformed into a protagonist by the group in a conflict whose origin in false representation is hidden from them. The reciprocal imitation turns to enmity when actors forget the original motivation for their differences and increasingly focus on each other. In spite of the fact that the origin of violence is the mimetic desire for the same cultural object, the tragic loss of the memory of the origin constitutes the monstrous double that produces greater and greater physical violence and ultimately death.[30]

Second, in terms of the monstrous double, Bigger bears the same name and is identically addressed as is his family and the American community. In the novel, the latter represents the Chorus. This meaning is symbolically indicated by the title of the novel: *Native Son*. It means that Bigger is an American son. I will not exaggerate the similarities between Bigger and his accusers; after all, the significant social differences are Bigger's race and class. However, in the text Bigger monopolizes innocence; the institutional actors—including Bigger's family and community; the black church, represented by Reverend Hammond; the criminal justice system, including the coroner and jury—all monopolize guilt. Bigger then is charged with a crime he did not commit. He did not intentionally murder Mary Dalton. By the time Bigger is confronted with his fate, he, like Oedipus, is joined in the manhunt. Bigger has become certain that he is guilty, and that is why he decapitates and burns Mary's body; that is why he kills Bessie; that is why he refuses to answer Buckley directly regarding his innocence; and that is why he is certain he is dead! This analysis of Bigger's violence necessarily requires the acknowledgment of the guilt of the Same. It is often noted that, according to Nietzsche, "God is dead." What is often omitted in the commentaries on Nietzsche's text is "We have killed Him—you and I! All of us are His murderers!"[31] The violence the commentators see as Bigger's is in fact shared by all.

The interpretation of violence that Foucault and Girard contribute had already been perceived by black intellectuals, including Wright, Frantz Fanon, Eldridge Cleaver, and Cedric J. Robinson. It was Fanon who suggested that internalized violence, taught by the dominators to the dominated, would follow the process of being expressed by the dominated against the dominated, and ultimately expressed by the dominated against the dominator.[32] It was Cleaver who first "practiced" rape against black women, and when his rape techniques had been mastered, subsequently raped white women.[33] It is Bigger who first expressed his acquired violence against his best friend, Gus, at the pool hall in preparation for Mary, and who subsequently purges Bessie, who equivocates on the rebellion. Hannah Arendt similarly pointed out that violence is retained by the powerful (the state), and pointed to the historical necessity of purges after the revolution.[34]

"MAX'S EYES WERE FULL OF TERROR"

There is a sociology in the literature of Wright's *Native Son*. Specifically, Wright's sociology makes social-psychological and political-economic contributions. It is clear that Bigger is both inside and outside the social system.[36] While Bigger distrusts the Daltons, he has, nonetheless, accepted their basic material culture. How do we explain this? Max is Wright's character who represents the Left in the text. However, even Max is unable to come to terms with that part of Bigger which contradicts his world view that eventual class revolution is a scientific fact. How is it that Bigger challenges the Left by being more of a leftist than the organized Left?

The significance of Gramsci's intervention in Marxist interpretation is indispensable for the interpretation of Bigger. The Gramscian intervention allows us to transcend the notion that sociology and Marxism differ over economic determinism. There is a debate over Gramsci's central concept of hegemony. Clearly, his usage of hegemony has three denotations. The first model denotes cultural and moral leadership exercised in civil society, where the state is the site of coercive power in the form of the police and the armed forces and the economy—the site of work disciplines—the cash nexus and monetary controls. In the second usage, hegemony denotes power exercised in the state as well as in civil society, where educational and legal institutions and the police become increasingly important in the hegemonic process. In the third usage Gramsci drops the distinction between the state and civil society, and he sometimes defines the state as "political society" and "civil society."[37] I am using "hegemony" in the broadest sense, as an order that maintains dominance not simply through a special organization of force but also because it goes beyond its narrow interests to exert a moral and intellectual leadership, making compromises within limits, with a variety of allies who are unified in the historical bloc. The historical bloc represents the basis of consent to a certain social order in the web of institutions, social relations, and ideas.

Stuart Hall has contributed to the concept of hegemony by pointing out that hegemony is never a moment of simple unity but a process of unification that is never totally achieved. The constructing of a social identity is part of the hegemonic/counterhegemonic process. Raymond Williams, too, has argued that a totalizing hegemony is impossible. I agree with these definitions of hegemony and believe the fabric of hegemony has gaps wherein struggle and negotiation are possible. It is the "fabric of hegemony" in which Bigger has become ensnared. These questions never arise for him: Are the values, beliefs, and materials of the dominant group ethical? Should they be reproduced? After all, hegemony signifies the authority of social and cultural forces that are able to win the voluntary consent of the ruled because the ruled accept their subject positions for the sake of an opportunity to indulge certain pleasures and desires.[38]

Max's problem in representing Bigger stems from the fact that Max perceives himself as Bigger's teacher. He never sees clearly that he, too, is a supremacist; that, as Malcolm X put it, "The Russian Revolution was white nationalism." For this reason, Max has accepted the hegemonic view of criminality and interacted with Bigger as if he were a member of the lumpenproletariat, a dreg of society. In his relationship with Bigger, Max believes he has a therapeutic function. Could Max represent Bigger? Could Max save Bigger's life? Clearly, he could not. However, Bigger has to realize that Max cannot save him. Therefore, by the novel's end we are confronted with Bigger's acceptance of his fate: "'I didn't want to kill,' Bigger shouted. 'But what I killed for, I am.'" Bigger causes terror in Max when Max realizes he himself is more a part of the status quo than he had thought. Bigger suspected all along, "'What I killed for must've been good!...I didn't know I was really alive in this world until I felt things hard enough to kill for 'em.'" Perhaps Foucault was correct:

> Power must be understood in the first instance as the multiplicity of force relations immanent in the sphere in which they operate and which constitute their own organization; as the process which, through ceaseless struggles and confrontations, transforms, strengthens, or reverses them; as the support which these force relations find in one another, thus forming a chain or a system, or on the contrary, the disjunctions and contradictions which isolate them from one another; and lastly, as the strategies in which they take effect, whose general design or institu-

tional crystallization is embodied in the state apparatus, in the formulation of the law, in the various social hegemonies.[39]

SUMMARY

Foucault's understanding of power precludes an interpretation of the dominated as passive and absolutely powerless. Historical sites of contestation available for African-American men will be considered in the next chapter. In this chapter, some general principles emerged from this cultural analysis. In the racist caste/class U.S. system, totalitarian roles are normative in family structure. The most "deviant" of the African-American group are those whose form of consciousness reflects classical Stoic technologies of the self. African-American men who are most deviant will express righteous indignation and so are least likely to internalize self-degradation. Institutions must function to perpetuate violence on, and to teach violence to, African-American men. The universal proclivity of mimesis expresses a particular form in which imitation of capitalist values results in heightened violence.

In the U.S. experience, African Americans monopolize innocence. They have emotionally and intellectually joined in their own manhunt and have politically positioned themselves to the left of the organized Left.

Since this cultural analysis integrates philosophical, spiritual, scientific, and logical categories to inform its perspective, it follows the tradition of the Afrocentric scholars. The Afrocentric perspective is communal, holistic, and spiritual. In the next two chapters I will document the Afrocentric way of knowing by focusing on an oral, as opposed to a written, data-collection strategy.

CHAPTER 2

The Failure of Reason and Black Males in the United States

The problem with the social understanding of black males in the United States is that the theories which inform our understanding of them are unrealistic and our goals are equally unrealistic. The standard theories of black male deviance obscure the historical reality of black males being forced into criminality. Forced criminality, viewed as a historical process, results in a black counterculture that will likely fail to correct itself through economic solutions. The common goal of social agents is to solve the problem of criminality in the black community. The image the agents share of this criminality is a landscape of poverty and a subject of deficit: boys who are poor, living in the ghetto with a family from which the father is absent.

Some believe the boys and men have deviant body types and low educational achievement ability.[1] The powerful role models the males see for themselves are black pimps, hustlers, drug dealers, and street-corner men within their communities; they see black athletes and entertainers, soldiers and prisoners as outside of their communities.[2] Even the progressive literature stresses the economic factors that prevent black males from developing middle-class attitudes and lifestyles.[3] It is doubtful that free and just economic participation in U.S. society will necessarily change the cultural values of black Americans into what whites find pleasing.

In this chapter I intend to (1) raise salient methodological problems in the study of black male deviance; (2) assess the idea of black progress in the United States with respect to relative deprivation as a process of crisis; (3) characterize the U.S. crisis in legitimizing differential stratification rewards as resulting in the continued reproduction of a culture of black resistance; and (4) trace the history of black forced criminality and its repercussions. I maintain the perspective that culture is political and represents real, lived human relations in which race and class relations are inextricable.

SALIENT METHODOLOGICAL PROBLEMS

The popular U.S. ideology holds that with an increase of income, the social values black Americans hold dear will change, producing a mythological society in which individuals receive social rewards based on merit rather than race, class, and sex.[4] Implied in this reasoning is the belief that middle-class income results in white middle-class role behavior. In spite of the fact that the historical evidence contradicts this view, it is vigorously maintained in the social sciences literature and generally in the culture. The studies that attempt to count numbers of criminals and delinquents and to examine their rearing and economic backgrounds, as well as other personal characteristics and attitudes, ultimately fail the test of providing an emancipatory social theory.

An emancipatory theory would indicate the ways in which black males might realize their full potential in a society structured to accommodate the "unity of diversity."[5] Some theories intentionally, and others unwittingly, support a specific form of unacknowledged political domination. They do this by denying the central contradiction in the development of black life in the United States: that blacks have been systematically formed as criminals by authorized agents in a politically organized social system that claims to be a more perfect union of liberated and equal human beings. My analysis of this development focuses on the black struggle to gain equality. It is a struggle about what equality is to be at any given moment. This means that in the final analysis, the empirical studies that quantify the study of black male deviance have a covert therapeutic agenda. Their goal is to cure the very victims of oppression they work so assiduously to identify, maintain, control, and improve. These students of deviance do all of these things while earning ever-better incomes through their administrative performances.

PROFESSIONALS/MANAGERS

It is not enough to theoretically appreciate the deviant males or to have sympathy for their choice to become deviants. This alleged choice is possibly the result of the economic and political history that has functioned, and continues to function, to limit conscious individual choice. Aside from the economic and political history, there is also a mythic history. Political economy alone will not suffice to satisfy oppressed groups. If there were realistic choices to be rational, all might choose to be authentic, altruistic-voluntary practitioners of the Golden Rule.[6] The historical condition of forced criminality produces a dynamic communicative discourse between the black underclass and the institutionally situated professional/managerial class charged with the management of the status quo. Fueling this discourse is the condition in which race and class have become virtually synonymous; they are empirically inextricable.[7]

For the purpose of understanding this perspective, it is important to stress that the professionals/managers represent an elite group located both inside and outside the race-class group—they are both white and nonwhite. The nonwhites are particularly interesting insofar as they represent a small social stratum that is gathered from the oppressed masses and retained primarily to articulate the values and ideas of the oppressing class. The black elite belong to this group and assist in administering the underclass in the context of Western liberalism. In a real sense, they are the "good black boys" of the American Empire. The popular press and the ethnicity theorists promote an impression that there has been a major increase in this group.

The proportion of black families in the middle-class range (with real income between $15,000 and $24,999) declined from 26 percent in 1972 to 23 percent in 1975 and was down to 19.5 percent in 1991.[8] Family income is a partial indicator of the size of the group of black professionals/managers. It would be necessary to consider which jobs include decision-making authority to determine whether the employee is a professional/manager. Although the professional/managerial class is a relatively imprecise stratification category, it consists of the upper levels of the black upper middle class. Their jobs have status and prestige, as well as incomes that range between $20,000 and $45,000 per year. Most of the blacks in this group are middle-level managers, primarily in government jobs without full decision-making power. Census data for 1980 indicated that 6.6 percent of all professionals/managers were black, whereas blacks were 12.6 percent of the total population. In 1990, 18 percent of all civilian black employed males were reported to be professionals/managers.[9] It is important to stress that not all of these so-called professionals/managers are indeed real professionals/managers. Many are employed in adjunct positions, giving the impression that agencies and corporations have met egalitarian standards. Usually there is a white male of power who retains the real decision-making power over the person of color occupying the professional/managerial position.

One example among many of the black professionals/manager's ideological orientation was the national news report on Joe Clark, the former black principal of Eastside High School in Paterson, New Jersey. Mr. Clark expelled sixty "failing" black students by the 1987-1988 academic year. Since he had become principal in 1979, he had suspended 300 students, fired a black basketball coach for talking during the singing of the school's alma mater, and locked the school's fire doors in violation of a court order. The reward for Clark's referring to troubled black youth as "knuckleheads and parasites who plunder and lurk in alleyways" was a commitment from the Reagan administration's domestic policy chief, Gary Bauer. The White House would hire Clark if the school board was "foolish enough" to fire him.[10] Presumably Mr. Bauer's offer did not require that Clark apply for a job; nor was it necessary for him to be evaluated by a personnel committee.

It is hard to understand how rational-legal bureaucratic administration operates, given Bauer's offer. Equally unclear is the nature of an institutional merit system in this case. What is clear is the ideological commitment Clark exhibited to the system, in spite of its flaws. For these reasons it is clear why the culture makers decided that Clark's story should be turned into a screenplay. Notwithstanding Hollywood, the most prominent systemic flaw is that even if the black student graduates from high school and finds a job, he/she will earn significantly less than white cohorts who have no high school diploma.

There are additional systemic flaws that make the behavior of most deviant black males appear more rational than the behavior of most professionals/managers. The difference between black and white income is a fact that is impossible to mask from the black masses. Black family income was approximately 56 percent that of whites in 1990, down from 60 percent in 1971.[11] What is more debilitating is the difference between black and white income when educational and occupational levels are considered. Contrary to the idea that rewards are distributed in society on the basis of merit, educational achievement fails to distribute equitable income at each level of schooling. Black men's education results in much less income than does white men's.[12]

The ideological position of the dominant professionals/managers is incapable of resolving these contradictions. It would be similar to asking two teams to play a game of basketball while crediting one team with two points for each goal scored and the opposing team with one point for each goal scored. Naturally, antagonisms would develop between the two teams as a result of the unequal rewards for similar work. Eventually the oppressed team would stop playing the rigged game because there would be virtually no chance of winning. The professionals/managers respond that standards are in place, and that the oppressed groups have failed to meet the standards. The history of these alleged standards does not substantiate the professionals/managers' claim of fair play.

The professionals/managers may be identified on the basis of their commitment to the myth of meritocracy. On the other hand, it might be clearer if we organize the professional/managerial group into social categories of those who cooperate, compete, coerce, and advocate conflict and exchange.[13] While various social situations will result in the existential expression of any one of these orientations of social interaction, it is reasonable to assume that personalities tend to consistently perform roles in a specific mode. Cooperative professionals/managers are indifferent to the inherent contradictions in the social order that cause black males great stress. They adhere to the goal of making the system work as it is currently organized. They often advise blacks to work hard and not to be too ambitious in their dreams. Above all, blacks must stay in their social place.

Conflict professionals/managers advise the black community to struggle for a greater share of social goods and resources through working against the powerful white social structure. Those professionals/managers who joined the civil rights and Black Power movements are examples of the conflict mode of interaction.

Professionals/managers who work in the exchange mode adhere to the policy of voluntarily doing something for blacks with the expectation that a reward will follow. White teachers in inner-city schools frequently behave in this mode.

They teach their students to behave accordingly.

A clear example of the coercive professionals/managers is inner-city policemen. They usually force the youth to adhere to the group wishes for the status quo. It appears that conflict professionals/managers comprise a group that provides the greatest potential to promote positive social change.

But overall, the professional/managerial class projects fear of its inability to contain resistance in the underclass by creating the mythology of meritocracy and writing a mythic history of black respectability. Through denial, the professional/managerial class absolves itself of responsibility for the perpetuation of black inequality. Through the culture of resistance, the black males view the professionals/managers as being "in on the take." Teachers in the classrooms, central-city police, and the various urban social services agents are on the front line of the entrenched battle between black culture and the professional/managerial culture. Knowing the black community is commonly understood as disreputable, the professionals/managers have to mediate between "just doing my job" and the socially constructed category of inferior deviant black males.

SOCIAL CONTEXT

To understand deviant black males, it is necessary to be sensitive to the social context that produces them. It is also important to understand the roles available on the stage of their social life. The males will audition for specific roles and will be offered them if their performances are sufficiently reliable to produce the criminal career. The landscape of the "ghetto" or "internal colony" is interesting as a backdrop of inequality. The available roles for black males provide myths that they usually internalize during socialization. Social class might provide some insight into differences between one group of males in opposition to others; that is, social class is only one element determining inequality in society. The lifelong process of socialization to become a black male in the United States means more than preparation for a class or income. It includes the commitment to remote goals, ambivalent moral moods, and expectations of the divine good being manifested.[14] To be an American black male is to live a value system and worldview that has been created within the context of a social history. There is a functional role for the mythic black male. The myth is often taken literally in a society to codify belief and morality in order to structure social action.[15]

FAILURE OF PROGRESS

America's paternalistic culture is more threatened by male action than female action. America, being both sexist and racist, has historically subjugated black men because they can take the place of the male oppressor. White men of power anticipate that black women will, at best, escape their defeminization and develop as an attractive sex object with a social class, power, and status comparable with those of subjugated white women. Black men pose a primary threat to white males as laborers, entertainers, sports competitors, sexual competitors, and military competitors. The interest of white men favors a peculiar form of dehumanization and subjugation directed toward black males. Notwithstanding this motive, black females' roles require them to accommodate the consequences of classism, racism, and sexism as well.[16]

The system of black male subjugation is an issue of income, status, and power; simultaneously, black males inherit and produce a different cultural voice than white males—and this latter factor is equally important. If we approach the economic factors from a sociological point of view, it will expose the expression of black frustration and protest in black culture. At every level of the economic hierarchy, blacks are discriminated against. This means that if any stratum class group (lower-class, working-class, middle-class, upper-class) is examined, blacks will form an aggregate at the bottom of the stratum. At every level of stratification, blacks will be concentrated at the bottom. There is additional segmentation at the bottom of these class fractions as well, since black women, black elderly, black handicapped, and black youth will be positioned at the bottom of the black aggregate in each class.[17] Lower positions in the stratification hierarchy have, by definition, less power and status. Also, the resulting inequalities of daily living present distinguishable differences in style and quality of life. And differential rewards in the labor market produce jealousies, antagonisms, and protests on the job between workers and against professionals/managers. Conflict is also produced within the professional/management ranks due to their internal inequalities.

Failing to understand this relative poverty may result in the specious reasoning that blacks have made social and economic gains since the civil rights and Black Power movements. The reported gains in white-collar employment between 1960 and 1990 do not take into consideration inequalities in discretionary decision-making power and relative salaries.[18] This failure in reporting inequalities also eliminates the possibility of understanding developments in black culture, particularly the black male contribution to resistance elements within the culture.

THE "UNDERCLASS" AS A CULTURE OF RESISTANCE

Black culture has become inextricably linked to resistance and protest, redefined over time by professionals/managers as criminality. Today's so-called underclass black family culture, education, employment, crime, and life itself are a composite of resistance. Black professional/managerial institutions are unable to veil the illegitimacy of the goals of such culture makers as professors, editors, novelists, orators, preachers, and politicians, who chant the propaganda of increasing the black piece of the American pie. The problem with such reasoning is that American values, beliefs, institutions, and structures are based on distortion, appropriation, fraud, and militarism. How can we ask children, particularly children of color, to make a commitment to such an invidious system? Yet we confuse the moral universe with just such a hypocritical request.

When the historically oppressed groups in the society reject popular propaganda drives—"Don't drink and drive," "Just say no," "Don't make a baby you can't raise"—the system, spearheaded by selected professionals/managers, resorts to brutal coercion and the distortion of blaming the victim. The U.S. government employs similar techniques of coercion in foreign policy when nations like Cuba, Nicaragua, and Angola reject the claim of U.S. moral superiority. To pursue coercion, U.S. policies use economic sanctions that mean hunger and limited shelter and health care, and military sanctions that mean immediate death and destruction. How can the United States monitor national elections in the Philippines when there are questionable elections in Chicago?[19]

The legitimation crisis is real to most black males. One example of this crisis occurred when a black male youth, engaged in an argument with a high school counselor, pulled $900 in cash out of his pocket and asked the counselor how much money he had on him. The counselor responded that he had $26. The counselor explained to the student that the money he had would not begin to pay the legal cost if he were arrested. The student told the counselor that "his people" had already considered that eventuality and made arrangements for such a situation. The unavoidable lesson of this story is that the student has a reasonable understanding of U.S. cultural and institutional systems.[20] He understands that money has become the omnipotent cultural production, and ideologies adhering to the moral justification of the system are merely rationalizations committed to the perpetuation of master-slave relationships. The persistent theme of liberation in black culture, particularly among its youth, has developed as a "pop hedonism" exposing the inherent contradictions in reason—not just technological society but a revolt against reason.[21] The outcome of this revolt against reason is endemic to the larger society: marriage and family, schooling, working, and dying indicate the deep-rooted protest and resistance.

In 1990, at least 46 percent of nonfamily, and 52 percent of family, black households were headed by women. The majority of blacks over the age of eighteen were not married. Divorce rates alone underestimated the extent of marital dissolution. Separations were nearly as common as divorces among blacks. In 1990, 53 percent of black men and 59 percent of black women were not married. Most black children were born out of wedlock and reared in poverty; 86 percent of black youth lived in poverty.

REJECTION OF KEY INSTITUTIONS

The nuclear family is no longer the model applicable to black families. The decline in black nuclear families is not simply due to the fact that blacks are unable to support the luxury of marriage and family; it is also due to a gradual disenchantment with the ideology of the nuclear family since 1925; male-present households were the norm between 1880 and 1925.[22] Whatever the impact on the growth and development of black culture, it remains clear that many blacks have rejected the ideology of the nuclear family. It has been reported that nuclear family organization is central to economic organization.[23] This ultimately means that while black neo-extended families, or network structures, are more egalitarian than nuclear family organization, there remains the contradiction between the black family and what is needed for economic success in the United States. It is likely that the rejection of the nuclear family is in fact a deeper rejection of capitalist economic organization.[24]

In an equally powerful way, black culture has rejected U.S. education. In New York City 72 percent of black males drop out of high school. Nationally, the rates for the same population have ranged from 21.6 percent in 1968 to 11 percent in 1991.[25] Twenty-five percent of black children are being raised by high school dropouts. However, black women fare better with urban education, resulting in a greater number of black females in college. In 1981 more than 128,000 more black females than males graduated from college. At this rate, there are now 1 million more black female college graduates than black male graduates.[26]

One wonders if American education is an important factor in economic success. The most successful and famous black Americans are very often among the least and most poorly educated, particularly among the self-employed businesspersons and high-profile entertainers. Black males, in particular, have not failed to make this observation. The empirical literature documented this observation years ago—it is old news: rearing background is the best predictor of educational success, in spite of test scores. Parents' location in the stratification hierarchy is the best predictor of future income.[27] It is logical to reason that the rejection of education is probably related to the rejection of inferior work roles in the capitalist economic organization; but the rejection of cultural orientations may be just as important.

Black males give little legitimacy to the labor market. In the decade between 1972 and 1982, labor market participation of black males declined from 79 percent to 75 percent. There were 425,000 adult black men who either never entered the legitimate labor force or were dropouts. In 1982, over 2 million of all black males between the ages of twenty and sixty-four (29 percent) were either unemployed or not in the labor force. In 1991, 37 percent of black teenagers were unemployed, compared with 16 percent of white teenagers. In 1990, the unemployment rate for blacks was 11 percent. Blacks made up 11 percent of the labor force in 1990 but constituted 22 percent of the unemployed.

It is estimated that 25 percent of the income of black youth comes from crime. Much of black labor is criminal labor. In 1981, there were more than 2 million arrests of black males. In 1978, blacks were 25 percent of approximately 273,000 persons in state and federal adult correctional facilities, and another

60,000 black males were in local jails. In 1990, black people in the United States accounted for 12 percent of the population and 29 percent of persons arrested for crimes; 45 percent of all arrests for murder, forcible rape, robbery, and aggravated assault were black; 34 percent of all arrests for burglary, larceny, theft, motor vehicle theft, and arson were black.[28] Robert Staples summarized the situation thus: "Many blacks do not consider America to be a fair and just society, hence feel little obligation to obey its laws....The fact that America and South Africa rank as the world's largest jailers of racial minorities in the industrialized world, gives eloquent testimony to the role of race in the criminal justice system."[29]

Black males have indicated a consistent estrangement from the American social system. The strongest evidence of this sense of estrangement has been increasing homicide and suicide among black males. The highest death rate from accidents and violence is among black males, compared with any other race or ethnic group. In 1985 there were 153 deaths per 100,000 black males, and 98.6 deaths per 100,000 white males. Black males die from homicide at a rate almost six times that of black females. In 1978, more than one-third of black male deaths resulted from homicide in the group between twenty and twenty-four years old. Between 1970 and 1979, there were over 78,322 black male homicide victims. There is a spiraling suicide rate among young black males. Suicide is the third leading cause of death among young black males. Black males had a 1979 rate of 11.6 suicides per 100,000, an increase from 8.0 per 100,000 in 1970; in 1989, it was 12.2 per 100,000.[30]

The popular media have not addressed these symptoms of systemic fraud; instead, they have advertised and pontificated a moral ideology concerning teenage pregnancy and the use of drugs. Their message is clear: We are not concerned with the life chances or quality of life of blacks. We are concerned with the lifestyle that black culture promotes when it costs us money. It is, therefore, far better for blacks to spend their depressed incomes buying the junk offered in the "legitimate" market rather than junk offered in the urban domestic street market. Social policies have no goal of generating solutions to the child-rearing dilemmas blacks face. The real policy goal is to stop black procreation, thereby reducing welfare costs. Apparently black males are not interested in either the economics or in the principles. How did this alienation and resistance develop?

SOCIAL PRODUCTION OF BLACK CRIMINALITY

Economic and physical deprivation is part of the black American experience. However, it is also part of the experience of people of color in many parts of the world. Take, for example, the blacks in Kenya. Over 1 million persons live in the largest city, Nairobi. Many languages are spoken in the city, including Swahili, Bantu, Kikuyu, English, French, and German. Religions that are practiced include Protestantism, Roman Catholicism, animism, and Islam. Various racial and ethnic/tribal groups constitute the population, and the annual per capita income is $290. The symptoms of economic and physical deprivation are significantly different if we compare black Americans with black Kenyans. Yet, Kenyans do not experience high rates of black-on-black crime. They do not experience nuclear family disorganization, as do black Americans. Violence and suicide are not particularly salient in Kenyan culture. Drugs are not widely used, although they are easily available. Still, black Kenyans are poorer than black Americans, and their stratification system appears to be a rigid tribal caste system.

The social histories of the two cultures might explain the significant differences in future research. The concern here is with black American cultural history, which may be organized in three phases of resistance: slavery, urbanization, and black pop hedonism.

Slavery

Black American criminality had its origin in organized plantation slavery. As one slave made vividly clear:

> I suffered much from hunger, but much more from cold. In hottest summer and coldest winter, I was kept almost naked—no shoes, no stockings, no jacket, no trousers, nothing on but a coarse tow linen shirt, reaching only to my knees. I had no bed. I must have perished with cold, but that, the coldest nights, I used to steal a bag which was used for carrying corn meal. I would crawl into this bag, and there sleep on the cold, damp, clay floor, with my head in and feet out. My feet have been so cracked with the frost, that the pen with which I am writing might be laid in the gashes.[31]

Slaves contributed the first authentic U.S. literary genre in the form of the slave narrative. Those narratives are criminal literature, revealing the cultural conditions necessitating the path of criminality.[32] If the slave Frederick Douglass had not become a thief, he might have perished. Had he been an animal, nature would have provided him with the necessary biology and physiology to withstand the elements of nature. There was nothing natural in the organization of plantation slavery. It was an orgy of human degradation, indecency, and debauchery. Consequently, the master class lost all claims to moral authority, either publicly or privately. Corrupted in the very foundation were American religions, politics, the military, education, medicine, and family life. Systematic plantation slavery attempted to reduce the slaves to mere animals, which eliminated any moral claim the master class or their agents might ultimately make for their institutions. This means that the accusation of racism remains a current and present theme of resistance.

The resistance of the slave and plantation slavery's socially constructed criminality of the slave developed as the legitimate moral force in the United States. As such, the subterranean black culture became an essential feature of U.S. culture. Forced to steal food and clothing to survive, forced to lie in order to cultivate reading and writing skills, forced to deceive in order to associate with the master class—all this represents the foundation of U.S. society. Out of those conditions developed American culture and black culture. Black Americans have a heritage of criminality that later resulted in Malcolm X posing the question of how African Americans could expect the criminals downtown to pass some sane legislation to correct their crime uptown. The intention of the slave system was essentially economic in the sense of generating labor, but the cultural repercussion was protest enveloped in the social and moral universe.

The slave protest took two essential forms: passive resistance and violence. The general works on slavery, labor, and the Negro; the journals and travel accounts of Southerners and of visitors to the slave territories; and the biographies and autobiographies of slaves indicate the nature of slave resistance. Those accounts illustrate three patterns of adjustment that formed a cultural statement of righteous indignation and cemented a system among blacks legitimating resistance. The slaves slowed the work, they destroyed property, and they malingered and self-mutilated their bodies. Of more significance, they created a language to communicate the culture of resistance.[33]

Following the Civil War, there was an attempt by the master class, both planters and merchants, to reconstruct the master-slave relationship, despite having lost a war and witnessing the colonization of the South by Northern carpetbagger governors. The result was economic impoverishment for both black and white farmers, landowners, tenant farmers, sharecroppers, and merchants. The merchant-landlords eventually gained political and economic control over Southern society and instituted the Black Codes. The Black Codes were both legal and extralegal rules that functioned to keep black laborers who desired to leave the South from migrating to other parts of the country. The landed class contrived, partially through the instrumentality of the Black Codes, to keep blacks poor and on the plantations. They developed an absolutely fraudulent criminal code system and executed legal and extralegal methods of coercion.

The Black Codes reinstituted a system of free labor. Violators were hired out to work, and whites confiscated their wages. The Black Codes penalized people who had "no lawful employment or business"; who were "unlawfully assembling together"; who refused to work; who did not support their family; who used obscene language; or who missed work. Those arrested would have their labor sold by local law officials who then extorted their wages. In short, the Black Codes were criminal.[34] If blacks attempted to leave the South, they were often lynched or thrown into jail. By 1887, the Ku Klux Klan was strong enough to keep the Southern caste system intact. This was only ten years after Republican Rutherford B. Hayes was sworn in as president after defeating Samuel J. Tilden by one electoral vote. One of the issues at the time was safeguarding the rights of blacks. However, this was not to be the case; the issue was superseded by the question of whether the country could regain the ability to settle presidential elections without using force.[35]

Blacks responded with the production of work songs representing the fusion of gospel music and the work experience. Later the work songs developed into the blues, which laid the foundation for jazz. The first authentic U.S. music form was black music. The work songs told the story of protest against labor exploitation while simultaneously delimiting the contours of African-American culture. An example is "Spike Driver's Blues," which tells the story of the John Henry legend.

According to one version of the John Henry legend, John was a steel-driving man whose wife, Polly Ann, completed his railroad track-laying job when he became ill. The legend relays the message that the black hero John Henry struggles against the class relations of the emerging industrial order by challenging his "captain." In addition, the hero fights against the race order that attempts to define him as socially inferior to white males.[36]

Also in this version of the John Henry legend is the drama of African-American values organizing male-female relationships in the context of labor exploitation. Historically, black women worked alongside black men, often doing the same work. The legend also addresses the relationship the worker establishes with his tool. Thus, rather than having a "red blanket" to indicate John Henry's sickness, he has a painted red hammer. John Henry and his wife are the victims of labor exploitation during the transition from slavery to massive black urbanization. The plantation slavery system had been reconstituted under the conditions of the old South. Urbanization required new methods of organizing African-American labor, and the central organizing agency shifted to the jails and penitentiaries.

Urbanization

Blacks became increasingly urban as the Northern industries attracted them to meet low-wage labor demands. The Southern economy pushed blacks to Northern and, in turn, Southern cities. Urbanization resulted in the colonization of blacks in the cities. They were relegated to ghettos, where jobs were scarce and social mobility limited. Herein lies the development of the urban domestic economy. This economy marketed leisure products for the surplus labor pool of blacks who had time on their hands. The domestic entrepreneurs sought to make available prostitutes, drugs, hair and beauty care, entertainment, fashion, street education, and the like. The ruling class attempted to thwart this development. Increasingly laws were instituted to control and dominate these economic adventures. Initially, from 1890 until 1920, the Gilded Age, attempts to clean up the cities were organized by the Charity Organization Movement. Its chapters were located in the major cities and were usually associated with the organization of labor.

One example involved George Pullman, the builder of railroad sleeping cars. He founded a company town outside of Chicago where his workers and their families were required to live. Pullman attempted to instill in his employees the values he held dear, including the elimination of urban vice, obscene literature, gambling schemes, and contraceptives. The paternalistic techniques of creating social purity were eventually disseminated throughout the country and became increasingly directed toward the African-American population. During the Gilded Age, a "friendly visitor" would arrive at a black person's door with the explicit task of transforming the African Americans to share her own values and moral standards; to make them more like middle-class whites. This movement was national, but Jane Addams of Chicago became one of the most notable among the "charity workers" when she founded Hull House in 1889 and when her book *Democracy and Social Ethics* was published in 1902.[37]

It was important for U.S. whites to control the agenda of moral discussion from police departments to schools in the cities. An example of this need was realized when Marcus Garvey attempted to educate the masses of blacks on the streets regarding black nationalism. Garvey was sent to prison in 1923 for using the mails to defraud in raising money for the shipping line he had created. Blacks have always been sent to prison in disproportionate numbers; the "nigger box" from plantation days developed as the state-controlled prison system.

Out of the new prison order developed prison literature, which expressed the fraudulence of the U.S. criminal justice system. Chester Himes, a major writer working in this genre, depicted the new state-run socialization's effect on black manhood. Unlike Frederick Douglass, the slave who stole clothing and food, Himes had a twenty-year sentence for armed robbery—he stole money:

I grew to manhood in the Ohio State Penitentiary. I was nineteen years old when I went in and twenty-six years old when I came out. I became a man, dependent on no one but myself. I learned all the behavior patterns necessary for survival, or I wouldn't have survived, although at the time I did not realize I was learning them.[38]

Prison literature exposed U.S. culture and its fraudulent institutions. Ice Berg Slim, Malcolm X, Eldridge Cleaver, George Jackson, Angela Davis, Martin Luther King, Jr., and many other writers indicted and protested against the U.S. system while documenting black American cultural resistance.

Pop Hedonism

Today that protest continues in the form of hip hop (rap) music. It is a racial and social geography of pop hedonism in which the youth are "dressed to chill." One early group was Grand Master Flash and the Furious Five. What were they furious about? "The Message" is their song that tells the story of desperation in the life of black youth. The political economy of "The Message" is that black youth has been pushed to the limits and has arrived at a point where they are considering social revolt.[39]

An examination of the national discussion on rap music reveals the dynamics of cultural appropriation, which is the attempt of the privileged group to control and earn profits from the cultural productions of a dominated group. Appropriation is a historical technique of Euroculture that controls the presentation of the subjugated. At the same time, the dominators reap the maximum profits from the cultural creations of the dominated. The path of least resistance is to select an artist or group to represent the interest of the dominators and to use the media apparatus to identify and promote the "proper" art form. This has been the pattern in each of the art genres African Americans have created in the history of their U.S. oppression.[40]

One notable example of the appropriating process developed in the case of rhythm and blues music. The majority group attempted to establish approval for the rhythm and blues art form by promoting Duke Ellington and Fletcher Henderson of the Northeastern big-band style which appealed to whites because the artists relied on white orchestral styles. However, unadulterated rhythm and blues music persisted while being marginalized by mainstream critics. The music industry managed the marginality of the art form. The Southwest sound was kept primarily within the domain of the "race" record labels; companies like Okeh Records and Black Swan Records would make the "race" catalogs accessible in the black neighborhoods. Unadulterated rhythm and blues artists were committed to swinging the sound with a rugged presentation. Such blues singers as Jimmy Witherspoon and Joe Turner promoted the "shout" technique; they would scream over the brazen rhythm sections and brass sections.[41]

The techniques of unadulterated rhythm and blues challenged the ascetic, republican, Puritan, and Protestant values of the United States by introducing fury, outrage, and passion into the African-American worldview. Futhermore, indecent and erotic lyrics contributed to a music that became a non-Western art form. A tradition of antagonism between African-American culture and the contrived "American" culture developed where blacks were so entirely segregated and in an oppressive situation. American culture is contrived in the sense that it systematically excluded non-Eurocentric norms and values. African Americans would often have to voice political concerns through music because their political participation was precluded.

As in the case of the other African-American cultural productions, rhythm and blues advanced a communal usufruct that was in direct contradiction to the value of private property promoted by the U.S. political order. The lyrical lines of one rhythm and blues song often appear spontaneously in other songs. The African-American tradition was to borrow lines and communicate them within the rhythm and blues community, which meant that a song called for an answer. The audiences of the rhythm and blues performance were expected to shout one-liners during the performance. Both the traditional African narrative form and the traditional African call-and-response technique were essential for the rhythm and blues art form.[42]

What was most important about the rhythm and blues history is the ways in which it stood diametrically opposed to the U.S. political value system. The blues text stressed mockery, sarcasm, tragedy, and accusation that were masked by melancholy. These same elements of value were present in work songs and in the jazz tradition, and served as the foundation for rap music. The narrative style of rhythm and blues music followed a strict ritual. For example, in "The Boll Weevil Blues" the weevil is the formidable enemy of the cotton planter; the cotton planter is the enemy of the cotton picker. The struggle in the blues song between the weevil and the "captain," who represents the planter class, finds the picker patronizing the weevil. The weevil then becomes the symbol of liberation and a site of political contestation.

Rap music resulted from combining a set of developments in rhythm and blues, including the essential African narrative, the call-and-response ritual, and communal usufruct, then pushing these themes to limits to which the African-American art form had not been taken before. For one thing, rap music relied on "sampling," which is the process of taking rhythm and blues music and writing rap lines over the music. This act is probably the most subversive in terms of using such a practice in a political economy that has private property as its strongest commitment.

In the popular media there has been an unrelenting effort to identify a "message to the mainstream" in rap music, as well as an accompanying attempt to appropriate hip hop culture. Rap music first made crossover status on Billboard's chart in 1986, when the group Run DMC's "Raising Hell" remained twenty-six weeks on the top ten list. The artist L L Cool J was on the charts forty-seven weeks with his hit "Radio," but its highest rating was number six. The most notable feature of these two major rap productions was their universal appeal, which was unusual for hip hop culture and rap music. From 1979, when rap first appeared, it was understood that its lyrical forebears were The Last Poets, Gil Scott-Heron, Muhammad Ali, black toasts, signifying language games, and the dozens (yo mamma) games.[43]

By 1990, the popular media had ideologically appropriated rap music when *Newsweek* stressed the contribution of the crossover "rap lite" music of M.C. Hammer, Stanley Kirk Burrell, and the white rap artist Vanilla Ice, Robert Van Winkle. Rap lite attempted to remove politics from music, but found the task an absolute impossibility. Despite the fact that M.C. Hammer's lite music was number one on *Billboard's* chart for twenty-one weeks, his music was historically grounded in both Rick James's and Marvin Gaye's earlier hits. Hammer's "U Can't Touch This," the big hit of the album, sampled the contestations of James's "Super Freak" and Gaye's "Help the Children."[44]

The political space of contestation opened by rap music remained substantial in spite of the popular media's attempts to control both messages and outlets. The media waged a major war against the lyrics rap artists created, which in many cases declined to name-calling. For example, when Peter Watrous reviewed "Public Enemy's Politics" for the *New York Times*, he concluded, "Great minds they're not."[45] Even if the critics did not engage in name-calling, they concertedly attempted to erase the meanings of contestation in the lyrics of the rap works.

The reviewers generally attempted to place the lyrical meanings in the context of the language of the U.S. convention of denying racism or in the racist convention of describing African-American culture as jester behavior designed to entertain white patrons. One example of the latter was in a *New York Times* article that concluded, "Hip-hop music itself rarely incites its listeners to anything beyond dancing, clapping, and chanting along. One of the rappers at Nassau Coliseum, Doug E. Fresh...devotes his raps to positive messages. Kool Moe Dee has built a persona as a comical braggart...Eric B. and Rakim's main message is that 'Eric is King.'"[46] Cultural critics committed to the agenda of a white social order promoted the view that rap music was violent, nonmusical, offensive, untrue, ignorant, misogynist, childish, and a continual set of equally pejorative characterizations.[47]

What the critics overlooked was the inability of their unilateral agreement to change the political message of the rappers, which represented a struggle to speak in an oppressed voice. As has been indicated, the voice essentially reproduced the historical themes of the African-American struggle. By 1992, rap music came under major attack from the ideological apparatus when hard-core rap overwhelmed the white attempts to select proper rap music through award-giving and media bombardment. Leading the assault from the rappers' perspective were the Geto Boys, NWA (Niggers With Attitude), Public Enemy, Ice Cube, Sister Souljah, and, to a lesser extent, 2 Live Crew.

What these rappers had in common was a critical, though not necessarily comprehensive, assessment of the historical development of the United States and its unending attempts to socially control African Americans, forcing white cultural values on the black community. In addition, the contours of the rap music followed the African-American tradition from slavetimes to the present: the most significant aspect of the lyrical form is the hidden message. Historically, the message has been misinterpreted by whites, who attempt to decipher the meaning of black language while lacking the necessary cultural preparation. For example, the term "bitch" in the white world is a gender-specific word; in African-American culture the term is gender-neutral. Moreover, a phrase such as "I'm not going to have to take my baby to the dentist in the morning because I'm going to knock all her teeth down her throat tonight" may have nothing to do with male-female relationships. In fact, "my baby" is generally understood as the U.S. government. In error, the dominant media have consistently interpreted such language as sexist.[48]

White America was faced with the eruption of the perennial double standard: white artists had been allowed to present risqué productions at their pleasure, but black artists felt that they were unfairly sanctioned by white power. The first time this situation confronted rappers occurred when two members of the group 2

Live Crew were arrested in Fort Lauderdale, Florida, after a concert for singing lyrics that a state judge ruled obscene. The second was when the rap group from Houston, the Geto Boys, had their album withdrawn on the eve of its release by Geffen Records because the lyrics were considered to be explicitly violent and sexual. And the third incident was the charge of anti-Semitism against the group Public Enemy when one of the group's members, Richard Griffin, accurately pointed to a relationship between the state of Israel and the fascist Republic of South Africa.[49]

The black middle class generally agreed with the white media—or, if you prefer, the state ideological apparatus—that there was a problem with these black youth—despite the fact that many of the most popular "youth" rappers were in their mid-thirties and some were over forty. While the black middle class was engaged in the liberal-integrationist politics of their historical agenda (led for the most part by Jesse Jackson), President Bill Clinton saw the opportunity to appropriate the black political agenda represented in the rap music through two strategic moves. First, he worked for the elevation of Jackson protégé Ron Brown to Democratic National Committee chairman and subverted Jackson's authority by pitting Brown's conservative posture against Jackson's "left" tendencies. Second, in June 1992, at the national meeting of the Rainbow Coalition in Washington D.C., Clinton accused Sister Souljah of being a black racist and suggested Jackson's complicity in her "reverse racism." These tactics represented both historical and typical white male behavior toward African Americans.[50]

At the same time, Public Enemy's major hit from their *Apocalypse 91…The Enemy Strikes Black* album, "Can't Truss It," moved to Billboard's number one position. The song told the story of animus of the white males and their willful betrayal of black trust. The song presents images of slave ships and the transatlantic slave voyage, Malcolm X's position on nonviolence, the countercultural presentation of African drums, white men as wicked and "haters" who taught hate, unfair white judges, and the fact that blacks cannot trust whites. Finally, the lyrics shout, in traditional blues fashion, "We are men!"

This analysis illustrates that the culture of black resistance has been consistently tied to the attempt of the ruling class and its professional/managerial class to criminalize black Americans. Each phase in the historical attempt at forced criminality resulted in myriad black cultural indictments exposing the fraud. Like the colonial societies in Frantz Fanon's analysis, U.S. society "is not a thinking machine, nor a body endowed with reasoning faculties. It is violence in its natural state and it will only yield when confronted with greater violence."[51]

SUMMARY: REPERCUSSIONS OF FORCED CRIMINALITY

Given the social organization that produced forced criminality, the concept of the underclass has not been fully developed in the sociological and social welfare literature to meet the needs of this analysis. Ken Auletta described the underclass as persons who feel "excluded from society," who reject "commonly accepted values," and who suffer "from behavioral as well as income deficiencies." Auletta goes on to describe the bottom stratum of the stratification hierarchy.[52] His definition is clearly a value judgment and, more properly, an economic definition of the underclass. A sociological definition of the underclass must consider relative poverty and relative deprivation, which will assist in explaining an aspect of the black community protest behavior in the working, middle, and upper-middle classes. I am suggesting that relative deprivation assists in explaining the perpetuation of the resistance aspect of black culture across class strata. A conscious fraction of each class feels excluded from society and views commonly accepted values with a jaundiced eye. As James Baldwin often stated, "To be conscious and black likely means to be in a constant state of rage."

Therefore, it is not only an issue of equal distribution of the wealth when discussing black male deviance, it is an issue of American fraud, an issue of relative poverty, power, and status and the repercussions of that condition. At bottom, it is an issue of the clash of two often contradictory cultures. Those two cultures are unified in a system where the dominant values of the more powerful purportedly represent the dominant values of the general society.

The professional/managerial class projects a fear of its inability to contain resistance of the underclass, creating the mythology of meritocracy and rewriting a mythic history to reflect egalitarian and universal values. Through denial, the professional/managerial class absolves itself of responsibility for the perpetuation of black inequality, population transfer, and genocide. Instead, that class revels in the luxury of technological production, claiming themselves to be young and coming professionals, while adhering to the values of acquisitiveness, selfishness (consumerism), and violence.

In contrast to the power the professional/managerial class has vested in it to administer criminality, the underclass persistently challenges the rationality and legitimacy of the systematic administration of containment, specifically the administration of education and justice. Those institutions became "total," and in fact totalitarian, in their administrative functions. Their increased technology allows for expanding ability to accommodate ever more diversity while simultaneously reducing human freedom to bureaucratic methods.

The agents of educational administration are primarily concerned with creating the definition of black males as "unprepared" for education, good jobs, and promotions. Because of their deviance, they are in need of "reform" and "rehabilitation," but in fact they have never been socially understood as humans with human personalities. Black males have remained a source of embarrassment throughout U.S. history. The pride black males have in themselves is at odds with the embarrassment shared by many blacks and whites alike as a result of the males' socially constructed disrepute.

Social commitment among black males is nonetheless encouraged by the professionals/managers in order to persuade the former to play the game of academics and athletics. However, the black males' consciousness is submerged by the historical vestiges of injustice, oppression, and structural inequality. They view the professionals/managers as being "in on the take," in the exploitative and genocidal social relations that are produced at the mental and material levels. In the next chapter I shall examine the process of the production and reproduction of resistance in African-American culture.

CHAPTER 3

African-American Temporal Refusal

As I argued in the last chapter, African-American culture produces influential cultural elements in response to its subjugation. The historical theme of the African-American protest stance has been reproduced in the context of the essential meaning of being black in the American experience. In this chapter I shall examine the temporal refusal of black males, which is influenced by African-American culture. I am not suggesting that culture is the only factor producing black personalities. Neither am I suggesting that only African-American culture determines the personalities of black men. Rather, I am arguing for the necessity of acknowledging the molding influence of African-American culture in the production and reproduction of black male consciousness.

METHOD FOR ANALYSIS OF TEMPORAL REFUSAL

No one in the "legitimate" world wants to know what black male deviants think. Nor do they ask them to give their reactions to particular criminal stories. For instance, black males are aware of the responses that they are expected to give to such stories. They have a cultural heritage of techniques to perform normative expectations. In the situations in which they are placed, they must, given their experiences, select, check, suspend, regroup, and transform the direction of their statements and behavior.[1]

I am using a method of studying the group that records their natural stories in everyday conversation. Researchers who engage the group cannot know if their preconceived ideas are correct or if they are getting truthful information. Instead, the researcher should rely on the mythical history and biographies created by the subjects. Otherwise, the researcher runs the risk of obfuscating the natural facade that the group under study creates, and the natural setting, by introducing political considerations into his or her study. The appearance and the manner of the researcher might significantly, for example, alter the manner of responding and, in short, the response to the situation.

To generate mythical histories and biographies, the researcher should become immersed in the culture of the black males, go to the places they go, and become involved in the action in which they are involved. In this way, the researcher can come to see the world from the viewpoint of the group. It provides the opportunity to listen to the natural stories the group members tell in their daily uninhibited conversations. Stories are narrations of an event or series of events that take on a mythical character. The myths organize the worldview for the community. Myths transmit the important style of life which is appropriate for group members with similar mind-sets or for members who are cast in similar social situations. This method takes on the world from the viewpoint of the subject rather than from the perspective of an authority. The myth is organized in rituals that express the goals of the social group.

I began systematically collecting African-American myths in various research roles in the 1980s, when I joined a northern California research team that interviewed black males in public schools, on the streets, and at a community agency designed to work with African-American males in street environments. I recorded and transcribed interviews for over five years. Using theoretical guides that had emerged from the study of black communities, I sought patterned themes from the conversations with black males. The interviews were conducted in focus groups where the research strategy was not to bring a theory or questionnaire format to the group but to allow the interviews to flow in the oral tradition. I met each group with different opening statements, and the replication assumption was that each focus-group session was a one-time event. The interviews with the teachers were one-on-one meetings using the same replication assumption.

Following the focus-group interviews, I identified sections of the black community where black men gathered to exchange communications, play basketball, and sell drugs. I maintained debriefing notebooks in which I recorded highlights from my conversations with the men. Conversations probed what was occurring in the scenes being observed. I observed family life, spectacular incidents in the community, and similar kinds of stories. Later, I repeated the participant observations in Minneapolis, Washington, D.C., Dallas, and Chicago. The data presented represent fifteen years of ongoing community research seeking the relationship between African-American mythic structures and cultural rituals.

RITUAL

Ritual behavior is group communications in addressing the human condition. Those behaviors are meaningful in the sense that the goals of the group are often expressed through rituals. Max Weber's "style of life" is more than the categories "matters of taste" and "appreciative standards" of "appropriateness." Reinhard Bendix wrote: "Weber's specific objective was to analyze the social conditions under which the charismatic inspirations of the few became first 'the style of life' of the distant status group and eventually the dominant orientation of a whole civilization."[2] To accomplish and maintain group membership, a commitment to the group's collective style of life is necessary. The commandments of the group become the individual's duty or, as Weber described it, his "sacred honor." The significant rituals that inform a style of life for deviant black males are the disciplines of heterosexuality, it's-a-white-man's-world, and the trickster. The agents of social control are committed to the rituals of I-caught-a-bad-nigger and isn't-it-a-shame.

Heterosexuality

Black males are oblivious to the full significance of their development of masculinity. Socialization of black males in the United States sends competing messages to them. On the one hand, they are encouraged to identify with the privileges of masculinity, while at the same time they are encouraged to remain boys for the rest of their lives. Generally, it is a choice of career paths where many males believe it is either "ball" or "time." They realize that any career choice will result in discrimination; that they will be unable to go as far as "white boys." A cultural form of ambivalence toward masculinity is obvious among black males. Claude Brown's classic *Manchild in the Promised Land* provides an example:

> The first time I heard the expression baby used by one cat to address another was up at Warwick in 1951. Gus Jackson used it. The term had a hip ring to it, a real colored ring. The first time I heard it, I knew right away I had to start using it. It was like saying, "Man, look at me. I've got masculinity to spare." It was saying at the same time to the world, "I'm one of the hippest cats, one of the most uninhibited cats on the scene. I can say 'baby' to another cat, and he can say 'baby' to me, and we can say it with strength in our voices."[3]

Brown's point should be discerned with care. Cultural constraint in the male's masculine socialization is not necessarily a fear of being called a "sissy." The males are primarily concerned about the possibility of being exploited by peers, authorities, systems, or situations. They are responding to the oppression and repression confronted in those kinds of interactions. Black males must save face in the face of brutal social images. They know that "sissies" are fair game for exploitation, as are their sisters. The males are careful not to jeopardize their birthright of masculine privilege by becoming as exploitable as females are in society. When the males' desire for full masculine privilege is affronted by repressive authorities, they react, bringing into action their cultural dicta. One black male illustrates the meaning of "sissy" by suggesting that his sister was not a sissy, nor was anyone in his mother's house:[4]

> See, I doubt if somebody will grab me because if they grab me they got a fight. My mother didn't raise any sissies in the house. My sister, she can fight. She's nineteen. I know this dude that jumped on me. She whipped him so bad they had to take him to the hospital; he had a concussion.

It's-a-White-Man's-World

Commitment to deviance in the context of the dimension of forced criminality features a ritualized response on the part of black males. They are alienated from the cultural values of the propertied and professional/managerial elite. This is most clearly illustrated in contacts the black males have with police. The police are often referred to as "the man" or "the rollers." "The man" has a double meaning. First, it refers to the most prominent sexual power in a given situation. Second, it refers to the dominance of white men of power.

Black males are primarily concerned with avoiding shame and guilt in situations with the police. Their relationship with the police operates in a way similar to the relationship of police to colonized and neocolonized populations in Third World countries. While most Americans believe that the police function to protect and serve the community, black males most often perceive the police as settler agents whose intentions are to "set up," "hold down," and "roll on" the community. To avoid embarrassment, shame, and guilt—in short, emasculation—the males seek to neutralize the militarylike systems that occupy their communities. An example of this perception of the police relationship to the black community was expressed by Huey Newton:

> Because Black people desire to determine their own destiny, they are constantly inflicted with brutality from the occupying army, embodied in the police department. There is a great similarity between the occupying army in Southeast Asia and the occupation of our communities by the racist police....The police should be the people of the community in uniform. There should be no division or conflict of interest between the people and the police. Once there is a division, then the police become the enemy of the people. The police should serve the interest of the people and be one and the same. When this principle breaks down, then the police become an occupying army. When historically one race has oppressed another and policemen are recruited from the oppressor race to patrol the communities of the oppressed people, an intolerable contradiction exists. The racist dog policemen must withdraw immediately from our communities, cease their wanton murder and brutality and torture of Black people, or face the wrath of the armed people.[5]

The myth of the police was communicated by a young black male, giving insight into the ritualized behavior on the part of both black males and the policemen:

One night I was walking down [the street] on my way to the house, and I seen my cousin and them [the police] in the washhouse. OK! Then a helicopter starts flying around me and stuff. They put the light on me and I just kept on walking until I got into the washhouse. When I went into the washhouse, see, I had some gloves on me, and I said these fools might want to come and get me. I handed my cousin the gloves. Just about a minute after I did that, I was standing up there and the police came in there checkin' me. So I said, "Ah, what seems to be the problem, officer?" He said, "Which way did you come down here?" I said, "I came down [the street]." He said, "Well there's a lady up the street who says you were messing with her car." [I said], "Do you see a bumper jack or something?" Then he asked me do I want to go down the street. I told him no, on the grounds it might incriminate me. I wasn't messing with the car. I always keep gloves; I might have to bust a nigger up. I don't want to mess up my hands on those hard-ass niggers. After that, soon as I go walking down the street, blood [the police] said, "We're going to get the lady to come down here"—where I was. So he got me standing in front of this big picture window like some kind of criminal or something. Then this other policeman comes down the street and tells him that the lady says that I was the one who did it. So I said, "Fool, I ain't no criminal." So they ran a check on me. So they said the lady said wasn't nothing missing out of her car. [The policeman said] "We're going to let you go, but I'm going to take your name and send a record of you to the police." I said, "Go right ahead"; they're never going to see me.

The legitimacy of the police is a constant issue among black males. They view the police as capricious actors in their communities. The neutralization process must in some way include an understanding of the males' view of capricious police behavior. The police techniques of interrogation often implicate them in the assumption that black males are guilty until they are proven innocent. After all, the police must build a case against the suspected males if they intend their charges to hold up at a court hearing. The fundamental technique the males employ is to view the legitimacy of the police as an anarchic mode of social bonding. They believe there are few rational justifications for the search, seizure, and interrogation often engaged in by the police. As one black male said:

In a sense, [the police] just come and stop you for nothing. That's how they shot my buddy. Me and blood [my friend] were supposed to do something that night. We were going to the [local disco club]. But I didn't get a chance to go, so I messed around and went over to my girlfriend's house. Now the police say he had a B.B. gun and that's a lie, 'cause blood didn't have no B.B. gun. None at all. Blood didn't carry no gun: anybody...carried a gun, I carried a gun. I'll shoot a nigger in a minute. The only thing that I got with me now is these bricks. First of all, if you seen two white boys coming at you with guns and told you to freeze; ain't showed you no identification, what are you going to do? Looking like hippies! They might thought you had burnt [exploited, usually in drug deals] them. Or might have sold them something, and they might want their money back. So they told [my friend] and he took off. They shot him up. They say they shot him about thirteen times. They unloaded on him. They shot him in the head, in the back, on the side, two times in the chest; shot him like a dog, and then tried him justifiable homicide. It's just like Dan White; if it had been a nigger, they would have hung him. Go down there looking for justice and that's what you find, just us. Whole bunch of niggers in them jail cells. Yeah, I was there [at the funeral]. I was a pallbearer.

In fact, black males form a position of opposition that results directly from their social experiences, which undermine the normal methods of institutional control. For example, prison has lost effectiveness among many black males fundamentally because it is assumed a priori in the black community that its men will at one point or another become involved with the criminal justice system. As one young male indicated, "Naw, jail ain't nothing. I got relatives in jail; ain't nothing going to happen to me." The consequences and power of this myth reverberate throughout the community. Those studies from black intellectuals that point to the fraudulent nature of the criminal justice system are clearly grounded in the mythic perception of the black community. In this myth, the conclusion is that the system and its agents, the roles and structure, all function as social techniques of domination that primarily employ deception and mystification. In short, the techniques of domination are viewed by the oppressed as fraudulent.

The Trickster

Authority has always been a problem for black Americans. As one commentator indicated, "It is not the dominator who constructs a culture and imposes it on the dominated. This culture is a result of the structural relations between the dominated and the dominator."[6] A form of anarchy emerges because the authority must use fraudulent social relations to maintain the system's legitimacy. We have seen mystified and, when viewed from the black perspective, contentious authority functioning as legitimate authority in racist U.S. history. This history is not regional but national. We have also seen the persistent revolt against U.S. social control at the level of black culture and its values.

An illustration of this theory is that black and white cultures respond differently in public situations where authority is involved. Black culture confronts a public view that sees its distinctive racial, cultural, and linguistic features as a source of public embarrassment. White culture comes to social situations with a cultural heritage associated with procreating "the lovely white." Black culture comes to social situations with an attitude of having something to prove. This need is perpetuated by the black cultural code that states, "A nigger ain't shit." Most persons in the black culture know the myth and operate on it in their general appraisal of situations. The more closely the black male is associated with the delinquent and deviant labels, the more certainly we can depend on his operating on the nigger myth.

Black males view their social promotion as pilgrims engaged in struggle. On the other hand, white males view their condition as a status of privilege, comfort, and harmony. Even rebellious white youth have the privilege of the race to clean up their image and rejoin the mainstream. If white persons engage in acknowledged criminality, the treatment they receive from the system is different from the treatment meted out by the authorities to blacks. Black persons believe they must fight for a place in given situations, while white persons believe their status is guaranteed. Often, blacks display an argumentative mode of conduct in the common situations that arise during the normal day. Authorities are disarmed by the level of aggressiveness. They view the aggression as poor preparation for the rigors of civilized manners and style and as due to deficiency. The authorities will point to biological, psychological, social, or cultural differences; they seldom reason that the differences are ideological and political. In fact, the authorities have developed additional techniques to contain black cultural "mau-mauing" in the resistance produced by black culture.

While whites value commonplace and dull posturing in reference to their social achievements, blacks value sport in their social presentations. Achievement is considered a matter of course by whites, who believe the myth that hard work pays off. Many blacks will refer to the myth of the "sporty life"— social accomplishment should be done with adventure where style and chance determine goals. When black males say that they have "scored," they mean that they have accomplished an intended goal in antagonistic circumstances. To "score a lid of dope" is similar to "scoring on that babe" or scoring in a class. White males believe that they score only at play; black males play to score. These distinctions appear to be true even among white criminals. The issue is that the historical conditions producing criminality are different for the black and white groups. Black criminality is sui generis in the U.S. experience.

Black males rely centrally on the myth of the player, hustler, or playboy as a model for the expression of style and manner. The authorities view those roles as pretentious displays of virility. Each role is fundamentally a labor market orientation. For the black males there is a great insecurity about their labor market roles. This insecurity translates into more aggressive behaviors on their part. White males feel a greater security in their labor market performances partly because the history of the U.S. political economy has provided affirmative action for white males. They have not had to compete with black males for jobs because black males have always been excluded from the best jobs. Even today, this legacy is with us in the sense of relative deprivation.

The orientations to masculinity of black males are not directed toward contributing to gross national production; they are tied to domestic labor production. The occupations are service-sector work, where street culture serves as a highly competitive environment snared with the antagonisms inherent in systems where individuals sell their labor in a "free market." The goal of the black males' activities is to earn money, material goods, and pleasure where all three are in short supply. The males carry culturally transmitted trickster techniques to enhance their competition in the urban domestic street markets. We shall see how the trickster technique functions in street communications.

Communication in urban street markets requires rituals of performance and "fronts." Information sharing is done through "signifying," where the communicator makes a verbal or gestural front that enables observers to place the communication in context. The observers are called on to agree with the performance of the communicator; that is, they engage in certifying the situational provocation of the communicator. If agreement exists with the social construction of the communicator, the observers initiate the ritual of "cosigning," where language and gestures of agreement are exchanged. The males will make statements such as "Right on" or "Sho' you right," or engage in hand-slapping ceremonies like "high five."

In a deeper sense, to signify means to repeat a sign that retells a folk tale: "Blood, it's a white man's world, he is out to crush the studs." To certify the sign is to admit awareness of it in the moral universe: "Sho' you right, black." To cosign means to affirm the messenger, the message, and the way of communicating: "I'm down with you, blood." Usually the symbols are performed in the setting of "jive talking" or "kicking it." For those communicating it becomes a matter of "keeping the faith."

Construction of social reality in the urban street markets always includes turn-taking. A turn to express reality is taken and not earned. Actors in black culture are expected "to take his," which is done through "woofing" and "dissing" (dismissing)—the communicator attempts to convince the audience that his understanding will stand before challenge. Black males who fail to do so will be viewed as less virile with respect to achieving the rewards of money, respect, and women. These exchanges require the careful management of aggression. The game for them is "to keep it all together" by remaining "cool" or by "chilling." In essence, the goal is to maintain peace in spite of the fact that violence is understood as a real and possible alternative.

Black males are also taught, through black male socialization, to portray docility. But their masculinity is tied to the ability to transform their docile appearance into a weapon against oppression. The grandfather character in Ralph Ellison's *Invisible Man* expressed this cultural dictum: "Live with your head in the lion's mouth...I want you to overcome 'em with grins, agree 'em to death and destruction, let 'em swoller you till they vomit or burst wide open."[7]

Black males who view themselves as "niggers" produce a moral commitment to the trickster image, which is justified by their condition of forced criminality. To be a nigger entails more than operating as trickster only toward white authorities. It includes making adjustments in a variety of interactions, in fact, toward peers, too. The nigger is hard and bad, possessing extraordinary sexual power. At the same time, the nigger is docile, a hard worker for a style of life reflecting consumption of the better things in life. The most respected pimps, for example, will work long hours to maintain their images and business organizations. At the same time, they are expected to be well-dressed and have impressive cars. The individual pimp's role is usually to be an adversary to other pimps who represent potential threats to his territory. The important ethic operating among pimps is to always avoid embarrassment.

Whether black males are involved in pimping and pandering, drug dealing, robberies, or prostitution, occasionally or on a regular basis, they rely on the trickster mode to accomplish the exchange. The ideal trickster is a magnanimous character whose intentions are malicious. Black males' malevolence is guided by the nature of the work they must do: simply, "it's a jungle" where every man is expected to take ideal and material power, given the opportunity. Charles Silberman wrote an excellent description of the black trickster.[8] For our purpose, it is important to stress the black cultural themes, given the historical and temporal (that is, transitory) reasons, of a commitment to those values.

The malevolent aspect of the trickster personality is directly related to the human condition which requires that the males either work or starve. That is, in a capitalist society, money is treated as the medium of the exchange of commodities, and labor is treated as a commodity. Most of society limits what is understood as legitimate. But black males have had to revise legitimacy to make sense out of their reality. Life becomes "that fast life," where a "quick trick" emerges as the means and ideal of the good life. Easy money is the ultimate symbol of success; and easy money is always fast money. It is certainly clear that reciprocity and redistribution are factors in the trickster's function; however, they do not represent the dominant aspect of the trickster's relationship, which is exchange. In fact, reciprocity and redistribution are primarily employed at the political and ideological levels of interaction.

The trickster's concept of time orients leisure differently than does the time concept held by propertied and professional/managerial classes. The latter's advantage stems from the fact that they have access to legitimate means for leisure expression. Black males create activity that will generate money in an environment that denies equal or meaningful labor force participation. Time is consumed earning the most money possible from an economy too poor to provide secure jobs with basic benefits.

Black culture disseminates a set of trickster techniques to contend with the necessary disregard of civility to reproduce inequality, imparting to its community a rebellious style: "You might be poor, but you can always be clean." The appearance of leisure and of conspicuous consumption might at first cause us to reason that an anti-work ethic exists among black males. We realize with closer observation that the domestic work of the males is hard work, accomplished with a facade of leisure.

The males, for example, who sell marijuana on the streets of the major cities are representative of the trickster mode. When the marijuana arrives in their neighborhoods, it is in bulk form. The marijuana must be weighed and packaged for distribution in the community. This work is tedious and requires attentive measures. The small packages must be distributed to a team of street hustlers who must compete in the street market with spontaneous techniques, such as two-for-one sales, or by "fixing up" (increasing the weight of) the package. In addition, the individual seller must be on constant lookout for plainclothes and uniformed policemen. The male selling marijuana on the streets feels stress—primarily because the police or a rival might "jump out on you" at any time. There is additional stress from the risk of missing a customer.

The dealers' language reflects the stress of the exchange. When dealers approach a potential customer, they will commonly set the boundary for the exchange: "Blood, it is hot out here." This indicates that the police are suspected of being in the vicinity. At the same time, the dealers must advertise their products, "This is the best lovely [a treated form of marijuana] in town." Regardless of the quality of the marijuana a street dealer is selling, he must unload it. This condition intensifies the trickster activity on the street. Poor-quality marijuana sells best where the seller can remain unknown, and the dealers will have to make a judgment when the issue arises.

IN THE SCHOOLS

Mythological systems that operate in the society have meaning not only in the streets but also within the social institutions. The schools are perhaps the best example we may observe to acquire some understanding of the conflicting cultural systems. Deviant black males take a countercultural attitude, with contracultural potential, into the classrooms. Countercultural groups deliberately and consciously oppose certain aspects of the dominant culture; contracultural groups constantly attempt to substantially disrupt the total operation of the system. Generally black males view each relationship in the terms of contextual conflict. As one high school student indicated: "Oh, when I tried to go to school, they wouldn't let me go to school. So I ain't thinking about those people."

The conflict is constantly repeated between the teacher and the student. The teachers and school administrators are the professional/managerial group in the schools. The meanings of the professional/managerial group are bound to conflict in a general sense with the meanings constructed by the oppressed community. For example, another high school student was asked what characteristics he thought contributed to good teaching. He responded:

> I think a bad teacher is one of those teachers who constantly like to see you in trouble. I saw a couple of girls get into trouble just for lighting up a cigarette, and that was on the football field. They made it up that they were smoking weed in the boys' gym.

The black male deviant students view the authority structure as illegitimate and consistently reaffirm the mythic construction that the system employs fraudulent methods in its administration. In this case the accusation, "They made it up," is based on a generalization that the agents of control tell lies to maintain their authority. The students' perspective is in line with the cultural baggage transmitted in the mythic system. They think in reference to the cultural baggage when they subject themselves to a world reality that, in a historical and temporal sense, views them as inferior. We may extend the observation and suggest that marijuana smoking is a status symbol for a large segment of the deviant culture. Moreover, the political aspect of marijuana should be considered. Marijuana is, like tea, a natural resource but, unlike tea, is not brought to the international market through the processes of cartel and trust. I do not intend to trace international trade processes and the exclusion of particular products. However, there is some justification in the view of oppression with respect to these products that finds support in the world economy. This points to the structural nature of the opposition and to the complexity of reading the mythic constructions.

Occasionally the conflict surfaces in name-calling. In each instance the antagonisms between the potential deviant and the teacher will emerge, develop, and abate. Each situation may occur and be over immediately or continue for days, weeks, or years. One student reported a name-calling incident that developed over several days:

> Yeah, I been suspended once. Getting into it with the P.E. teacher. He called me a few names and I put a few back at him. I was asking him about my grade, and he act like he didn't want to take care of what I wanted to know....I don't know exactly what he said, but he said something. It wasn't my name, so I guess it was racial. I was talking to one of my partners and he said he might of marked [me] absent. So I said, "No, I'm here, Jack." He said, "My name ain't Jack." I said, "I wasn't talking to you." Which I wasn't, so he didn't have nothing to say to me if I wasn't talking to him. So it went on, and then we got into it. A couple of days after that they called me down to the office about my referral. [The vice principal] said he'd have to suspend me for a couple of days for talking to the teacher.

Notice that the student is steadfast in repeating his innocence. The teacher can implement his decision by suspending the student. However, the suspension does more harm than good—primarily because the student reaffirms the fraud of the power relationship that suspended his education in favor of the situational comfort of the teacher—a teacher who was not a member of his community. The student comes to feel that his community has no control in the schooling process. One student confirms this feeling by pointing to the teacher's control over equipment:

> I can see where you carry things too far, and then there's no recreation except to play basketball. Like they have a weight room here and you can't even go in there unless you're playing football, and then you got to be on the football team.

The black male student reasserts his masculinity in the daily rituals in the school, bringing the cultural-myth baggage into play. We certainly are unable to deny that the school is involved in producing athletes for the university athletic system. It is clear that the schools must use their limited resources to feed that system. So while the average student will admire the university athletic stars, at the same time the average student will also perceive the inequality and exploitation necessary to produce the star athletes for the university system. One student summed up this orientation by justifying the "bad day": "Right, when I have a bad day I don't even go to class. I had one today. I go mess with them. They say something to me [and] I'm ready to get off on them."

The figurative myth "to get off on them" is an explicitly masculine expression. The customary usage for the phrase is in the context of a male "getting off on" a female, which refers to an orgasm. The orgasm serves as an analogy for power plays in the mode of the sporty life. "Getting" implies a process of rise, turning point, and fall; while "off" implies completion, fait accompli. For this reason it would be an error to understand the black cultural orientation as merely countercultural since often those expressions are contracultural. The goal of this student is to substantially disrupt the total operation of the system.

The student computes each situation in terms of his previous impressions. Then he reacts according to his judgment of the situation. Judgment is a process of considering how his actions will be immediately received, as well as the stream of events and the likely form the scenario may take. A student illustrated that he was aware of the "white person" myth from his cultural tradition. Of more significance, he illustrated that in a confrontation with a teacher he dreamed an extravaganza, introducing his mother and probation officer as a supporting cast onto the stage because he refused to be dominated and held in the underworld:

> I don't like being talked down to, especially by a white person. I don't like the things they try and do to you. She [the teacher] used to try and suspend me for coming in the back area too soon and just silly things. She acts like you're so much shit. Then we had a big talk with her; my

mother and probation officer. After that she didn't seem to bother me much.

The teacher's mythic dynamic and structure relay the message that the black students and their kind are despicable characters, and the student's mythic system convinces him of his worth. The student believes that many of the circumstances are lamentable. As another student expressed the condition:

But [the teacher] just like trouble. [My friend] had a basketball jersey. Somebody lost it. He found it and wore it to school one day. [My counselor], [another teacher], and [the teacher] were there. [The counselor and another teacher] tried to pull [the teacher] off [my friend]. [My friend] wasn't going for it, so [he] swung back. I feel like when my mother and father tell me, if a person swings at you, if he's man enough to swing he's man enough to take a punch, and that's just what he did. He swung back, and they had paddy wagons up there at the school; they had something of everything up there for him. He was ready to give the shirt up. But no, [the teacher] just had to go on and rush him 'cause he was talking. He rushed him, tried to grab him, and he swung at him. I don't know if it landed or not. I know [my friend], he's big. I say he weighs a good 195 to 200 pounds and he plays football. [The teacher] is about the same weight and height and everything. He didn't care. He wanted to see him kicked out of school anyway. They didn't take [my friend] away. His father rushed up there immediately. Took off from work. His son almost had a scholarship from that school. This is what [my friend] was talking about. He's a senior. We're suppose to go to the seniors for help when we're in the school; school problems or any kind of problems. He said that's one thing that you don't do; you don't never get into trouble with a P.E. teacher 'cause they will try to ruin your scholarship. They're trying to ruin you any way they can. He said, "I was fixing to give the man his shirt right off my back, the man just had to rush me, so I just took a poke at him, too." If he had rushed me, that would be the only thing I would do.

Harry Edwards has elaborated the definition and process of the "macho hustle" in U.S. culture. He argues that black masculinity is hustled by the white patriarchy. The relationship transforms the black male role into that of a prostitute to masculine institutional systems—athletics, the military, and prisons—where macho is the dress needed to pass through the forms; the more the better.[9] Here, we clearly see the significance of the athletic myth at the school. Generally, the athletic myth is applied to basketball and football players among black males. Let's briefly examine the basketball metaphor, since the role of athlete is essential to the socialization of black males.

The basketball metaphor signifies developing rote excellence as opposed to cognitive reasoning. The "hoop" implies a more stringent confinement to accuracy than a sport where the score is accomplished in open space. There are at least two profound themes underlying the basketball myth. The first is related to the reality of the prostitution relationship that is supported by the economically based structure of the game. The second is related to the ideology of rote excellence that is required to emerge as a star in the game. For black males the game systematically reinforces the ideals of their national experience of assumed criminality.

While the student believes that basketball is his means to legitimate success—which, incidentally, is relative success because the job on the average lasts only for a few years—the chances of the student finding success through this masculine institution are infinitesimally small. There are more than 10 million black males in the United States; there are fewer than 300 professional basketball players of any race. The improbability of success, including the fact that professional sports is work for the young, suggests the structural hopelessness of the situation, to which the students are oblivious.

In my studies, the pervasive black male dream was to play basketball. One student said:

I'm a go to about a four year college....Study basketball....Yep....Study how to play basketball real good and get good grades and get out of college....I'll say anything....I don't know, I just want to go in college and take ball. I don't know yet; I just want to play basketball while I'm in college.

Another stated:

Go to college. [local community college]. Because I know the coach there, and he'll help me out on my grades, and then I will advance into pro basketball. Yes...jump shot....[I am] 5'9". I can shoot jump shots— too small to go inside. I can't dunk on somebody bigger than me.

The idea was put forward by many other students. Another student expressed his frustration:

I plan to get a scholarship. Yep, if the coach would let me play basketball and quit sitting me on the bench like he did last year. On the team I was on this year, there was about two [blacks], or something like that. And then I start talking about it 'cause I feel like I can beat everybody out there who's the first in basketball. I know I could. If I play right now, I could beat every one of them.

It is a pressing problem to explain the students' position in terms of conventional logic; we could point out the errors in their reasoning and so disregard the meaning of their statements. We may not as easily disregard their social reactions on the basis of their reasoning. The students are merely acting on their understanding of the mythic symbols that are presented to them. Since both the student and the community view the basketball myth as an official way to success and value its standard, the student must be challenged by the reality and social structure of the game. The national game has become dominated by black men in concert with the current way of explaining black masculinity. The nation is distressed because the major issue in the National Basketball Association is that owners acquire white stars to appease their middle-class customers. The game has become referred to as "African Hoop Ball" and other derogatory names, which denotes diminished status for the game compared with other major sports in U.S. society.

In the black male imagination, basketball is not merely a conscious and deliberate opposition to Eurocentric values, or merely a way to participate in wholesome competition. In general, for black men, one element of basketball is to disrupt the total operation of the system. This results in real conflict in the organization of the NCAA and the NBA. There was, in recent times, a rule making the slam dunk an illegal play in both organizations. The excitement of destroying the backboard during play has necessarily been accommodated in both organizations. This change developed in situations of conflict where the slam dunk could not be contained. For these kinds of reasons, basketball must be understood as both contracultural and cultural. Within the transitory system of constraints, black men seek to destroy the power relationship of the organization of basketball. The power relationship is, intentionally or unintentionally, primarily organized so that black men are the performers and white men have the intellectual function.

Leaving basketball aside, we find the relationship between black parents and the school's professional/managers also to be a source of resistance. The black male student believes that his parents are as important as the primarily white teachers and coaches are presenting themselves to be. I am not indicating that the students are unimpressed by the teachers' abilities to accumulate, exchange, and circulate commodities; this, in fact, may be the students' central motive for going to school. The students are clearly impressed with the hegemony of the teachers. But the student, in spite of the capital arrangements, believes his symbolic father image to be the highest symbol of virility, just as the teachers believe their symbolic father's image represents the strongest masculine symbol. We could speak about students whose father image has fallen in their eyes; but this issue is aside from the immediate concern, which is to idealize the black student's relation to the father symbol. The point is that a mythic father symbol exists among black males. One student demonstrated his belief in his father's virility as related to his academics:

> I can sit down and start writing. I could write an autobiography on Abraham Lincoln, if I read the book, and put it in my own words. But when I take it back to school and get a grade on it, it'll come out a D.

My mother and father would help me on it. They were good in school. My father, the way he talks to me, it sounds like he graduated from high school; but he didn't—that's how much insight my father has. He knows what's happening. He listens to the news. He watches channel 2, 5, and 7, ten o'clock news, eleven o'clock news, either channel it's on, he's going to watch the news. My father had to come up to the school one day. I think I had gotten into some trouble. He knows what's wrong in the school. He really wasn't worried about the trouble, 'cause I had a fight. He said, "You can take the school and everything else and shove it. If anybody puts their hands on my son, my son has to fight."

The teacher steadfastly stands with a commitment to the traditional ideals handed down through the hegemonic order, while the students steadfastly demonstrate a commitment to a set of nontraditional values and grope for margins to wage a counterattack. One student indicated the conflict:

I got kicked out of [school] 'cause of the P.E. teacher. I came in late to class one day and he kept watching me. I asked him if he had a problem. He answered me in a smart way. I said, "I wish that you would move and go on upstairs so I can put my clothes on." He walked up on me and I was about to hit him. But I said, "Man, if you don't get off me, you might get hit." He said, "You come in my class late again, you're going to be out of my class." I asked him again would he leave so I can put on my clothes. He started talking, so I said forget it. After P.E. he said, "Go to the office." So I didn't go the office, I went home; but I didn't tell my mother and them about it. I missed school for two weeks. Just didn't attend. So I came back to school and went to homeroom, where they took down the attendance. Soon as they took down the attendance, [the dean] he called the police. They had about five or six cars out there. Threatening the teacher. We had a black something like supervisor for black students and she said, "Wait a minute. You called five or six police for this little boy?" She said, "No, he not going anywhere, I'll take him home, and we're going to get his mother." We go back up to the school and [the vice principal] tried to get in between. Half on my mother's side, half on his side. My mother say no. She was calling him so many [names]. We talked until twelve, from eight that morning till twelve. They sent my name to the student placement officer, and he wasn't on the [vice principal's] side. He said no, that was bullshit. I got kicked out, and [the placement officer] asked what school I'd like to go to. I asked him if I could go to [the local reform middles chool]. So I went there and graduated from [there]. I think the most fun I had when I was [there was] when they elected me "Student of the Month." The most aggressive student helping the Board of Education. I stopped nine riots; nine fights that could have turned out in riots. They were black and white; and I think Arabian and black.

The black males consistently question the teachers' commitment and sincerity. To them, the teachers' commitment to them and sincerity in educating them are questionable. The black males feel that the teachers are at the schools simply to earn a paycheck. To them, the teachers just do not care. One student presented the pervasive sentiment:

Oh, the teachers in class don't care if you don't come in there. They give you work that you don't understand. They don't want to help you. They put it on the board and don't give you no instructions how to do it, and when you ask them, they get mad. You get smart, 'cause they don't help you; they just don't help you; they send you out.

Another student poignantly represented the prevailing sentiment: "Teachers don't care if you go to class or not; they got theirs."

The teachers' role functions to make the black male students conform to the hegemonic vision of people of color. On the other hand, the students are on the scene to establish an improved quality of life for themselves and their families. The blacks must become "bad" in order to express individual autonomy in the schools. The "bad" posture is an analogue to earlier phases of race and class inequality in U.S. social life. The slave had little to look forward to but unending work. That condition transformed the slave into a brute in the sense of being degraded, dirty, poorly fed and clothed. To traverse the slave experience meant, as we have seen, that the slave had to lie, cheat, and "steal away" to freedom. The slave was forced to become criminally bad. A similar set of circumstances was at play in the period between the Civil War and World War II, when convict labor was widely used in U.S. towns and cities through the convict-lease system. When black males come to school, they have a perspective as part of their cultural baggage that is grounded in this history, expressed in their myth system, and acted out in their behaviors. The students think in reference to the cultural baggage when they subject themselves to the world of reality, which is constructed to see them as inferior. This contradiction was mentioned by one student:

I mean, in order for me to stay in the class, I had to come in and start charging this man. That's why I started calling him all kind of bald heads, and stuff like that; but if I wouldn't say nothing to this fool, he tried to send me out of class. He was white.

The experiences in the school are in actuality set in a community context. In the community a sort of informal policy toward the school emerges. The systemic contradictions that are reified in the community were represented by one student's mythic account:

They just told me, "Here, nigger, take this." I didn't have no say-so about it or nothing. So one time my mother came up here and [she] looked like a student. She was standing on one side of me and I'd walk into class. He [the teacher] just stops and looks at me like I was crazy, and she seen that. I looked at him, and I turned around and looked back and said, "Do you see what I mean?" She flipped out!

I-CAUGHT-A-BAD-NIGGER

The most conspicuous ritual engaged in by the professional/managerial administration is the activity of systematically organizing and justifying the failure of black males. The fact is that most crime is committed by the professional/managerial class. In spite of this, most arrests and prosecutions are suffered by the underclass.[10] While it might be reasoned that the professional/managerial class provides a necessary service in society, it is more difficult to make a cogent argument that it is motivated by altruistic motives.

Most professionals/managers are in the presence of the underclass primarily to support an ever-increasing standard of living. This means that regardless of the other interests they have, if their salaries are taken away, they have little reason to remain administrators over the oppression of the underclass. Notwithstanding all this, the values of hard work, loyalty, strength, discipline, religiosity, fitness, patriotism, and character are essential to the professional/managerial agenda. However, those values function according to the specifications of racist mores and traditions. The racist mores are significant in that they are distinguishable from the folkways, which do not share moral overtones. Given such a context, the value orientation of the professional/managerial class is applied to make the black males understand their status in society as confined to a caste/career of limitations and diminished potentials. The professional/manager's central technique of domination is to initiate status degradation ceremonies employing traditional assumptions about the disreputable black male.[11]

In black culture we are left with the profile image of the professional/managerial agenda in Richard Wright's novel Native Son. The protagonist, Bigger Thomas, is described in the story's newspaper account as a "Negro sex-slayer...looks exactly like an ape...gives the impression of possessing abnormal strength...is about five feet, nine inches tall and his skin is exceedingly black....His lower jaw protrudes obnoxiously, reminding one of a jungle beast."[12] While it is hard to imagine the five-foot-nine boy being the animal he is described to be, it is relatively easy to understand how Bigger is imagined by the professionals/managers. Bigger supposedly has the profile of a criminal. The work of the professional/managerial class is similar to the earlier work of the missionary in colonized countries: the colonizer must transform the heathen culture of the native into a supposed culture of repute. The professionals/managers are, for the most part, oblivious to the cultural vestige, since they have been trained to believe that their system of government is the best in the world, one in which persons are presumed innocent until proven guilty and individuals are rewarded on merit. The professional/managerial myth results in the anarchy of their administration; they operate as if black males are guilty of incompetence, overexpressed athleticism, rhythm, and deviance. The males, for their part, sense an indignation and a feeling that they have nothing to lose.

The police represent the most salient aspect of the contradiction between the contrasting commitments. The police are committed to reconfirming the ineligibility of the black male's claim to the imagined opportunities in society. When the police approach these males, they behave as if the males are criminal, and they proceed to interrogate them to establish their guilt or innocence. In fact, the police approach is similar to the approach used by the police in repressive states. Not only does the black community physically resemble Third World countries with respect to police occupation, rates of school attendance, provision of health care, and mortality and morbidity rates, but the professional/managerial attitudes toward the males are similar to the attitudes the settler class expresses toward the inhabitants in colonized Third World countries.

The police operate with suspicion drawn from a profile of males, and the black male ritual system corresponds to the police profile. The police use discretionary power in the apprehension, search, and arrest of the males. Black culture is under constant surveillance by the police state. A rite of passage for black males is the assurance that at some point they will be "checked" and "reported on" by the police. Naturally, their response is to "trick the man."

ISN'T IT AWFUL

In reference to secondary institutions, the teachers in the classroom play the most prominent role in the socialization of black males into the world of limited work and second-class citizenship. If a student and teacher come into conflict, the teacher has the greater legitimate authority, and thus has the greater potential to control the situation. Research in this area is reported by Delos Kelly, who points to educators as initiators of "status degradation ceremonies," applying non-academic standards, perpetuating academic and societal stereotypes, and the like.[13] Nevertheless, many will be surprised to realize that the teacher is as powerless as the student in the school relationship. The teacher as a professional/manager is occupying a structural role assisted by a myth system that produces a semblance of order in the nation.

One young teacher reported her desire to guide her students, which, ideally speaking, must result in disillusionment. The inner-city teachers' situation ultimately uncovers their powerlessness in the school situation. When asked how she felt about teaching at an inner-city school, she responded:

I like it very much, I would say. I enjoy working with kids and seeing

how they change, and also I will be able to guide them into whatever
they want to do. Give kids guidance is what I would like to do.

Her aim is to guide the students toward success. However, she has not been
able to meet her objectives. The urban black students' perception of success is
marked by a memory of real images of limited opportunities and violence. The
experience of being employed in uncertain domestic colonial labor markets and
the cultures that exist with them are vivid images in the students' minds that are
constantly being re-created. The teachers' memories of success, on the other
hand, are a story of regulation and reward—the experience of attending college
and landing a secure job.

One woman had been a mathematics teacher for six years, the past three at
her present school. After indicating that her work experience did not correspond
to her ideal, she indicated the physical toll the experiences took on her in the
form of headaches. This she accounted for in respect to disciplining students:

> [I dislike] discipline problems like everybody else. But sometimes it
> interests me a lot, too. When I meet a challenge, I really like to confront
> it and try to solve it. That could create a challenge situation, but most of
> the time it gives me a headache....I guess I like it moderately because
> there are a lot of discipline problems in certain classes, so that is one
> thing that really gives me a headache almost every day.

If disciplining students occasionally occurred the teacher would have met
her aim of imparting her view of wisdom and values to students. In other words,
if the students had challenged her only once and she perceived that her solution
had been the guidance to ameliorate the situation, she would have approached her
desire to repeat having her value system confirmed. But the conflict between her
discipline and the discipline of the students at last became two cultural forces
unwilling to give. The unmet need resulted in a tension that caused her headaches
over and over again.

The teachers are, for the most part, unaware of the competing disciplines.
They have been educated with a set of ideals in which they have placed both intellectual and emotional belief. Their background myths leave for them a reaffirma-
tion of the national ideals of hard work, loyalty, strength, discipline, religiosity,
fitness, patriotism, and character. So the teacher is placed on an antagonistic stage
where the perceived goal is a mission from God to inculcate the obstinate irreli-
gious, and thus unenlightened, with what is, in effect, the teacher's paternalistic
culture values. Thus, an immediate dualism appears: good us against bad them.
One teacher working with disadvantaged students pointed out her perceived role
to nourish the students with her acquired fatherly blessings:

> The main thing I like is the feeling I have an effect on the student, not so
> much that maybe their reading level goes up several points or their math

level will go up within several years...maybe one or three points, depending on the youngster, but the fact that I'm establishing a relationship with the child...positive one where he can see himself in relationship to his environment, society, and where he's headed, what his future goals are, what his future needs are, and I feel if I can make him understand that that's tremendously important because I think if anything... kids are given an impetus to stay in school....[They feel] discouraged because their abilities are really far below level....They see their limitations, and that can be very frustrating, because the desire to do well is there regardless of the youngster's handicap....It's difficult to get over the hurdle, for them to accept the limitation, but at the same time realize that there still is a potential within them, but to understand that limitation so they don't expect too much of themselves because that's unrealistic.

Of course the teacher has bitten off more than she can chew: the student already is aware of his relationship to his environment, primarily through the mythic constructs. Notice how this teacher has failed to take a critical look at the structure of the "slow learner" myth. The possibility that the tests which measure slow learners are rigged or that the system is rigged in the sense of discrediting slow learners does not occur to her. The teacher does not ask: Why is it that black students are disproportionately represented in slow learner classrooms across the country? Therefore, her desire to "make him understand" his caste/class career of limitation and diminished potential is in actuality her desire to make him desire her value of his place. It is of little wonder, then, to discover that she dislikes dealing with disciplining her students. One thing is certain, the teacher is the authority. As she indicated:

I think dealing with discipline is what I don't like, primarily because I'm a firm believer that the problems of discipline, not in all cases, but in most cases...are problems that should be dealt with at the home level... I often feel that the home is not willing to or able to cope with discipline, consequently that responsibility is put on the teacher in the classroom, which again means I'm working with a child who has a lot of problems, with that youngster, so that the other children who may have less of an emotional problem are being deprived of getting instruction during that period. And then I dislike that. It's a reality that I have to deal with, but I don't care for it. I don't feel it's necessary. I feel if parents would somehow handle a little more of that responsibility, it would be easier for the teacher.

The teacher does not realize that the students are at home and that they have no reason to make it easier for the settler class. She does not realize that the students' parents are in competition with her authority over their children in the sense of value orientations. She believes that the black parents are failing because they have failed to instill the values inculcated in her, in their children, as her parents had instilled them in her. Nonetheless, she realizes that her authority extends over the black parents by stating, "I've never made a home visit, no. Usually the parent comes in or it's discussed on the phone. I have not made a home visit."

The teacher's authoritative role allows her the privilege of calling in the parents to discuss any problem. She has no real interest in the student's home and community, aside from their functioning according to the specifications of her cultural traditions. She nonetheless is forced to face the fact that the parental opposition is real, because the community is applying pressure on the teacher. The situations around which these pressures surface in the black communities are repeated endlessly. One example of such a situation developed when a teacher was assaulted by a student with a radio. One teacher reported the incident.

[A teacher] asked two students to stop smoking, and it turned into a confrontation and he was assaulted with one of these radios...I don't think he was seriously hurt but he was hurt, and this was one of the students they had tried to suspend last year for an incident in which another student was beaten up and all three of the students were not suspended—all three of them were transferred out....This one's mother apparently has some political influence through [a community organization], and she got to someone on the board or something and the boy was not transferred. The same student! And so...that news got around. When I talk about the morale problem, it's that kind of thing that creates a very bad morale for both teachers and students to see that type of...it means that the on-site school administrators don't have too much authority and the teachers have virtually none...especially if it's a white teacher and a black student.

The teacher's role is structured to diametrically oppose black students', just as the cultural communities are fundamentally opposed. In fact, the teacher's reason for being in the black community is in opposition to the community's reason for being there. One teacher indicated this by pointing to the teaching profession as a way to send her husband through law school. It was not to supply the community with an additional lawyer—the chances of this are slim. She said:

Teaching was my primary choice as a profession. I think I was putting my husband through law school. ["You mean you became a teacher as a means of putting your husband through law school?"] I did here, yes.

The teacher is oblivious to the fact that her interests are white paternal interests. She believes that she can show the paternal structure a thing or two—introduce him to something he does not know. As such, she feels that the paternal authority is not quite refined enough. Because of this, she literally takes paternal standards and divides them into dark realities. A teacher concluded:

> The schools are disintegrating. The materials that we got in the 1960s are the ones still holding us. We haven't been able to get books at least since the big push on reading in the compensatory program....When we got a lot of reading materials, there hasn't been anything of that sort since....I know from my experience at [another community school] that $150,000 was poured into that school a year, two years, ago and the results were negligible. The reading scores kept going down. That was because the *Sullivan Reader* was the favorite of the superintendent at that time...who later went down and worked for the people that put it out....The politics of the school are hideous, and people become very demoralized....I am at the moment somewhat demoralized by that because you don't feel that you have any support from anyone.

Despite the fact that the school appears to be "disintegrating," in the view of this teacher, she believes that she might very well turn the situation around. In actuality this teacher has a commitment to the U.S. cultural system, and she is overwhelmed and disillusioned by the processes of the disintegration. She is following the paternalistic ideals to approach her truth, thereby confirming her being. Nonetheless, the structural contradictions emerge in the relationships with students as well as in relationships with colleagues and hierarchical authorities.

But the teacher is ambivalent about the paternal power relations, too. She feels that the system mishandles the relations in her area; that the system comports with the interest of the opposition too often. One teacher illustrated this feeling in the context of race issues:

> I have noticed in the last couple of years, since I came back from sabbatical, that the chaos of the central administration office is now reaching every place. For instance, my daughter, who is fifteen now, was in the second grade when the school busing started, so she was bused under one superintendent to—she's Caucasian—she was in a virtually all-black school and was bused to a Chinese school, which was all right. They enjoyed the bus ride. Then a few years later, another superintendent, while the schools were closed down because of the earthquake proofing, so she went to junior high school...under split session....Now we are in the process of redesign, which is a new word to describe the same old shakeup...I'm very much disillusioned with the people who run the school district. I think they are a bunch of incompetents, and I don't believe that the new people that have been hired, the minority people, are any better.

However, the teacher realizes that the game of schooling is the kind of game that is highly dramaturgical. One aspect of the drama is blame-passing. Blame-passing is necessary because the threat from the community is a real threat. One teacher aptly stated it:

> Defensive, the administration attacking, well, Mr. Johnson, who is the assistant principal, yesterday showed me proudly the results of this survey of students and faculty and parents that showed the two major problems of the school. One was poor student skills, and number two was incompetent teaching... [The survey] is designed to make things worse. That kind of blame-passing, everybody loves to do it. As I've just demonstrated by blaming the administration.

The teacher feels that if the institutional organization and popular commitment to the dominant cultural values were more regulated, the oppositional black community could be more adequately maintained. The teacher may be compared to the biblical heroine Eve during the Fall. Eve felt the need to transcend the knowledge of the order in Paradise to become as powerful as God, and the teacher appears to have a similar feeling about the school organization—to become as powerful as the administrators and politicians. The dominated community represents a threat by its very existence. It is the bottom, where the teachers must never be. But the administration and teachers must negotiate with a community that is constantly creating an ideological position, hoping to establish a covenant with the dominators. So, in one case, the community raises a point regarding high black suspension rates.

Suspension is a major tool the teacher uses to control the student. The issues are similar to those having to do with excommunication from the Roman Catholic Church. The community, like the followers of Luther, demands a greater emphasis on the salvation aspect of "justification by faith," pointing out stresses on the depravity of mankind. But in contrast, the teachers, like the Catholic Church, are concerned with "good works" and the external practices. The community wants the student to be the best at what he is, in accordance with their understanding of the concept of love. So the community "tacks the ninety-five theses on the door at the church of Wittenburg," which is to say that they question the legitimacy of the school's rigid guidance as if the teachers were on a mission from God. Moreover, the community faithfully believes in the value of their children by virtue of their being. One teacher said:

> The policy has been, apparently, we are told, that because of racial imbalance in suspensions...we mustn't suspend such a high proportion of black students....[This] may or may not contribute to the feeling that I get in the halls that the kids don't care because they don't feel anything is going to be done to them, no matter what they say or what they do, if they don't get caught. There is no authority that they feel can reach them, and they are aware of the change in policy.

However, recall that the teacher's sincerity and commitment to the students and their community has already come under question by them. Moreover, the attacks on the authoritative representatives are constantly being opportunistically exercised by the students. "Your job essentially has to be that of a policeman in situations where you don't know the kids and the kids hide behind the same anonymity. If you don't know them, they can do anything."

The alienated student and teacher express their separate views of cultural values. Both suspect a stranger in the village, that a seditious element exists in their environments that is contrary to their individual value commitments. The black role represents a "strike back" structure and function. Black males are not just striking out at teachers, they are striking out at physical structures, which are sacred places; they are tearing down walls. They are striking out more intensely than the teacher is striking out against the paternal order, but equally intensely as the dominant paternalism is smiting the dominated paternalism. The teacher is a witness of this struggle also: "The vandalism is demoralizing. There has been an attack on a student, he was killed here this year, and several attacks upon teachers by students."

The teachers are disturbed by the lost generation of students wandering aimlessly in the dark wilderness of the urban "underculture," and they are certain to ask, "Isn't it awful?" "Those kids bother me a lot, the wanderers through the halls. The disruption of classes because people are in halls who shouldn't be there. A lot of noise, and motorcycles."

Additionally, the teachers are aware that there are limits to the exercise of their authority. They realize that they must avoid confrontations where power is raw. One teacher indicated this point:

> [Before] if they didn't have a pass and they were out of class, and you said Get to class or What are you doing in the hallway, they would offer an excuse or they would certainly maneuver their way out and get going. These kids were not about to be moved from where they were standing, and they were not about to be quiet. Not about to produce a pass or a name. And any attempt to tell them something, they laughed in one case, and in other cases they walked away and started running. But one teacher is helpless to confront that kind of group activity.

The teacher must assess, compute, and react to the situations that arise. Each event requires all the actors' constant, immediate judgment. A teacher shared an event that highlights the situational process:

> Yes, they're belligerent, and they're not about to do anything, and it's really disturbing. If they know that you know them, it's a completely different matter. If you know one kid, even, standing in the hall with a whole group of them and you say, "Well, John, why aren't you in

class?" the rest of them are careful because they know they can be identified.

The students' invisibility has become a question mark for the teachers: it is an old metaphor in the black community. The teachers know that the characters with whom they interact are fake, but the teachers' sensibilities are often shattered:

> I have had several confrontations in the hall where I've told students to go to classes or to leave the building if they're not students, whoever they are....In one case I was verbally threatened and the dean was down the hall, and I got the dean and we came back and the boy—he [the dean] knew who the boy was—but the dean told me after that incident that there was nothing the school could do to these kids. The fact was, these people downtown had tied our hands in terms of dealing, punishing that kind of verbal assault. ["You mean you couldn't even reprimand the student?"] The dean reprimanded him. He said, "All right, Jones, you get up to class right now and I don't want to hear anything else." It was very severe; but in fact he did nothing but send the boy onto class, and then afterward he explained that this is the way things were.

The teacher is involved in a process that endlessly rationalizes the dominant myths and folk tales that prevail over the patriarchy's planned cultural transmissions. We have not said that black males nationally perform below grade level at a rate twice as high as black females in public schools.[14] But the teacher must recreate the image to clearly establish the culturally transmitted statuses. The teacher reasons, using the prevailing myths, that the black males perform below standard. It should be stressed that most black males are actually programmed to perform at their class and race position in the stratification hierarchy. They often refer to "what a nigger ought to do." They are referring to the roles expected of black males in U.S. social institutions.

One teacher explicitly states the roles:

> One of the major problems of the school...the fact that so many of our students are coming to this school with very low skills, and yet these are kids who are really bright, above average, who shouldn't really be having these problems. I really find it tragic because I personally don't know how much a junior high remedial math and reading program can do to help the child to catch up, because I imagine there's an enormous amount of discouragement the kids must be facing by not being able. Look at themselves and [they're] twelve years old and [they] still can't do this and still can't—no matter what the bravado and defense mechanisms are—I don't care....I've just seen that from the contact I've had

with these kids. I think it's a very, very serious problem for outside life. This problem, I think, is not peculiar to schools in [our city], not just...in our district. I'm not aware of the problems other minorities have. I think they have some problems, too, possibly because of language and maybe isolation, but I think it's really tragic. I've discussed this often with people, and I don't know what the answer is. I don't know what has happened where....I wish I could know the answer. I think [the superintendent] is right on track in that sense. [He argues to] have nothing but reading and math because once they have those basics, they can build a great deal of information on that and maybe that's what he's doing now. I hope it continues, because I think it is tremendously important.

The teacher is convinced of the disreputable characters of those for whom the mission is to inculcate in them the dominant professional/managerial values. Those values are reinforced in the form of secular mini rituals, all of which are repetitions of the creation of order. Estrangement from the order is visible everywhere. Policy is created to reconfirm the darkest convictions—"the school ain't no safe place to be." At one school, for example, a policy was instituted to keep the windows in the classroom doors exposed during class. The decision to implement that policy came about after the teachers expressed fear of being in completely closed rooms with the students. However, not all the teachers observed the policy, and as a consequence, the administration enforced it:

I refuse to keep my door open. The policy in this school is to also leave the window section of the door exposed, in the middle of the door there's a little window, and I taped mine shut with paper because students are constantly providing a disruption to the class and I find that irritating.

This is an example of ritual to re-create a margin of control that reconfirms the nature of the job. It convinces the world of the proposition that the students are indeed disreputable and must somehow be transformed. Thus, the teachers' main function is to re-create the dominant white values and convince the students to agree with them. Consequently, teachers tacitly attack the black community and challenge its cultural orientation. The myths, as we have seen, paint a dismal, if not intolerable, picture of the community. The teacher employs such images to symbolically underwrite the circumstances of oppression; but the teacher's concern with oppression is in actuality the teacher's oppression. The teachers are oppressed by the "generalized other" authorities, just as the students are. But the teacher has additional value in the cultural market. Modifying symbolic interactionist terms, the teacher has more legitimate "me," which increases the chances to legitimately express "I." Persons possessing greater objective power in self-definition have greater chances for expressing subjective power in a social situation. Such a person has greater freedom because, through the subjective expression, they command greater attention and respect from others. The opportunity to command respect is one way to achieve exotic or novel feelings; the chances are then greater for the subject to fuse with the object, resulting in more control and power over the external objects. Greater legitimate social power means more personally rewarding experiences in life.

The teacher may adventure into an exotic community to earn a living. The exotic community for the teacher is, in a real sense, comparable to dirt for a child. Children are fascinated by dirt. Often children ask their mothers, "Mommie, may I make a mud pie?" When allowed to do so, children will happily play in the dirt. However, when the time comes to discontinue play in the dirt, mothers often remark, "Now look at how dirty you are; don't get that dirt on Mommie." Adventure into an exotic community for the teacher becomes a source of feeling pleasure and of feeling the need to detach the self, or to clean up, after the job is completed. One teacher said:

> [One local school] was virtually all white when I started teaching there and when I quit…it had become maybe 20 percent black. Still very few Chinese at that point….After I left, a lot of problems because they bused the black kids in and they changed the boundary lines in rather odd ways….The school went downhill very fast, I heard, and at least partially because there was absolutely no tradition in that neighborhood of integration.

And another teacher revealed:

> I like teaching a lot. I like the response from the students. I like having different students, even though I feel stale teaching the same classes year after year, so I try to switch around. The students are always an element of novelty and interest; that human interaction is absolutely fascinating.

The teacher has a personal connection with the student insofar as he or she shares in a covenant of joy. This sharing can occur only when both teacher and student act within the limitations of their expected roles, act within their legitimate places. But the repressed energies are stored from the oppressed states of the actors keep surfacing, resulting in the constant posture of striking back. Even the teachers, however, have sympathy for the underworld the students must occupy. As one teacher presented the case:

> the extortion which I've heard about…[among]…the students. I've heard about these students being victimized. Students are victimized far more than teachers. I don't know how common extortion is in this school, but I know it happens, and the son of some close friends of mine

is deathly afraid of the back gate here because there's a very tough group of Chinese kids that ask for money. He's a little alarmed and wants to fight back, but hasn't yet. The situation is out of balance racially. There's no racial group that has control of anything and there is a lot of feeling, I think, among the kids, one they're really afraid of are the Chinese gangs, who appear to be much more vicious....the conduct that's so outrageous to many of the teachers is routine when it's on the streets....And the people [living] there are the victims of this kind of thing all the time and so that's what I see....That same kind of thing coming here.

In the end, it is the responsibility of the teacher to stand by the school. After all, the teacher is from outside the community, and the school space is like an embassy where the teacher practices diplomacy as an ambassador of prevailing values. One teacher made an internal criticism:

They're not right, many teachers. It's a complicated situation where the teachers are used by certain kinds of students and can't adapt to other kinds of students, so the teachers are sometimes not sympathetic, and after all, most of the teachers don't live in [this section of town]. They live in the suburbs. They wouldn't send their own children to this school. Even worse than the one that's hard on the kids is the one that doesn't give a damn. We have several of those.

The teacher reasons that the students are deserving of their ill fame, rotten through and through:

I'm not prepared in my classes for certain kinds of conduct—and I see it [policy regarding attendance] as an attempt to perhaps placate the black community....I see them and the Chinese kids from the—immigrant kids—and we have a bunch of white kids who are surf skateboarders who cut classes all the time, too. Incredible! The whole thing is that there isn't that kind of peer pressure to excel academically among these groups. It's not there. It's not oriented in the old traditional ways we expect our students to be, so that's where I see the problems. It's a process of acclimatization and they haven't all got it.

SUMMARY

In this chapter I have made the Afrocentric assumption that events occur once and only once. This idea was central to African art forms and became popular as the guiding idea of the jazz tradition. A form of the idea was introduced in sociological methodology by Anselm Strauss and referred to as grounded theory.

Additionally, the methodological strategy of having open-ended conversations promotes the oral tradition of African and African-American culture. African-American culture was understood in terms of myths and rituals that inform lines of action of the participants in black culture.

The historical development of African-American culture reflects essential elements of the culture through its mythic theme. Various members of the professional/managerial class struggle with subjugated black men to produce their socially essential criminality. African-American culture is rife with opposition to the organization and administration of white culture. In the next chapter I shall examine the theoretical understanding of the development, organization, and administration of African Americans.

CHAPTER 4

Colonialism and Black Male Deviance

The social structure of the United States has applied a variety of techniques that may be viewed as a massive interlocking formation of social exchange through a series of operations in which the highest hierarchical position enlarges its interest by using its authoritative gains to buy and sell additional interest on its margin. Essentially, I am describing what Antonio Gramsci referred to as "hegemony." Hegemony is an order by which a certain way of life and thought is dominant in a society in such a way that it informs all tastes, morality, customs, religious and political principles, and all social relations. In the next chapter I intend to clarify theoretical hegemony and how it has been applied to both race and deviance. In this chapter I intend to explicate the issue of deviance with a focus on its chief technique of domination, colonialism. In this sense, it will become clear that the other side of the order of privilege is a structure of hope for a world turned upside down, which I have referred to as contracultural action.

COLONIALISM

The major theories of racial inequality are applicable to the position presented here. I have chosen to use the term "structure" rather than "institutional racism."[1] The term "structure" is broader than "institutional" since it includes all of the social institutions. Of greater significance, as the description presented in the last chapter suggests, the organization of privilege is inextricably tied to the larger social structure in which contradictions emerge both at different sites simultaneously and at different times.

For the moment, I will turn my attention to one type of major theory of racial inequality to support the hypothesis that deviance and race relations structurally work to re-create inequality. The "colonial" model appears to be most fit to explain the relationship of deviance and race. Some will wonder why I do not employ the caste-class theory of racial inequality. There were two major contributions that seem to represent the caste-class school. The first was a series of books published in the 1930s and 1940s under the direction of W. Lloyd Warner. *Deep South* argued that both caste and class operate to limit duties, privileges, obligations, and opportunities socially.[2] Caste, moreover, created rigid barriers between group divisions, like prohibitions against marriage out of the caste. Class was seen as a system that allowed for social mobility. John Dollard, in *Caste and Class in a Southern Town*, pointed to a "high" caste and "low" caste, particularly with respect to "sexual gains." White men could have either caste of women, black or white; black men were limited only to black women.[3]

George Simpson and J. Milton Yinger, oddly enough extensively citing John Delorean, the former automobile producer who was implicated in a government cocaine sting operation, focused on to the economic subordination of race rather than the legitimation of biological and cultural deficiencies and differences.[4] Oliver Cox in *Caste, Class and Race* treated the caste system in India and raised comparisons and contrasts.[5] Nonetheless, the caste-class theories are not broad enough to explain why groups exercise privilege. These theories do not consider the political and cultural characteristics of particular groups. They miss the fact that race is socially constructed in the sense that there is doubt that a pure race exists.

It is problematic to construct a model of the relationship between deviance and race using the caste-class theories because they are ahistorical. While they describe particular relations in the South during particular epochs, they fail to tell us how the relations came about; nor do they tell us why the relations persisted. One possibility is that the relations are contemporary analogues to the system of slavery that predated them. Also, they treat class as "social" at one moment, to explain some aspects of privilege, and as "economic" the next moment. They fail to point out group interests that might be the source of class alignments. The colonial model appears to be a more precise concept when explaining how racial deviance is socially reproduced.

The framework of a colonial interpretation is the worldwide imperialism of specific capitalist nations, including European nations and the United States. It is commonly agreed that the capitalist expansion began in the fifteenth century and resulted in the majority of the nonwhite world becoming victims of the European colonial powers. Usually, social theorists refer to three forms of colonialism: external colonialism, neocolonialism, and internal colonialism. External colonialism involves management of a country's politics and economy by an outside colonial power. There are many forms of this. Neocolonialism is a contemporary form of colonialism in which, through revolution, colonized countries overthrow the colonizers, but the colonizers continue to direct the economies of the colonized through international capitalists and corporations. Finally, when there is a large in-migration of whites into a colonized country or a large in-migration of people of color into a colonial power's country that results in the control and exploitation of non-European groups, the country is internally colonized.

In the United States' internal colonialism, non-European groups are usually residentially segregated, "superexploited" in employment and wealth, and culturally stigmatized, and have some of their leaders co-opted by whites. At the start of the 1960s the colonial model was dormant, but during the 1960s and 1970s several major national groups converged and applied it to explain U.S. inequality. Perhaps the most important single group was the student movement at San Francisco State University, which advanced a coalition ideology grounded in the notion of a "third world." Of course, prior to that time an international anticolonial movement was set in place and was surging at the same time as the civil rights movement in the United States. Between January 1963 and December 1969, twenty-five coups d'etat took place in Africa. Some of them were neocolonial struggles, meaning that while the country had fought an earlier revolution against colonial bondage, it was still fighting class inequities in the "free" states.[6] The assimilation concepts came under question throughout the world, while in the United States the internal colonial idea became a highly prominent concept.

Abroad, Frantz Fanon, a black Algerian psychiatrist, published *The Wretched of the Earth*, in which he pointed to the social cause of all neuroses.[7] Fanon's work combined aspects of Sigmund Freud's theories with aspects of Marxist materialist theories. The neurotic patients he treated during his practice in Algiers presented symptoms that he thought resulted from the colonial relationship between Algeria and France. Fanon thought his psychiatric practice was a revolutionary activity. Albert Memmi, a Tunisian philosopher who had disagreements with Fanon, published *The Colonizer and the Colonized*, which discussed the entropy law of colonialism; the law states that colonialism is self-destructive and will cost mother countries far more than they have earned. He dedicated the American edition to "The American Negro."[8]

In the political atmosphere marked by the Vietnam war, there were several major spokespersons for the internal colonial concept. Eldridge Cleaver, Stokely Carmichael, Tom Hayden, Huey Newton, and Bobby Seale were in the national headlines, supporting the internal colonial postures.[9] Martin Luther King, Jr., also made continual allusions to the internal colonial model without joining the proponents—for example, in a speech at the 1963 March on Washington, when he said: "[From slave time] the Negro still is not free....On a lonely island of poverty in the midst of a vast ocean of material prosperity...still languishes in the corners of American society and finds himself exiled in his own land."

The social science literature also presented the colonial idea; it is best stated by Robert Blauner in *Racial Oppression in America*, a collection of essays that were published between 1969 and 1972.[10] Blauner stressed the colonial concept in order to question the "melting pot" belief that blacks are the latest immigrants to come to the cities and so, the reasoning goes, will eventually move up the ladder as the other immigrants did. Blauner questioned a more fundamental assumption of the assimilation model and the upward mobility privilege that had been achieved by the European immigrants. He pointed out that the entry experiences of the Third World immigrants were significantly different from those of Europeans. He delineated the level of discrimination that was systematic and structural in the experiences of the former. He pointed to black politics in the 1960s, which called for community control, cultural nationalism, and riots as a response to the experiences of the colonized groups.

Robert Allen also developed the colonial perspective in reference to black politics.[11] Mario Barrera, in *Race and Class in the Southwest*, used the concept to account for the history of Chicano inequality, with its features of institutionalized patterns of inequality and the role of political and economic interests. Barrera also discussed the history of race relations theories in the United States and drew insightful connections between them and the history of U.S. expansion. He discussed the material with great clarity and provided a collection of diagrams that systematically present the logic of the dominant theories.[12]

INTERNAL COLONIAL MODEL AND DEVIANCE

The internal colonial model offers a broad range of possibilities to explain U.S. inequality, but there are limitations to its analytical application. Is it possible for the concept to encompass the anthropological nature of humanity and explain the flux in the collective consciousness of labor in varying historical periods? For example, can the internal colonial model explain why some cultures colonize and others do not? Most theories of deviance or race relations do not connect their interpretations to the history of labor. Gunnar Myrdal is an exception, which accounts for the popularity of his contribution.[13] The fact that the colonial theory stresses privilege is important for understanding how one group exploits the labor of other groups. Privilege is created with the labor that produces it.

When we extend our eagerness to see the drama of political and economic interests at play in their entirety, we necessarily must draw a connection to the nuclear family as a form of colonialism in which the interests of the father are accommodated in exchange for his "protection." We may make an additional step down on our theoretical ladder and assume that the social psychology of individuals is illuminated through the use of the colonial model, similar to the way that Fanon saw the social causes of neurosis. As in Fanon's work, the concern of such a perspective is the resistance of a personality struggling against social and cultural inequality. This fundamental assumption becomes clear from an analysis of the structural organization of myths and rituals of African-American culture.

The theories of delinquency have paid considerable attention to the "class" problem. Nonetheless, scholars of deviance avoid the use of a Marxist interpretation of class, which stresses the relationship of groups to the relations of production. (The class delinquency theories were grounded in the concept of anomie, so they paid little attention to class interest.) However, they pay a great deal of attention to structure. The major representatives of the anomie theorists are Albert Cohen, Robert K. Merton, and Richard Cloward and Lloyd Ohlin.[14]

Cohen applied the framework of Merton's anomie and structure theory. Merton pointed to the disjunction between culturally prescribed goals and the social structure that limits access to them. The limited opportunities are particularly intense for lower-class youngsters, who have little chance of gaining success. Cohen pointed out that the lower-class person lacks personal characteristics for success as a result of "class-linked" socialization patterns. A combination of barriers to success and class-linked personal inadequacies causes status frustration. Cloward and Ohlin placed a greater emphasis on the barriers to success.

Cohen enlarged Merton's theme by suggesting that the delinquent subculture offers a solution to the status problem for lower-class males who cannot achieve status in the structural way. Lower-class males use alternative subcultural ways to get that status. Cohen wrote that youths who break completely with the middle-class moral order do so because of "no moral inhibition on the free expression of aggression against the sources of [their] frustration."[15] He felt that breaking the "respectable norms is characterized by irrational, malicious, and unaccountable hostility." He concluded that we can make sense of such behavior only when we see its function of reassuring the subject against the inner threat to his defenses, as well as meeting the external situation on its own terms.

I have several reservations about this perspective. The central point is that these arguments use a make-believe definition of class. They treat class and stratification as if they were one and the same thing, which raises interesting theoretical problems. Because the aforementioned sociologists accept the stratification class concept, they are operating with several obvious "domain assumptions": that lower-class males have internalized the theorists' social norms, including success goals, and that they are motivated to achieve them; that the lack of opportunity for the males is society's fault; that the high level of status frustration is due to the disjunction of means and ends; and that the lower-class males create a delinquent subculture as an answer to their status frustration.

In contrast, why not suggest that the African-American lower-class males have not adopted the norms of the middle class because those norms oppose their community traditions and cultures?[16] There is no logical or scientific reason to think that some inherent feature of the dominant culture's value system is supreme. There are, however, logical reasons to think that African Americans will view the U.S. system of norms and values as illegitimate. Futhermore, to suggest that African-American men have made a rational and "respectable" choice to be deviant overlooks the history of the structural containment of African Americans. How, then, is it possible to experience status frustration in a social system in which sectors of the population are at best ambivalent about its norms and values?

There is another disturbing feature of the status-frustration argument; namely, status-frustration theorists overlook the role of the dominant group in socializing individuals to behave violently. Think of the many commercials, movies, and programs on television that communicate the acceptability of violence; think of the political pundits in both electronic and print media who call for the death of Saddam Hussein or Fidel Castro without compunction. Futhermore, the schools and the universities are the repositories of the socialization into violence through their sports programs, particularly football and basketball programs. The social rewards for acting violently, as well as acting-out violence, are celebrated throughout society as normal masculinity. The stratification class theorists have adopted the theme of frustration-aggression because they have overlooked the political role of theoretical work in oppressing the poor.

The stratification class theorists sought the class emphasis as a reaction to the differential-association theory, which, in turn, arose as a reaction to the ecological view. The ecological view generally held that lower-class communities are inhabited by heterogeneous, economically depressed, and highly mobile populations. Differences in value orientation give rise to confusion and uncertainty on the part of the young. They do not internalize normal moral patterns, and the result is that delinquency and criminality develop in them.[17] The differential-association theory emphasizes exposure of black males to criminal values in the high-delinquency areas. It sees deviance as the result of the excess of definitions favorable to violation of the law over definitions favoring conformity to the law.[18] Walter Miller contributed to the status-frustration theories. Although he should not be considered a status-frustration theorist, his contention is that lower-class deviance is directly a product of a distinct lower-class culture, rather than of the exposure and reaction to the middle-class value system.[19] But the stratification class theorists failed to revise their notion of class, accepting the class definition tradition from the competing stratification and pathology theories. It is here that I differ with the former. For my purposes, Marx's notion of class adds more clarity to the explanation of the reproduction of African-American male deviance.

MARXIST CLASS AND STRATIFICATION CLASS

Marx's concern with class inequality and class conflict was not connected to an interest in describing how societies are stratified, or how rank differences among actors affect the structure and functioning of the social system and of specific institutions, or how position in the social hierarchy determines individual or collective behavior. These are all legitimate sociological concerns; the problems with these theories are well known among social scientists. Marx's class analysis has the advantage in the explanation of deviance because it is designed to explain structural change in a society characterized by the capitalist mode of production.

Marx developed a dichotomous scheme wherein two classes, owners and producers, are defined by their opposed functions in the productive process. While his view comes close to the class-linked analysis, there is a significant contrast in their purposes. For the stratification theorists, class is designed to map out the pattern of inequality in a society at a given point in time so that they may empirically test hypotheses about deviant behavior. "Class" is used to denote an aggregate of persons who happen to have similar amounts of one or more "deviant" attributes. Ralf Dahrendorf wrote that the term "stratum" might be more accurate in reference to the stratification class concept:

> Whenever classes are defined by factors which permit the construction of a hierarchical continuum, they are wrongly defined; i.e., the term has been applied wrongly. Status, ranking by others, self-ranking, style of life, similar economic conditions, and income level are all factors which define social strata but not social classes. However one may interpret, extend, or improve Marx, classes in his sense are clearly not layers in a hierarchical system of strata differentiated by gradual distinctions....Class is always a category for the purposes of the analysis of the dynamics of social conflict and its structural roots and as such it has to be separated strictly from stratum as a category for purposes of describing hierarchical systems at a given point in time.[20]

It is not my purpose to explain here why U.S. social scientists have not taken Marx's definition of class seriously; why they have chosen to index and class-link their observations. Marx was concerned with differential property relations to the means of production when he used the concept of class. His concept of class is inextricably wedded to his understanding of the fundamental institutional features of capitalist production. It is not just a label but expresses the involved interaction of meaning he uncovered from the opposing dichotomous standards.

If we say that some "deviants" are of this and that stratified class, we will be asked, "What is the structural source of these classes?" The stratification class theorists answer that it is the outcome of the individual ability to command rewards for individual marketable skills and services available to them. Merton and Cohen see society as a distribution system that allocates rewards in response to economic flux in supply and demand in the market for talent, trained ability, and hard work. This cannot explain the relationship between race and deviance; nor does this theory explain how it developed. These theorists blame the victim for lack of ability or talent and, in a subtle way, they imply that inequality is needed to attract and retain the qualified people for good positions.[21]

Marx's conception of class is not an objective thing; it is a figurative idea as a medium for understanding conflict. In fact, he used two class terms: "social class" and "political class." His social class is probably closer to the stratification class definition. Political class was used more often in respect to organization. But in either case, central to his concept of class was the idea of exploitation at the point of production.

Marx used "exploitation" to refer to a situation in which the surplus product of a society is controlled by a group that effectively excludes the actual producers of that surplus product. Exploitation is the resistance against democracy. For Marx, it was the method of exploitation that distinguished the privileged class under capitalist organization from other forms of social arrangements. Marx pointed out that all societies have had conflict and exploitation. Marx and

Frederick Engels wrote: "Freeman and slave, patrician and plebeian, lord and serf, guild-master and journeyman, in a word, oppressor and oppressed, stood in constant opposition to one another, carried on an uninterrupted, now hidden, now open fight, a fight that each time ended, either in a revolutionary reconstruction...or in common ruin."[22] For Marx, class was always the appropriation of the surplus products. Capitalist exploitation was different because "it has pitilessly torn asunder the motley feudal ties that bound man to his 'natural superiors,' and has left no other bond between man and man than naked self-interest, than callous 'cash payment.'"[23]

A discussion of Marx's theory of class is far too complicated to take up in its entirety here. Nonetheless, this brief appraisal brings focus to the concern with the class issue in the deviance literature. Some contemporary Marxist theorists, neo-Marxists, post-Marxists, and Marxologists are dissatisfied with the original class concept and have attempted to refine it, making it more applicable to an analysis of modern capitalist organization.

Erik Wright presented one contemporary view in "Class Boundaries in Advanced Capitalist Societies."[24] Wright found three major classes of society in advanced capitalist systems: capitalists, workers, and petty bourgeoisie. He argued that each of the major class interests contradicted the interests of the other classes. He stressed conflict on the job over the opposing interests and roles that the workers played. Barbara and John Ehrenreich wrote "The Professional-Managerial Class," in which they described the classical class distinctions, but argued that a "new" class emerged during the late nineteenth century and grew primarily through the college and university system, producing a group of professionals/managers. For the Ehrenreichs, the professional/managerial class comprises people who work with their minds for a salary to reproduce capitalist culture and its relations. While their class is not essential to bring about the capitalist relations, it functions to control, shape, and regulate economic, political, social, and cultural relations.[25]

CLASS AND RACE

The scheme of class boundaries developed by Wright and the Ehrenreichs best explains the reproduction of black deviance. The Marxists, nonetheless, have severely overlooked the race variable in the general discussions of the connections between race and class. It should not be expected that race has been seriously treated in the deviance literature; it was overlooked by the liberals and the Marxists alike. For the most part, liberal scholars treated black culture as a deviant form of American culture. The civil rights movement in the 1950s and the unrest of the 1960s, with the attendant rise in a commitment to black nationalism, resulted in U.S. reformers giving more attention to race. The Left became involved in a broader discussion of the objective history of the "Negro Question."

In 1963, the Socialist Workers Party (SWP) claimed the black nationalist movement held erroneous perspectives on revolution. Prior to that time they supported Leon Trotsky's interpretation of the revolutionary struggle, which argued that support for black separatism should be based on black concentration in the U.S. trade union movement. The SWP distributed a pamphlet titled "Leon Trotsky on Black Nationalism," in which he pointed to the persistent black language as an indication of an embryonic nation analogous to the more backward nations of tsarist Russia, and in which he advocated that revolutionists should properly struggle for self-determination. The SWP had used the concept "revolutionary integration" for the "black belt," realizing that the race issue had not been adequately codified in the National Socialist movement. Much disagreement was aroused among the various socialist groups. The *Spartacist* editorial board argued in July 1963 that "The Negro people are not a nation, rather they are an oppressed race-color caste, in the main comprising the most exploited layer of the American working class. From this condition the long sequence has come that the Negro struggle for freedom has had, historically, the aim of integration into an egalitarian society."[26]

All of this debate on the landscape of a socialist movement consistently betrayed African-American trust. This betrayal was analogous to the betrayal by Stalin of the international socialist community, when Soviet state capitalism reaped profits assisting Mussolini in the war against Ethiopia. Added to this sense of betrayal was the opportunism of the socialists in the United States in reference to the Scottsboro case. Simply stated, the socialists pursued a policy of secret infiltration of black organizations, which they referred to as "boring from within." It became clear that the boring from within failed to develop a "national minorities" socialist tradition. Rather, the socialists themselves became more dogmatic in their practical applications of Marxism. Even Lenin and his advocates pursued the dogmatic logics.[27]

Much of the Marxist scholarship on race is dealt with in an insensitive way. There is no Marxist theory on race and race relations that flows in a succinct, analytical way. Cedric Robinson's work represents a major attempt, but he has been virtually ignored in mainstream Marxist theory building.[28] One school of Marxist orientation holds that U.S. capitalism no longer has the obsessive need to perpetuate racial divisions. Eugene Genovese pointed out that a strong relationship between racism and capitalism existed, particularly during the nineteenth century, but since World War I the relationship has become less salient.[29]

Other Marxist scholars who have taken the race problem under consideration have asked questions about what processes result in blacks remaining at the bottom of the U.S. stratification system. Paul Baren and Paul Sweezy pointed to three groups of factors: (1) private interests that might gain from cheap labor, ghetto landlords, white workers who do not have to worry about black competition; (2) race prejudice, which functions to release frustration and hostility that arises out of the class system among white society; (3) declining demands for unskilled and semiskilled labor.[30] Michael Reich similarly argued that the existing capitalist class benefits greatly from racial inequality.[31]

Oliver Cox, in *Caste, Class and Race*, contributed a widely recognized argument that the relationship between race and class was a colonial one. Originally published in 1948, the book argued that contemporary race relations grew out of the colonial systems developed by the Europeans after the fifteenth century. Cox argued that racism was an ideology contributing to the function of the colonial system by keeping labor and resources in the position to be exploited. He contended that racism grew out of the need of the planter class, which was the ruling class, to keep freed blacks exploitable. To accomplish this, policy had to be generated. Therefore, in Cox's view the capitalist class was served by the race ideology in two ways: (1) it provided a surplus labor pool and (2) it created tensions among workers.[32]

With respect to the race and class theories, a growing number of sociologists are concerned with labor-market segmentation and class fractions. The concept of a dual labor market is the basis of the market-segmentation theorists. This group of researchers conceived two caste economies: one for mainstream America (primary), another for the "wretched" minorities (secondary). While the primary labor market provided jobs with security and mobility, the minority workers were forced to take seasonal work and other low-security, high-turnover, and dead-end jobs in the secondary labor market.[33]

The labor-segmentation theorists come closest to my interpretation of the creation of African-American deviance. They broadened the concept of class and considered other personal characteristics related to inequality. They pointed to the interest of the capitalist class in stratifying the work force through the factory system. The secondary labor market, in short, includes high-risk groups like minorities, youth, women, elderly, and gays and lesbians. However, only a few of these researchers have been interested in sexual and racial segmentation.

Nicos Poulantzas suggested that class fractions needed more attention. A fraction is a further division within a stratum-class hierarchy. Class fractions account for particular role differentiation related to political and ideological relations. Poulantzas primarily focused upon fractions in the hierarchical occupational structure, rather than variables like age, race, and sex.[34]

The conception of race and class in this book is tied to the earlier explanations, but extends them because of my concern with the paternalistic/race interests that stretch through every form of social relations, from the earliest forms of social organization to the contemporary late capitalist organization. My interest will become clearer in drawing the connection between Marx's social class and Freud's object consciousness. Learning to appreciate things in the environment is embedded in the early personality of individuals. Individuals select different things for the investment of emotional significance from an array of activities, objects, and ideas (cathexis). Cathexis occurs with familial objects as well as with collective class objects—all of which are in themselves ideological. By this, I mean they are soaked with interests through and through. This perspective allows examination of deviancy in ways that are not usually pursued. The perspective avoids the liberal stratum- and class-linked problems with ideology and equally avoids the Marxist elitist interpretations that cast Marxist theorists as priests of the revolution. As has been discussed, the Marxists have promoted forms of supremacist logic in both practice and theory. In the examination of power in U.S. history, it is important, as Michael Omi and Howard Winant have written, to conceptualize race as a fundamental causal variable.[35]

There is an irony in my perspective on African-American deviance. The sociological literature related to African Americans has tended to treat black culture itself as deviant. Mainstream sociology legislated black immorality at a time when it was severely needed for capitalist interests. Let us turn our attention there for a moment.

RACIAL OPPRESSION AND DEVIANCE

Two central themes that have appeared over and over again in sociology are humanism and value neutrality. These ideas are deeply embedded in Western philosophical history as well, and they emerge in the field of sociology as the ideal ethical laws. The arguments are apparent: since sociology is the discipline of human action, the objective study of human relationships, value judgments are not supposed to enter into conclusions of sociological study. Of course, white men of power were responsible for writing what they considered to be objective sociology. Their value judgment of the objective became problematical, since they argued that no value judgments were to enter into their scientific approach.

An instance of this kind of contradiction appeared in the sociological literature in which the researchers' insistence was to classify blacks in a way to assist the powers that be in their interest to sustain their supremacy. The black scholars responded that aside from the gathering, classification, organization, and verification of data, the dimension of re-creating supremacist logics was a matter of fact.[36]

To suggest that sociologists make value judgments in their work provokes a concern. Why is it in the interest of sociologists to do so? We may suppose that each researcher will be motivated by particular circumstances, and so the thinking is that differences in motive will range from unmindfulness to callous calculation. The value-free doctrine's objective meaning was summed up in Alvin Gouldner's now famous words from his *Coming Crisis of Western Sociology*:

> The value-free doctrine is useful both to those who want to escape from the world and those who want to escape into it. It is useful to those young, or not so young, men who live off sociology rather than for it, and who think of sociology as a way of getting ahead in the world by providing them with neutral techniques that may be sold on the open market to any buyer. From such a standpoint, there is no reason why one cannot sell his knowledge to spread a disease just as freely as he can

fight it. Indeed, some sociologists have no hesitation about doing market research designed to sell more cigarettes, although well aware of the implications of recent cancer research. In brief, the value-free doctrine of social science was sometimes used to justify the sale of one's talents to the highest bidder and is, far from new, a contemporary version of most ancient sophistry.[37]

If this is the case, central to the value judgments sociologists promote is the opportunity for them to do so while having the privilege of a position (job) and publication outlets. As a field of study, sociology is a social relation involved in making culture. Culture functions to assist in the reproduction of economic relations. The economic relations appear in sociology as an extension of the domestic colonial interest in capitalist expansion, and an extension of white patriarchy's will to power. Although it is commonly argued that sociology should be kept separate from politics, including not only ideological beliefs but also power systems and power struggles, how can this be done? The cosmetic line drawn between politics and knowledge has resulted in real reaction from the intellectual community with the rise and demise of the "New Left" and ethnic, sex, and race studies.

This fact became clear for the liberals on Thursday, May 16, 1969, in Berkeley, California, in connection with the events surrounding the "Third World" mood. Preceding the May events, various minority student groups had begun a colonial interpretation of their social positions. They debated whether the Third World concept helped them to explain U.S. inequality. That morning about fifty street people gathered in People's Park for a demonstration to take over the 250 x 450-foot lot. They had suffered abuse at the hands of the Berkeley Police more than a month earlier. The university was determined to reaffirm its legal rights of ownership. For one thing, the people were considered dramatically outside of the prevailing order, powerless, by the corporate order because they were labeled "street people." The university was proclaimed in a "state of extreme emergency" on February 5, 1969, by Governor Ronald Reagan because the "Third World Strike" confirmed the rebellious mood and the justification to maintain order. About 200 police from Berkeley, Alameda County, and the campus arrived between 5:00 and 6:00 A.M. The police were equipped with nonlethal and lethal weaponry. They forcibly erected an eight-foot fence around the park by noon.

Meanwhile, a rally on the University of California campus in front of Sproul Hall convened with approximately 3,000 people. The president-elect of the student body spoke; he was later indicted for inciting a riot. The crowd moved toward the police at one point during his speech. The police fired tear gas, causing the crowd to scatter. The crowd threw bottles and rocks. At another location, a city car was burned. More police came. Somebody threw a rock. Police fired into the crowd. James Rector died, and another man was blinded.

Before the day's work had been done, more than ninety people had been injured by the police. Tear gas hovered over the campus, and the main library took at least six buckshot and three .38-caliber bullets.

The chancellor of the university, Roger Heyns, was out of town. His principal vice chancellor had gone to a regents' meeting in Los Angeles. The regents responded to the events by announcing, "It is of paramount importance that law and order be upheld." The governor said that the street people took the lot as an "excuse" to riot. A city councilman said that the lot had been a "hippie Disneyland freak show" while the street people used it.

The next day, 2,000 National Guardsmen appeared in full battle dress, armed with the usual weapons of war. Helicopters were in the air. Berkeley was on fire! Berkeley was occupied! In some odd way the spirit of the Third World Strike and the outcast street people congealed into what the authorities called "the senseless violence." Nonetheless, the liberal community thought it over. To them, the park had been a haven for drug addicts, sex fiends, criminals, and revolutionaries. Now the police were "clumsy and inefficient," and the people were invited to negotiate through a responsible committee. After all, a man had died.[38]

The reappraisal unsurprisingly appeared in the sociological literature. Jerome Skolnick cited William Kornhauser on the reappraisal of the definitions of collective violence: "The readiness to assimilate all politics to either order or violence implies a very narrow notion of order and a very broad notion of violence...what is violent action in one period of history becomes acceptable conflict at a later time."[39] Skolnick redressed the analysis of collective behavior with the broader conflict definition of violence. After the experience of the Berkeley occupation such a revision could be advanced.

The situation at Berkeley occurred one year after the May 1968 events at two French universities, Nanterre (near Paris) and the Sorbonne. Classes and examinations were boycotted, and eventually there was a workers' strike that questioned the whole mode of social organization in France. While the French situation had little impact on state power, which was the initial goal of the students and workers, a contribution was made to the social sciences. Two Frenchmen who emerged as theoretical leaders were Louis Althusser and Michel Foucault. They raised a number of important points for oppressed groups to consider: (1) institutions in the society interact with one another to reproduce the oppression of targeted groups; (2) the educational institution is the chief ideological machine in late capitalist societies; (3) the ruling ideology that needs greatest attention is the assertion that individual choice and responsibility are factual; (4) it is necessary to provide agency for underdogs so that they may speak in their own voice.

The reappraisal of the traditional concepts questions the conventional external view of underdog groups, and it questions the victim-blaming by ideologues of the status quo. With the underdogs, African Americans have purportedly been objectively studied, defined, and explained. It is in the objective (passive) tradition that blacks have been studied in sociology. The tradition, interestingly enough, illuminates how whites, even radicals, oppress the voice of minorities by attempting to speak for them.

THE DEEPEST, DARKEST SUBCULTURE

The central concept of the objective tradition is the idea of "subculture." The idea implies a political distinction between deviants, subjugated social classes, racial and ethnic groups, and the "normal" population. In a way the "sub" prefix is a sociological euphemism for counterideological values. In other words, the mainstream values, from the point of view of culture makers, are not classified as such, which means that the values of the subjugated groups are not legitimate. The use of the "sub" prefix in sociological literature refers to some conception of individuals who have chosen particularistic rather than universal values. The reasons behind their choice are explained in various ways by sociologists. However, the political implications of the term are unavoidable. One political dimension is also apparent in the concept of "suburban," which implies environments of particularistic values rather than "normal," "universal," and "rational" values. Futhermore, sociological language is often associated with its class interest. Concepts like the "sub" prefix function to buttress the established order. The "sub" prefix also has been consistent with the rise of ideological reaction, posed as alternative conceptions of race. By using the "sub" prefix, limitations are placed on what may be said in a political system where majorities rule. In fact, the subculture concepts underwrite the claims of Nathan Glazer and Daniel Patrick Moynihan that black culture is nonexistent.

The long-standing claim of traditional sociology was the agreement that black culture does not exist.[40] The assertion was that blacks have no distinctive collective creations, no separate group patterns, and no shared traditions of their own. The view is found in sociologist Nathan Glazer and urbanologist Daniel Patrick Moynihan's book *Beyond the Melting Pot*: "It is not possible for Negroes to view themselves as other ethnic groups viewed themselves because—and this is key to much of the Negro world—the Negro is only an American and nothing else. He has no values and culture to guard and protect."[41]

After fierce reaction from minority and minority-aligned scholars, Glazer and Moynihan revised their conclusions in a new edition, in which they contended that they did not really mean what they wrote in their first presentation. They pointed to their original error being grounded in "the authoritative scholars, among them E. Franklin Frazier." Frazier had been one of the most celebrated African-American sociologists. White men of power often look for perspectives from within the ranks of black people to promote or excuse supremacist logics.

Moynihan and Glazer claimed to have ignored "African survivals," and they acknowledged that the new contributions of "Afro-American and Black studies" challenged their generalizations. They admitted that they overlooked African history. Their new ideas were framed along the same lines as the pluralist observation that very little assimilation had happened in the "melting pot." But, ironically, Glazer and Moynihan condemned the separatist view that argued for "racial purity" in social institutions. They concluded that "Out of American origins, one can create a distinctive subculture." The subculture could account for organization that might or might not have been connected to African heritage.[42]

The sociological view that black Americans have no specific culture of their own was originated by the early apologists. The apologists justified the slave trade on the basis of that philosophy. The modern liberal version of this position is found in the Swedish political economist Gunnar Myrdal's *An American Dilemma*.[43] The book was written during the Great Depression and was a cultural production in the development of the justification for World War II. Myrdal's concern was to treat "the Negro problem." His book reveals the interesting consciousness of part of the liberal mind, which was torn in ideological contradiction. His work attests to the fact that liberals were confounded by African Americans. The book might have been more accurately titled *White Dilemma*. In fact, although Myrdal tells us that we are going to explore a "problem deep in the hearts" of Americans, we are not introduced to that subject until after nearly 900 pages of the book, where finally we are in "The Negro Community." He declares: "American Negro culture is not something independent of general American culture. It is a distorted development, or a pathological condition, of the general American culture."[44] Myrdal reported, and paused to remark on, the instability of the black family, the personality difficulties, the high black crime rate, the poverty of black recreation, the tendency toward emotion among blacks, and on and on. At the beginning of the book we are told that the author is committed to neutrality and humanity; by the close of the book we feel that we have been to another all-white-power political session. The subjects have been transformed into deviant objects by Myrdal; his scholarship is brutally inhumane, despite the fact that his work is required reading for anyone in a graduate program related to race relations and is considered progressive.

Myrdal equated culture with whiteness, and this resulted in his treating race prejudice and strata ("class") prejudice as if they were the same thing. Because Myrdal was particularly optimistic about the mobility possibilities in the black American experience and particularly certain about America's move toward equality, he overlooked the concepts of caste and race prejudice. Myrdal's and his students' optimism concerning race relations has not proved to be justified. Racism as an embracing ideology has remained as the key organizational theme in this society. Racism is empirically identifiable in the culture through the visible conflicts in linguistic patterns and mythological systems. Liberalism's "realistic view" of assimilation is plagued with an adherence to self-righteousness and self-importance. The apologists' notions are still lurking in the liberal mind, which results in liberals like Myrdal being hopelessly white. To be hopelessly white is to be incapable of recognizing white privilege and power.

E. Franklin Frazier is the respected authority from whom Myrdal drew his foundation theme of nonexistent black culture. Frazier argued that the experiences of passage and slavery altogether eliminated black culture. He thought that only a minority of the black population maintained authentic cultural patterns; eventually even those were displaced: the mixed bloods became a "false" middle-class hiding behind exaggerated pretensions, and the rural folk became debased urban dwellers.[45]

Frazier almost resorted to name-calling to point out how degrading black social institutions had become. He concluded that the blacks' moral and emotional commitment to their institutions had been completely destroyed. The families lost cohesion and now existed in disorganization, where the individual was demoralized, breaking the restrictions against "immoral" sex conduct.[46]

Frazier was a black American sociologist and professor at black Howard University. His works are beautifully written, and his ethnographic data are quite engaging. His shame and guilt are equally engaging. His constant fascination is with the waste of human life, with immorality, delinquency, desertion, and broken homes. In the last chapter of his *The Negro Family in the United States,* "Retrospect and Prospect," he concludes that the black slave mother passed on the traditions of the white institutions that she had acquired from being the "protectress" of the master's children and that gave rise to the maternal family organization. He explicitly states his specific interest: "That the Negro has found within the patterns of the white man's culture a purpose in life and the significance for his striving which have involved sacrifices for his children and the curbing of individual desires and impulses indicates that he has become assimilated to a new mode of life."[47]

It is not hard to understand Frazier's "black skin, white man" interpretation of black American culture; but today we realize that, through interrogation, it is possible to discover the "black skin, white mask" reality. Frazier joined the forces of cultural imposition and confirmed the disorganization and deviance of black life by failing to recognize a legitimate cultural conflict. He repeatedly stressed the immorality of black life, as though the black form of consciousness were some dismissed part of humanity imbued with the tragic yoke of inferiority. Futhermore, a school of assimilationists followed his line of reasoning, "waiting for Santa Claus" in the midst of "Santa Claws," expecting blacks to emulate immigrant models, pulling themselves up by the bootstraps.[48]

The assimilationist construction of social reality requires questioning. Each immigrant group and each minority or "colonized" group had its own set of experiences. We may say much the same of each deviant group.[49] Many Irish came to America primarily in the face of British colonialism, and a minority came as a result of Ireland's potato famine. Many east European Jews came in the face of pogroms; they were refugees who fled in family units with no intention of returning to Europe. Others came as lodgers, with the intention of returning home after their American adventure, and they spent little energy investing in language, culture, and institutions. The early immigrations from China, Italy, Japan, and Mexico were primarily of this type, and can be compared to the modern Puerto Rican migration patterns. There were others who came to America in positions of privilege. The Germans and the Scandinavians are examples of immigrants who acted on privileged information and treatment when they settled in America. Others were forced and subjugated in the arrival experience. The African Americans were denied their national identities; their languages, cultures, institutions, and religious beliefs were subjected to systematic destruction by the plantation system. The Native Americans were forced to live under conquerors who perpetuated migration instability and the decimation of them. Each racial and ethnic group must be examined individually to view the roots of oppression and privilege.

Even after the realization of the political aspect of both assimilationist and pluralist thought, a group of "realists" still attempted to classify black American culture as deviant, needing special treatment. The realists sought to present themselves as willing colonizers with political developments that offered "poverty programs" for the poor under the banner of liberalism. But what prevented African Americans from respecting the programs was a black culture which recognized that white generosity had its limits. Blacks commonly viewed the programs as a way for whites to create jobs for themselves by defining African Americans as deviants needing the special and dominating attention of whites. In fact, the brilliance of John F. Kennedy's campaign for the presidency was the strategy to use the poverty programs in the context of federal machine politics. But, as Frances Piven and Richard Cloward made sufficiently clear, Kennedy reversed every promise made to the blacks to accomplish his presidential victory.[50]

The central point of the realists was the repetition of Weberian stratification theory applied to black Americans. They paid little attention to Marx's theory of class. The caste-class and ethnic-class systems were the tools they employed, depending on whether the blacks lived in the North or the South. Realist intellectual influence culminated in the development of a stratificational approach, in which each class was supposed to have its own distinctive lifestyle and subculture. The stratum that blacks were assigned repeats the real class interest of the scholarship: that they are "pathological," "deviant," and "disorganized," while the higher (white) strata are "healthy," "stable," and "respectable."

Melville J. Herskovits differed from the realists by drawing connections between "Africanisms" of the past and the unique cultural patterns of African Americans in his now famous book, *The Myth of the Negro Past*.[51] Herkovits contradicted the prevailing opinion of black inferiority, but his work suffered diminished potency in the face of the pluralist, assimilationist, and realist positions. In fact, the trend in the social sciences was to overlook the racial category, preferring to look at class relations.

The leading work in the tradition of the class explanation of racial inequality was *Black Metropolis*, by St. Clair Drake and Horace Cayton.[52] The authors focused on urban blacks in Chicago from the Great Depression to World War II. They treated the "great migration" of blacks from the South to the North as if the blacks were a homogeneous social group. The internal differences in the black communities were conceptualized only in terms of class, omitting the synthesis that would best explain the peculiar black presence. Their caste-class theme followed the Euro-American view of economic order and morality, and from that point of departure, they assumed the black experience necessarily reflected similar values. Any references to culture in the index are to American culture. Their error was influenced by the white male canon of social investigation. It served the purpose of reducing black folkways, mores, and sanctions to the overbearing cultural regulations of the republican and Puritan ethics, while simultaneously reducing Euro-American contact with aspects of a black and elite university-trained reality.

Drake and Cayton distorted ethnicity and race by treating the two as if they were synonymous with social class. They viewed segregation as the conscious act of black Americans to accommodate the "cherished" lifestyles of the white middle class. Because black lifestyles depart significantly from the values adhered to by the white middle class, blacks segregate themselves. This thinking made it easy for the social sciences to promote the "low-class" arguments of poverty. These arguments were called cultural poverty theories. Cultural poverty theories diminished racial and ethnic concerns by focusing on a new poor-man lifestyle stereotype for blacks. The reaction came quickly from critical social scientists like William Ryan, who wrote: "So what?"

Suppose the mythical oil millionaire behaves in an unrefined "lower class" manner, for example. What difference does that make as long as he owns oil wells? Is the power of the Chairman of the Ways and Means Committee in the state legislature diminished or enhanced in any way by his taste in clothing or music? And suppose every single poor family in America set as its long-range goal that its sons and daughters would get a Ph.D.—who would pay the tuition?…The simplest—and at the same time, the most significant—proposition in understanding poverty is that it is caused by the lack of money.[53]

The ideology of cultural poverty did not cover the sore of American justice. Racism eats away at U.S. political organization; the evidence is overwhelming in the national experience. Black expression, in the sense of the "nigger" kind, became a broken Jacob's ladder that needed only a few rung adjustments to fulfill its function for the liberals. Once again, in the adjustment process, black culture was subjugated by the culture makers in social scientists' garb.

The misuse of the class concept in these traditions does not mean that persons in those traditions were suggesting that class is an unimportant variable in the explanation of racial oppression and deviance. As stressed earlier, the Marxist view of class seems best suited for analysis of African Americans for the previously stated reasons. This discussion of the class concept merely highlights the political role social scientists play in the economic organization that re-creates inequality in U.S. race relations. It also points to the real misery people experience as a result of the imperial arrangement that appears to be centrally organized around race in the world class order.

Earlier I mentioned that Herskovits departed from the mainstream view of treating black culture as a deviant subculture. In fact, his work engendered a movement grounded in the idea of cultural relativism. The cultural relativists attempted to counter the ethnocentrism of the mainstream doctrines by pointing to ethnic distinctiveness and divergence from mainstream norms. They countered the moral judgments of the privileged objectivists. Extreme relativism is synonymous with value neutrality. Yet ultimately, extreme relativism fails because it does not embrace the poverty and suffering of the victims of inequality, race prejudice, or deviance. Extreme relativists fail to point to the intended acts of an idealized black culture; they merely describe black culture in more attractive ways than those previously presented.

One cultural relativist was Charles Keil, whose study *Urban Blues* was an ethnography of the urban blues singer as culture hero. Keil stressed the urban blues singer's value system: the blues singer emphasizes "trouble," "flashy clothes," and "sexuality." He asserted that the hero was a mythic cultural model of maleness that was highly valued by the poor and was relatively independent of the mainstream cultural view. Keil clearly was attempting to establish a black cultural tradition.[54] He failed, however, to mention the possible political significance of blues production.

The major reaction to Keil came from Elliot Leibow, in *Tally's Corner*.[55] Once again, black culture was viewed from the "problem" perspective. Leibow saw pathology in black culture, related to the inability of black men to earn enough money to support a family. He pointed to a purported weakness in black men: they exploited their women. He concluded:

> From this perspective, the streetcorner man does not appear as a carrier of an independent cultural tradition. His behavior appears not so much as a way of realizing the distinctive goals and values of his own subculture, or of conforming to its models, but rather as his way of trying to achieve many of the goals and values of the larger society, of failing to do this, and of concealing his failure from others and from himself as best he can.[56]

Leibow associated his study with the issues most often raised in the history of conservatism. What has always been important for conservatives has been the "natural order" of inheritance rights, which they associated with the "natural" organization of nuclear families. The conservatives argued that privilege must be inherited and passed down from generation to generation. Leibow overlooked the political significance of his culture study of the black street-corner problem. The supremacist logic of his argument was clear, but nowhere in the study did Leibow discuss the political function of racism in the perception of his subjects' alleged actions as "concealing failure."

The next major study of black culture came from a Swedish social scientist imported to study black communities. The study was published as *Soulside* by Ulf Hannerz, who attempted a pragmatic liberal perspective to determine what was different about ghetto life.[57] Hannerz was careful to call attention to the fact that the ghetto personality was not monolithic. He claimed to have focused on the central tendency of style of the peculiar community. He was concerned only with differences, not with similarities. In fact, if he encountered similarities he discarded them from consideration in testing his hypothesis.

Hannerz concluded that black culture is "ghetto-specific culture," and that the cultural poverty point of view was best suited to fit black behavior. His concept of ghetto-specific culture is similar to the concept of the "culture of poverty," which Oscar Lewis and Walter Miller saw as the central contributing factor to delinquency and deviance.[58] The ingredients were the same, too: the conflict between the sexes; dominance of women; the fear of trouble in the environment; interest in dance, music, and religion; and hostility toward white America.

Moreover, Hannerz's substantive interpretation of particular phenomena is flawed. For instance, his interpretation of "playing the dozens" was that the boys disrespected the mother image.[59] He believed that the boys were fighting for their honor. It might be equally cogently argued that they were fighting for the honor of their mothers. Furthermore, the function of the dozens game might enhance guilt management about the fact that their mothers were also victims of the domination and so were susceptible to public dominating experiences. Rather than acknowledge the possible confidence-building function of the dozens for black manhood, Hannerz preferred to interpret the rituals in terms of the pathology of black men. He turned a beautiful ritual into a sordid deficit; he transformed a fortune into a misfortune. His study is a brutal explanation of black life and its meanings. The interest that goes protected in the technical language of his art is doomed to failure when confronted by the counterperspective of the black community.

The pattern of assigning black culture to pathology and deviancy status gave rise to a concern for the linguistic patterns of African Americans. Those studies created the category of "Black English." The tone of the language studies was in the tradition of Herskovits's work, but the language studies extended the pathology analysis to both the linguistic and the body-language interpretations. The linguists were more sensitive to black cultural expressions, although their reasoning highlighted the "primitiveness" and "exotic pleasure" in black expressions. For instance, one study of black cultural time during this period was titled "Time and Cool People," as if to suggest some leisurely anti-work value in a pejorative sense.[60] Many of the studies appeared with words like "rapping," "jiving," "down," and "jungle" in their titles. For the most part, these studies posed the black culture issue in terms of "standard" and "non-standard" English. The term "standard English" did not refer to British English but to Northeast U.S. English. "Non-standard English" referred to Black English.

The dominant view in this body of literature once again affirmed black deviance. The model is referred to as the "verbal deficit" hypothesis.[61] Its argu-

ment is that the well-documented failure of many black children is due to impoverished or retarded language abilities. The verbal deficit theories argued that a
poor environment produced black children who did not hear "good" English,
which caused them to be impoverished in their modes of verbal expression. The
deficit hypothesis claimed that blacks use "giant" words and cannot formulate
complete sentences; that they display conceptual ignorance; and that they do not
know the names of common objects.

A sympathetic group of writers refuted the verbal deficit thesis, pointing to a
biculturalism of the black experience. Those theorists focused on the correction
of misunderstanding between the two cultures. They believed that if the authorities just learned about the nonstandard dialect, they could better manage the
black community. Roger Abrahams's *Positively Black*, for instance, made an
attempt at explaining the misunderstood black culture in an effort to educate
whites about "lower-class black life." He concluded that the problem was an
intercultural conflict about intentions and meanings. In his study, whites were
portrayed in balance and blacks were portrayed in conflict. He developed the idea
of "men of words," in which strife, coercion, competition, and exploitation were
the underlying values for black culture.[62]

Thomas Kochman, in *Black and White Style in Conflict*, maintained the tradition, with hopes of contributing to "social change." The value of Kochman's
work is that he points to "cultural factors which shaped the patterns and attitudes
that blacks and whites brought with them to the communication situation."[63]
Others have followed the tradition in particular ways; many of them have
attempted to discard the deficit, deviancy, and pathology models, but few of them
have been entirely successful.[64]

It is in the interest of the black community to debunk the theories of nonexistent black culture and their claim of black subcultural deviance. Moreover, it is
important to recognize that conflict and strife also exist in white culture. In fact,
competition and imperialistic expansion, that is, trouble and aggression, are the
most salient qualities that built the nation. The class order built by imperial
aggression depends on race to organize its structure. The greater a group's power
to control the social, economic, and political order, the greater interest the group
has in the right to exploit and control other groups.

It is not hard to imagine why the liberals in Berkeley suggested that the
"deviants" at People's Park talk it over in legitimate, democratic, and pragmatic
ways after the occupation. The evidence was clear that the friendly benevolence
of the powerful had been demystified in the streets as a real situation of coercive
oppression. The occupation of Berkeley also reaffirmed the principle, so often
repeated, that power is never voluntarily given up by the oppressor, but must be
demanded by the oppressed. Furthermore, like May 1968 in France, the Berkeley
situation resulted in minimal social change, regardless of the theoretical revision
in the social sciences.

This point was the root of the coalition development that marked the 1983
March on Washington, making it distinguishable from the 1963 event. Many of

the limitations on the psychic history of the nation during the 1960s had been diminished by the rise of the feminist, gay and lesbian, elderly, and handicapped movements, all aimed at the interlocking social mechanisms of inequality. Moreover, the resistance of each of the oppressed white ethnic groups had, in particular ways, been organized in terms of the examples set by the earlier movements.

An instance of this observation results in a significant, eye-opening contribution to the relationship between race and crime. Paul Takagi and Tony Platt, in an article titled "Behind the Gilded Ghetto: An Analysis of Race, Class, and Crime in Chinatown," analyzed the racist and ideological roots of explanations of Chinese-American crime.[65] The authors highlighted serious historical problems with the culture-personality theories, which ultimately blamed the victim for criminality. They drew careful distinctions between organized crime of the primitive accumulation varieties and street crime.

Another instance of the academic theme of coalition politics as a method to overcome histories of oppression appears in Angela Davis's *Women, Race and Class.*[66] Davis acknowledges the history of sexual coercion and attempts in very broad ways to relate that history to the history of U.S. slavery. She points to the need to draw a distinction between the black women's movement and the more general women's movement. These clarifications have led to a theoretical reformulation of race relations literature, in which racism is becoming increasingly viewed as the independent variable in the sociological models of inequality.[67]

Many of the white revisionist writers have focused on humanitarian ethics for the social sciences and the historical and apparent policies of those sciences to benefit the wealthy through the exploitation of the poor. The revisionist writers seldom question their privilege. It is as though they do not recognize the ways being white has been beneficial in their lives. On the other side, the attractive force for black male deviance is located in the affinity of the oppressed in their differential rate of association with the environments and conditions of oppression. It is my argument that the very production of the deviance language reproduces sites of resistance on the other side of the unrecognized privilege of whiteness. African Americans produce an adaptation to the circumstances of what some commentators refer to as scientific racism. I previously referred to the black adaptation as contracultural. I do not mean to suggest that black culture is a pure ethnographic form existing outside of history. But we should not diminish the fact that black cultural innovation challenges the usual function of social guilt working as social constraint. In other words, black culture is a site of contestation based on the perception of legitimate discontent.

COLONIAL CONFLICT AND DEVIANCE

The social history of African Americans in the United States is a contradiction between capital and liberty. In its most radical form, this contradiction might presumably result in contributing to the annihilation of capitalist democracy as the world has known it; or, at very least, one may expect the contradiction to contribute to a change in U.S. relations of production and the concomitant ideas of liberty. This development in black consciousness is made vividly clear by the recent development of the coalition consciousness that has been a theme in African-American political sociology. I am interested in a theory of black male deviance and the colonial problem because it has meant a great deal to African Americans.

The study of black inequality suggests that its nascent form appeared in Africa at the hands of European foreign policy. The policy is adequately described by the myth of the colony; even more, the traditional moral order is associated with the rise of the colony, which is a persistent theme in Western cultural and economic history.[68] The myth of the colony is that the cultural values and traditions of the colonizers are universally correct and should be used to manage the lives of groups from different cultures. The colonial theme, combined with the ideologies of asceticism, passed on from the Middle Ages and the Puritan ethic of the Reformation, is representative of the development toward Protestantism and the Enlightenment. This development was underwritten by the economic force of private property, which was first given power by a process of primitive accumulation through the sanctions of the Enclosure Acts. The acts of enclosure separated the English peasantry from their land base.[69] The European conquest of North America and the later U.S. expansion to the Pacific, expropriating Native American and Mexican lands, is part of the same process in the accumulation of capital: it is the appropriation of another people's land base in the interest of the colonial powers' ruling classes for the purpose of acquiring surplus capital by changing that land base into increasingly concentrated private property.[70]

The colonial images are deeply embedded in the Western cultural psyche. The oracle of Apollo at Delphi, for instance, provides the principles of the ideology that were present at the chief international center in the ancient world. Its chief maxims were "know thyself" and "nothing to excess." In Herodotus's *History*, one is told the oracular edict. A young man named Battus, from the island of Thera, was concerned about a speech defect. Battus believed his speech problem would interfere with his ambition to become a powerful political leader. He made a pilgrimage to Delphi to ask Apollo's advice about overcoming the defect. Apollo surprised Battus, advising him to found a colony in Libya. Battus proceeded to organize a group and established the prosperous colony of Cyrene on the African coast.[71] European men with alleged defects were dispatched all over the world, spreading death and destruction wherever they went.

When a colonial power asserts its will over a community destined to become colonized, the colonial power must perforce gain control over the material conditions of the native inhabitants; it must displace the patriarchal relations of power and production operating in the host colony. The scenario must follow the pattern of gaining economic control over the natives' existence. This means that rents and taxes must be instituted that force the natives to raise wages to pay the assessments. Use of housing, roads, water, and other necessities of existence becomes mediated through capital. Profits, rents, and taxes become elaborated to socially sustain the ruling classes. Additional systems, such as jails and asylums, are established, providing jobs for the colonizers and containing the resistance of the colonized.[72]

Schools are established to socially create, perpetuate, and administer knowledge. The technological advances of the colonizing agents are introduced as a hierarchical system of culture values. Elite values and techniques emerge that stand in contradiction to the native value system. Thus, the colonizers provide jobs for themselves in cultural education, technique, and administration while they simultaneously control the social distribution of knowledge. Through the social division of labor, the colonizers are capable of denying the natives access to the information necessary for material and technological self-sufficiency.[73]

The colonizers also annihilate the culture of the colonized. However, many of the native cultural artifacts are valuable to the colonizer because of their market value. Those items are then appropriated into elite class values. If the natural resources have a market value and can be removed from the land, as is the case with gold and copper, the colonizers expropriate the resources, sharing the spoils of the colonial adventure with other imperial powers of the world capital arrangement. Meanwhile, the colonized remain to some extent oblivious to and powerless against the exploitation inherent in the processes of appropriation and expropriation until the moment in history when the colonial arrangement is challenged by the consciousness of the exploited.[74]

In U.S. history, the colonial ideology and its collateral ideologies travel on a kind of errand into the wilderness for republican ideas, which are represented in the American founding documents and biographies of great men like Thomas Jefferson, Benjamin Rush, Andrew Jackson, and others.

The question is simply: Did Battus ever fix his speech defect? The answer is not so simple, although the simple answer is an unequivocal no. The common explanations for the "white man's burden" of developing civilization were proffered by John Locke and Thomas Jefferson. Locke suggested that all children were born with minds like blank slates (tabulae rasae) on which experiences could be written that could serve as a reference throughout life. Jefferson suggested that all children were born with intelligence. The greater the intelligence, he thought, the greater the individual's sense of fair play. When examining Locke's tabula rasa one is threatened by the experiential information some personalities are accumulating and laments the cause of the depravity of people of color—not everyone owned property and was interested in supporting "law and order." On the other hand, when one institutes Jefferson's "moral sense," which requires intelligence, one quickly realizes that some of the nation's children possess natures that nurture cannot change. In either case, it is the colonized culture to which the republican imperialism sought to "extend the empire of liberty," and it is that culture which is necessarily striking back.[75]

BLACK SOLUTIONS TO INTERNAL COLONIZATION

The arrival of blacks in Jamestown in 1619, which eventually led to slavery is, by and large, the recapitulation of the colonial myth; its form is domestic, however, and is referred to as domestic colonialism.[76] The history of the applied colonial myth and its rituals in the United States was not only economic but also political, cultural, and social. Despite the evolution of black consciousness in reaction to the various elements of the colonial structure, an articulated comprehensive statement remained dormant until the 1960s. In fact, the Third World Strike and the Free Speech movement combined to dramatize the severe race and class contradictions in U.S. inequality. The colonial interpretation, as we saw earlier, became increasingly cogent as the contradictions inherent in the dominant contending explanations of social inequality were demonstrated to be inadequate. Blacks addressed inequality in historical phases that may be subsumed under the rubric of nationalism.[77] Five major historical forms emerged: political, economic, cultural, integral, and moral.

The political phase of black reaction to inequality stressed the founding of a black nation elsewhere. In fact, in 1854, at the Emigration Convention a committee was established to investigate the possibilities for the emigration of blacks to Central America, Haiti, or West Africa. The emancipation of blacks from plantation slavery curtailed the interest in black emigration. Emancipation failed to bring about black equality, however, and resulted in severe white reactions, particularly in the South, in the form of Black Codes and Jim Crow laws. Reconstruction sent carpetbagger governors into the South and transformed concern from political interest into the search for philosophies of economic excellence and black self-help.

The condition of blacks remained oppressed and depressed. A representative philosophy of economic development was in the ideas Booker T. Washington presented in his famous Atlanta Exposition address of 1895. Washington's philosophy stressed black cooperation with the white capitalist class, who managed labor competition in the Northern industrial markets. He urged blacks to "cast down your buckets" in friendship to the white power structure. Thereby, Washington reasoned, blacks would be hired by white employers once they had proven worthy. In the interim, Washington encouraged blacks to pull themselves up by the bootstraps through agricultural and technical education. Blacks became disillusioned with Washington's program in light of its major contradiction, which argued for agricultural and technical education at a time when the nation was becoming increasingly industrial.

Soon to follow was the era of cultural nationalism. This period was marked by its emphasis on demonstrating to white America that the history of blacks included major contributions to humanity. It was believed that the reconstruction of black history would raise the contradiction between American racial stereotypes and reality. Futhermore, the cultural focus was believed to function as an instrument of racial solidarity and pride for blacks themselves. Leaders of the

period included W. E. B. DuBois, Langston Hughes, Carter G. Woodson, Arthur
A. Schomburg, and Zora Neale Hurston. Later, the work of James Baldwin sym-
bolized the black disillusionment with the cultural nationalist era.[78] As we have
seen, most white scholars reacted to the period with works that denied the existence of black culture altogether.[79] And many such theories explained black life
as a culture of poverty and debauchery.[80]

The first contributor to an integral philosophy of black life was Marcus
Moziah Garvey, who organized the Universal Negro Improvement Association
and African Communities League (UNIA) in New York City in 1917. He was
born in Jamaica, and the UNIA was actually first organized in Jamaica in 1914.

Garvey's movement proceeded with the Great Migration, when blacks were
pushed and pulled from the South to Northern cities. Between 1913 and 1915,
more than 2 million blacks moved to Northern industrial centers. Even though
Garvey's leadership had an international influence, in the United States the
newly settled black Northerners were attracted to Garveyism. Southern crop fail-
ures and boll weevil infestation, combined with a wave of legislation forbidding
blacks to live in residential neighborhoods with whites, assisted in pushing
blacks to the North. In addition, the vestiges of Black Codes and Jim Crow
resulted in the most brutal atrocities. The National Association for the
Advancement of Colored People (NAACP) reported that during the year 1913,
the Emancipation Proclamation's fiftieth anniversary, seventy-nine blacks were
lynched. Shortly afterward, World War I placed heavy demands on Northern
industry and caused the suspension of European immigration. The factories needed the blacks and appealed to them through black newspapers and magazines.
More than 70 percent of the black population was literate, and the word quickly
traveled.[81]

The black arrival in the North was a U.S. nightmare. Naturally, blacks were
not prepared for the cold Northern winters. They arrived with very few personal
possessions. Secondarily, they encountered severe hostility from Northern white
labor, who felt threatened by the new black cheap labor. For example, on July 2,
1917, white labor in East St. Louis, Missouri, initiated one of the most vicious
race riots in U.S. history. Close to 6,000 blacks were driven from their homes;
estimates are that as many as 200 blacks died. Race riots exploded across the
country: Houston (1917), Chester and Philadelphia, Pennsylvania (1918),
Longview and Gregg County, Texas (1919), Washington, D.C. (1919), and
Elaine, Arkansas (1919). Ten thousand New Yorkers marched down Fifth
Avenue in a silent protest against brutalities and lynchings on July 28, 1917.[82]

Garvey preached black self-will during a period of black disillusionment and
despair. His perspective was Pan-African, "Africa for the Africans at home and
abroad," which cast God and the angels as black and Satan and the imps as white.
His movement was sheer drama, employing mysterious ritual and pageantry. His
dramatic imagination, in the context of creating revolutionary conditions, is a
model for any student of social change. Pomp and ceremony, parades, and titles
of nobility combined to create street theatrics that resulted in Garvey's collecting

millions of dollars in a short period of time. Garvey integrated philosophy, pragmatics, and economics by organizing factories and cooperatives. He developed a commercial steamship enterprise, the Black Star Line. Moreover, he commanded a private army.[83] The fall of Garvey came in 1925, when he was arrested and charged with mail fraud. He was deported to Jamaica two years later and died in London in 1940.[84]

The most pervasive resistance by blacks to their experience with American inequality and its colonial nature began in Detroit, when a man who became known as Mr. W. D. Fard arrived during the summer of 1930. Fard developed an integral ideology of the black condition both in the United States and internationally.[85] His teachings were grounded in the Bible and, later, the Qur'an. He also used the writings of Jehovah's Witness Joseph F. Rutherford, Hendrik Van Loon's *The Story of Mankind*, James Breasted's *The Conquest of Civilization*, and literature from Freemasonry. What was different from other blacks' programs was Fard's comprehensive explanation of the history and cosmology of the black race. His central task, in fact, was to bring his people to a knowledge of self. Fard prepared two manuals for his audience: *The Secret Ritual of the Nation of Islam*, which was passed on orally, and *The Teaching of the Lost Found Nation of Islam in a Mathematical Way*.[86]

Elijah Poole was renamed Elijah Muhammad and inherited the leadership of the movement after Fard's disappearance in June 1934. Internal political conflicts pushed Muhammad from Detroit to Chicago's Temple No. 2. His leadership became legendary, and his political power among his followers became unquestioned.[87]

The Nation of Islam was the appropriate historical black reaction to the continued U.S. experience of internal colonialism. The Great Depression left blacks in total disarray. Even if Garvey had not been arrested, the depression surely would have resulted in his failure. The hiatus between Garvey's and Fard's leadership provided a period for the Black Renaissance to congeal in the national black spirit. The Nation of Islam functioned to introduce rigorous moral standards. Nonetheless, the moral imperatives of the Muslims were ritualistic—as if preparing the black masses for a more advanced period of moral group behavior. In fact, the new morality of the Nation of Islam was a legacy from the period of moral giants of the nineteenth century, most notably Frederick Douglass. But the Muslims imposed repressive behavioral codes on their followers, "cleaning them up" for the work to be done.

The most powerful figure to emerge from the moral excellence of the Muslims was Malcolm X, born Malcolm Little in Omaha, Nebraska, about 1925. His father was an outspoken black activist and Garveyite who fled with his family to Lansing, Michigan, when Malcolm was very young. When Malcolm was six, his family's house was burned by the Ku Klux Klan. Finally, Malcolm's father was found dead with his head bashed and body mangled.[88]

Mass identification with Malcolm was high as a result of both his personality and his philosophy. Malcolm was streetwise: by the age of eighteen he had become Detroit Red, a pimp. He found himself in a maximum security prison, where a metamorphosis occurred when he realized that he was "ignorant." One of the members of the Nation of Islam converted Malcolm, and he remained loyal to the ministry of Muhammad for some seventeen years. In 1959, Malcolm made a pilgrimage to Mecca that resulted in another metamorphosis in his life. His vision of the white man changed from hate to love. He revised his perspective on international relations, carefully outlining the economic conditions of colonialism. Many Muslims reacted to him in anger, suggesting he had begun to "love the devil."[89]

In March 1964, Malcolm stopped associating with the Nation of Islam and formed his own organization, The Muslim Mosque, Inc.; later, its secular organization, the Organization of Afro-American Unity, was established. These organizations provided the instrument for Malcolm to disseminate his Pan-African and nationalist agenda. On February 21, 1965, Malcolm was assassinated. Almost immediately, a pervasive cult of Malcolm X followers, cutting across race and class lines, emerged both in the United States and internationally. Despite the internal differences about Malcolm within the Nation of Islam, one of his students, Louis Farrakhan, was appointed national minister. The moral, economic, and social disciplines Malcolm X advocated became a significant influence on other major black spokespersons, such as Huey Newton, Kwame Toure, and Angela Davis.[90]

The most influential moral critique of black internal colonialism was made through the theology of Martin Luther King, Jr. King brought Christian cosmology to the masses. The three major objections in Western thought to religion were proffered by Freud, Marx, and Nietzsche: religion as mass neurosis, as mass opiate, and as terminal. However, King taught the black masses that there exist moral persons in an immoral society, a society that fails to respect every form of human personality. King challenged the moral conscience of the nation through the satyagraha method of Mohandas K. Gandhi, by staging dramatic street scenes of social injustice. King told his audiences to behave in righteous indignation so the the whole world could witness the brutal inequality of segregation. The theatrics functioned to shame the agents of domination into an acquiescent position.[91]

King's freedom was a function of human love; he was well aware of the problems with the term "love."[92] Generally love is conceptualized by two apparently mutually exclusive ideas—the Greek *eros* and the biblical *agape*. King's conception of love opposed the emotional striving to attach the self to an object because of a need or a lack of need in the organism, to which the term "eros" refers; rather, he supported the emotionally charged effort to serve the object through the transcendence of individual interests and needs. While King recognized the existence of "the drum major instinct" (Alfred Adler) in the will to power (Nietzsche), he was unequivocal in his determination that the eros form of love was a perverted, destructive, and ultimately nihilistic energy. (King may have been asking too much of the average audience.[93])

Lawrence Kohlberg has argued that only a relatively few elite reasoners are capable of reaching transcendental understanding.[94] Thus, the aim that King modeled might be better described as a state of mind instead of being conceived as an emotion. Nonetheless, King's love appears to remain a self-satisfaction for an ideal state of equality; therefore, its genesis is narcissistic. But King's love was "productive love," in Erich Fromm's terms, and not a romance with the self.

King influenced a large segment of black culture, particularly youth culture. Among his students were Jesse Jackson and Andrew Young. It is interesting to note that despite the less than exemplary careers of both of these national figures, they consistently posture as moralists in their institutional roles.

CAPITAL AND LIBERTY

Capital is the antithesis of freedom. The relationship between capital and freedom is well documented in the history of social science.[95] Fundamentally speaking, capital relations of production produce alienation within the worker, separating the worker from what is produced and placing workers in competition for jobs and private property. The worker in the colonial situation performs forced labor in the interest of the ruling classes of the controlling imperial power. The imposition of nonvoluntary work produces a feeling of misery, since the worker is not fulfilling himself by doing the work; rather, he is denying himself in order to fulfill the desire of an oppressor. Capital work is not activity done to satisfy the needs of the worker, but is done as a means of fulfilling the needs of the capitalists. Therefore, the worker will compulsively avoid work, doing it only when forced to do so.[96]

This realization of the structure and process of capital relations demanded incorporation into mass black culture and into the philosophies of black liberation. It became a constant and prominent theme among the black culture makers. W. E. B. DuBois's flirtation with communism is a biographical connection between the critique of capital and theories of black liberation. Richard Wright, particularly in his early work, raised the Communist theme to a majestic metaphor as a "Bright Morning Star."[97] Ralph Ellison depicted the contradiction between scientific socialism and the need for communistic social democracy.[98] James Baldwin described the tyrant who rises in America, pointing to the contradictions of the capital relations in black urban life.[99] Alice Walker described the colonial process and many of its effects on the internal colonial culture.[100] Time and again the presentation of black criticism of capital relations is marketed to raise the U.S. social consciousness to a level based on moral grounds.

For the major black critics of American inequality, freedom does not imply assimilation. In fact, black nationalism appears to be the recurring theme. In the most general sense, freedom means release from the domination of others. This is the freedom to which black liberation is dedicated. Several of the Western ideas of freedom fail the black ideal in the U.S. experience. The Nazi and Fascist theory of freedom, so often heard in the internal colony, holds that where the conditions or opportunities considered by the powerful as necessary for the development of one's capacities exist, there exists freedom.[101] This idea of freedom has been shown, in an earlier chapter, to be a prominent attitude of white teachers in internally colonized schools.[102] In general, we may expect this to be the attitude of institutional authority in internal colonial structures, particularly where race presents itself as the central organizing theme in the class order.

Thomas Hobbes saw freedom as the state of being allowed to do what one desires to do and can do.[103] This notion of freedom remained inadequate for blacks because, historically, they were instructed that they were a priori incapable of realizing their desires. Prior to evolutionary theory, blacks were alleged to possess a defective ancestry because of the curse of Ham. Later the polygenists "proved," through a theory of cranial capacity, that blacks were less intelligent, and therefore should, on moral grounds, be denied opportunities.[104] After evolutionary theory influenced world thought in the second half of the nineteenth century, the Western biological and social sciences began measuring heads and bodies, often using their flawed research to politically support the proposition that blacks should be denied opportunities. At the turn of the century, white social scientists presented the intelligence quotient (I.Q.) as a hereditary function that measured intelligence through the mathematical procedure of factoring.[105] Clearly, it is often assumed, blacks should be denied opportunities because of their inability to achieve scores equivalent to those of whites on scientifically developed tests. The internal colonial position of blacks prevented them from a commitment to Hobbesian freedom, since their desires were suppressed by the interlocking white scientific domestic (internal) colonizers. What is more, there is no certainty about the bourgeois claim that group opportunity represents progress; nor that opportunity in U.S. society is a legitimate goal. These two claims are the postulates on which the Hobbesian worldview rests when it is applied to African Americans.

The conception of freedom as behavior that conforms to moral law failed blacks in their history of inequality. While Epictecus held that no wicked man is free, blacks remained committed to the idea that the social conditions were wicked. If blacks were to heed Thomas Carlyle's formula for freedom as "finding the right path and walking thereon," it would have meant yielding black humanity. Black creative consciousness found the most important task to be day-to-day resistance against social inequality. The forces of inequality remained brutal in their denial of black humanity. In fact, as the Frederick Douglass narrative makes vividly clear, the "right path" for blacks required that they become criminal to satisfy the basic human needs: Douglass had to steal bread and then clothing to meet his food and warmth needs. As blacks became increasingly urban the motif of the "bad nigger" guided the development of black human consciousness.[106]

Hegelian freedom is far more compatible with the black historical experience. Hegelian freedom is reasoned patriotism. In Hegel's view, freedom is the determination of the will by reason, accomplished through individual realization of perfection in and by the self.[107] Martin Luther King, Jr., adopted a Hegelian approach to freedom. Hegel viewed the state as the manifestation of the ethical whole and the actual whole of freedom. Therefore, the civil, political, and economic circumstances of the black population constitute a critical assessment of the ethical health of the nation.

The black struggle for equality and empowerment consists in abrogating the ethical rules of so-called civilized society. Much of the killing, raping, stealing, pillaging, and destruction, so well known in both black and white communities in the United States, is largely in the black case, the actualization of black resistance to patriotism. The colonial, and then later internal-colonial, vestige of killing the colony's father image (which was a necessary historical process to produce markets for capital) denies, and perforce contradicts, black liberation. The contradiction between the capitalist form of production and liberation evolved in black consciousness, expressing the forms of resistance more prominently. This resistance is a righteous indignation in the collective perception of black America expressed toward real forces of human perversion and the hegemonic need to produce black male deviance.

My understanding of black criminality is informed by the view that the punishment for crime in the United States is largely both symbolic and a booming business. The black prison reform advocate Mumia Abu-Jamal argues the symbolic nature of the criminal justice system when he asserts, "What I was thinking is that every prosecution is a public and symbolic act, a political act by the state to give the populace an illusion of control." Abu-Jamal elaborates his argument:

> Another figure that I read recently in the ABA [American Bar Association] Crisis in the Criminal Justice System Report is that there were over 34 million crimes, felonies, victimizations in America in 1986...Thirty-one million out of 34 million were never exposed to arrest, never went into the criminal justice system at all.[108]

The determination of who will be subjected to the criminal justice process is an issue for political sociology. The fact is that race, and not the rate of crime, predicts the number of inmates in U.S. prisons. States with high black populations and low crime rates have high prison rates, states with low black populations and high crime rates have low prison rates.

The prison industry is one of the largest in the United States. Dhoruba Bin Wahad, a leading prison reform advocate, said:

> The prison system in the United States is a booming business. It's one of the major growth industries in the country today—even in a period of recession. In New York State for instance, 85-90% of all the prisoners are Black or Latino. And they come from only eight communities in the entire state of New York....In New York, the majority of prisons are in

rural areas that are predominantly white and economically depressed....The solution to this depression is to build prisons in these
regions in order to employ people and bring in taxable income.[109]

SUMMARY

In this chapter I have stressed the ways that deviance and domination are
related in the African-American experience. In the realm of ideas, Marxism has
been a prominent perspective for the black intellectual leadership. However,
while the Marxist perspective provided a set of liberatory theories, practices, and
goals, the Marxists have yet to adequately address the issue of race. The key
technology in world history for the management of racial minorities has been
colonialism. Although colonialism has appeared in different classical, neocolonial, and domestic colonial forms, there was a specific colonial method.

The technology of colonialism was applied to African Americans and resulted in their developing strategies of resistance. African-American resistance was
treated by the agents of domination as "subcultural" social deviance. In the next
chapter, I shall examine how scientists theoretically conceptualized deviance,
and I shall suggest a tentative liberatory approach to the deviance label.

CHAPTER 5

Race and Theories of Deviance

The question of the relationship between race and deviance cannot be avoided. To fail to raise this question assumes that U.S. life has come to terms with the guarantees of equality that were laid down in the foundation documents; in the end such thinking would be an insult to many whites and blacks, as well as Asians, Hispanics, and Native Americans—all of whom have witnessed the disparities over time. Deviance is a social problem with its roots as deeply embedded in U.S. awareness as is its race problem. To say this, then, is to challenge the completeness of many of the extant theories of deviance and potentially to bridge a gap between micro action, such as the psychological and biological facts, and macro action, such as the economic relations between social formations and classes.

Furthermore, any social explanation of deviance must select a particular case, drawing connections between the wider origins of the deviant act, the actual act, the immediate reactions to the act, and the wider origins of the reaction.[1] Beyond these explanatory factors the theory in some way must offer a practical solution capable of policy implementation within the case's context.

The system of authority, that is, hegemony, in the United States reveals the way the quality of life is maintained along racial and sexual lines. The dominant ideas related to authority have inadvertently served the purpose of limiting the critical understanding of deviance in the U.S. experience by omitting the political sociology of deviance. In this chapter I propose to trace such ideas in sociology and illustrate a major deficiency in the ability to address deviance, particularly among black males. I believe that race has much more to do with deviance than has been recognized.

Contemporary deviance analysis may presume liberal freedom. The liberal perspective may act to reject the value of the black male on the basis of the definitions structuring the understanding of black males' form of consciousness. Hence, I shall consider some aspects of black male presentation within the context of deviance and suggest it as an equally cogent, though subordinated, competing theme in the authoritative (hegemonic) structure.

AUTHORITY

Classical sociologists have been constant in introducing authority into a social relation, by which they mean a voluntary or conventional interaction explicitly detached from its political connection with coercive power. They have sought to develop the idea of autonomous social authorities, which are independent of the modern state. Emile Durkheim argued a decline in earlier repressive types of society, for example, ones with a "familial base," where "it is [as] difficult to change from them as to change families" and a corresponding rise in the organic type of society, where "children no longer remain immutably attached to the land of their parents, but leave to seek their fortune in all directions."[2] Durkheim suggested a declining significance of the tradition of the elders that is supported by the social fact of the intensification of the division of labor.

The idea of autonomous social authority is also found in Max Weber's writings. Weber drew a distinction between power and the more "precise" sociological concept of authority. He defined power as "any probability of imposing one's will within a social relationship even against resistance," and authority as "the probability of securing obedience to definite commands from a relative group of men."[3]

Durkheim and Weber asserted that the social dimension of political "commands" provides obedience without coercion. They both acknowledged the necessity of the belief in legitimacy; consequently, they drew no distinctions concerning principles within authority. They established as sociological fact what had been thought of as anthropological principle: that religion, church, and family were losing their institutional hegemony and at the same time were buttressing, by a thwarting of previous social relations, the drive toward rational calculations of coercive power. Thus, the history of authority for them was the explanation of difference of type and of succession of stages in which the "normative" role represents the rational organization of highly integrated modern society.

Similarly, Vilfredo Pareto's conception of the circulation of the elites is a continuation of liberalism's assault on traditional authority. In Pareto's scheme the role of authority in modern society is a process of lower-class nonelites moving into the governing class; that is, the natural gain of the fittest political capacity.[4] For Pareto the highest achievers in any area of human production governed through force and fraud. Pareto differed from Gaetano Mosca insofar as the latter thought that the organization of the minorities was the process that resulted in the circulation of the elites. The classical elite theories of Pareto, Mosca, and Robert Michels share liberalism's attack on traditional authority.

More recently, Max Horkheimer's critical essay on authority and the family addressed the problem that the traditional perspectives raise, namely, that social authority was a characteristic product of the declining, preindustrial stage of Western civilization; and authority in some form remained as a striking feature of the industrial age.[5] Erich Fromm and Herbert Marcuse saw authority, in a general sense of affirmed dependence of the larger part of men upon the smaller, as a central category of all forms of society.[6] These conceptions identify a problem with the earlier formations of authority, but in concert with them is the obstinate liberalism that stresses a new form of authority definable by the voluntary submission of supposedly free individuals to natural, metaphysical, or psychic constraints. The psychoanalytic treatments argue that liberalism's conception of authority is actually a reified form of authoritarian control by a dominant social group.

RATIONAL AND CALCULABLE SOCIAL CONTROL

Fundamentally, the studies of deviance have responded, as assuredly as a Pavlovian dog, to the rule of the sociological tradition that asserts it is apolitical voluntary behavior and, more recently, social power of authoritarian control by a dominant social group. Many of these studies fall outside of the sociological discipline and are compiled by educational psychologists, working as administrators, counselors, and students of the subject in universities and colleges.

The dominant explanations of deviance from these professionals have a tendency to be, in one way or another, based on the psychometric or behavioral approach. Their tradition is mechanistic, and there has been a concomitant growth of industry that supplies test batteries and manuals, and in the agencies and schools conceptual categories such as "maladjustment," "school phobia," and "low self-esteem" are often used.

In comparison, the sociological literature on black male violence, delinquency, and deviance does not form a voluminous collection. The major concern of these works, however, is with the relationship between institutional experience and deviance, which is only one of the concerns of the educational psychologists.[7] Like the psychologists, the sociologists have tended to design their work within the framework of the dominant literature of their own discipline, and to concentrate specifically on the structure of family, culture, and school experience.[8]

The dominant literature on deviance in psychology and sociology is not necessarily germane to understanding the conflict approach being applied in this study. It does, however, share liberalism's revision of the concept of authority in differing ways. Currently, writers of this literature have developed into "problematic situation" photographers. For the most part, they are committed to naturalism, explaining the situation of a deviant as created when a person's behavior elicits interpersonal or collective reactions that serve to "isolate," "correct," "control," or "punish" the person engaged in the identified behavior.[9]

There are several reasons for arguing that the naturalistic "problematic situation" perspective is important. For one, it focuses upon "real" behavior as socially defined, and not on alleged characteristics of the behaving person or on some objective feature of the behavior itself. Furthermore, the naturalistic perspective pays close attention to the normative standard against which the judgment of deviance is made. Finally, it emphasizes collective responses to the behavior of individual deviants.

Edwin Lemert was one of the first sociologists to be interested in the role of social reaction and deviant commitment to the career of deviance.[10] He indicated that social reaction "starts with a jaundiced eye on the collective efforts of societies to solve problems of deviance."[11] Basically, this theoretical movement is concerned with the way being labeled deviant by a social audience, or by an agency of social control, can change one's conception of self, and possibly result in a situation where there may be a gradual adoption of deviant behavior. In the social reaction theories, authority is conceived as structured outside of its political relationship with coercive power, socially functioning as legitimate social control.

Another social reaction study, by Aaron Cicourel and John Kituse, drew from the phenomenology of Alfred Schutz and from Lemert's early work, contributing several structural features of "the social organization of the high school and deviant adolescent careers."[12] This research was designed to look at the ways school personnel and the related social organization defined adolescent behaviors and how these definitions became social types, that is, an invisible chart of role structures. Moreover, Cicourel and Kituse were interested in the effects of adolescent typing. They reported that "adolescent problems" fall under three categories: (1) academic-mentally retarded, slow learners, and the like; (2) conduct-delinquents, maladjusted; (3) emotional-low self-esteem, withdrawn. These categories form the basis on which the deviant career is launched. The organizational lines of action that charted the courses of these careers were then examined in terms of the records and officials in the institutions that were studied. Authority, in this study's context, remains consistent with the liberal sociological tradition. It nonetheless renders an excellent set of depictions of the processing of deviance within institutions.

Carl Werthman employed Anselm Strauss's qualitative research techniques of starting without a reference to a theoretical perspective in hopes of generating a grounded theory from the research experience.[13] The problem Werthman found was that members of black delinquent gangs create problems for, and get into trouble with, some teachers but not with others. Werthman's conclusion was that students do not accept the authority of authority figures as a given. Social actors will accept only authority that is viewed as legitimate. He argued that if teachers in schools assert authoritative claims over behaviors (such as dress and hair styles) to which the student has not conferred legitimate authority, or if the teachers impose authority in a mean style that projects the diminution of the student's "autonomy" and "style," the likely result will be misbehavior.

Werthman carefully documented his theoretical findings by using interviews with pupils and questioning them about issues such as student response to grades that teachers assign. He developed four categories that form the rules for grade assignment: (1) assigned fairly; (2) used as a discriminatory weapon; (3) used as a way to bribe; and (4) assigned on a random basis. Any assignment of grades on a basis other than that of fairness was viewed by the students as illegitimate and resulted in a corresponding reaction. The significance of Werthman's study is that it returns to the classical utilitarian argument that human action is rational—which was essentially David Matza's argument to demonstrate "the ineradicable element of choice and freedom inherent in the condition of delinquent drift,"[14] a point I will take up momentarily.

Werthman's contribution to the phenomenology of deviance was to highlight the symbolic interaction involved in its production, with an emphasis on the black student's view. Another advantage to his work is that it primarily focuses upon black juvenile males, who are seldom studied in sociology.[15]

In this phenomenological tradition, David Hargreaves, Stephen Hester, and Frank Mellor studied several British schools.[16] They generated eleven categories in which deviance is imputed by teachers in the course of delimiting the rules (e.g., by giving a command, by displaying sarcasm, by asking questions about behavior, and the like). They proposed that students are typed by teachers in three stages: (1) speculation, the teacher expects delinquency; (2) elaboration, the teacher imputes meaning to an ongoing set of behaviors in the "routing of deviance"; and (3) stabilization, the point where the teacher has a good idea about the student's conduct and finds little difficulty in making sense of his or her acts. The English study claimed to have added more substantive data than did Cicourel and Kitsuse—that is, it offered extensive quotations from school delinquents and analyzed in detail the events that the researchers saw in schools.

In spite of the fact that these theories of delinquency and deviance are of the most liberal persuasion, they share in the perspective that authority is a given in the structure. Werthman, who at least acknowledges that there is a differential distribution of legitimate authority, nonetheless argues that the role of teacher remains authoritative. Our question is: Is it possible to distinguish the functions of deviance studies along the lines of the management of knowledge? This question is centrally related to the interpretation of history and so requires a social philosophy of deviant history.

LABELING THEORY

In times of crisis people inevitably return to the fundamentals of tradition. The questions of the relation of knowledge to the world of experience are revived, often in conflicting ways. Thomas Kuhn referred to these conflicting currents as "paradigms," which are methods that use succinctly coded vocabularies representing ideal models with inherent assumptions. Each of these paradigmatic vocabularies, with its motives, can be thought of as standing in opposition to some other vocabulary.[17] A simple statement about the current debates concerning black male deviance is that there is a conflict between the turn-of-the-century social scientists, the positivists, who believed that social science should be structured like the physical sciences, and a growing number of labeling theorists and phenomenologists, who believe it should not. This debate is particularly advanced in the deviance literature, both in breadth and in depth. To bring some clarity to the issues the debate raises, I shall discuss some of the history of the philosophic traditions leading up to labeling theory. Using this discussion as a starting point, I shall then elaborate the development of labeling theory and propose a paradigmatic revision of theoretical and methodological perspectives grounded in a theory of Marxist hegemony that stresses cultural issues.

UTILITARIANS AND POSITIVISTS

The positivist tradition of viewing deviance grew out of a reaction to an earlier tradition of the Enlightenment that argued classical utilitarian ideas of the rights of men. The utilitarians maintained that people had to be protected from the authoritative excesses of social institutions.

However, in eighteenth-century England the system of punishment was capricious insofar as it did not adhere to any particular process of law. A settled ruling class could rule only through forms of judicial terror; year after year new capital offenses were enacted. In the heart of London great crowds assembled on the regular hanging days, and there were riots beneath the gallows at Tyburn for the possession of the bodies of the condemned.[18] This is not to argue that judicial history has progressed, but to point to real social circumstances that caused some to reason that every citizen entered into a social contract by agreeing to repress some of the individual's innately motivated greed for pleasure in exchange for social protection and peace. This meant that human relations could be weighted using rational principles. That is, men equipped with the same social information will necessarily respond rationally in order to derive the greatest amount of good with respect to social utility. It logically followed for the classical utilitarians to argue that useful activity should be rewarded, and nonuseful activity should be punished; that men were ends in themselves.

Classical utilitarianism makes four problematic assumptions: (1) that persons agree upon what is rational and what is not with respect to social morality; (2) that persons agree with the social distribution of property and the relations of production; (3) that any infractions against the social morality, economic distribution, or relations of production are pathological or irrational and are committed by persons who are (for various reasons) unable to enter into the social contract; (4) that the theorist of deviance, such as the social scientist, lawyer, or the like, has the criteria to access the difference between rational and irrational acts.[19]

All things being equal, the classical rational interpretation of human action might fit in the real world. However, under the banner of positivism, a group of social thinkers pointed out that all things were not equal, and so they reasoned utilitarianism was inadequate in explaining why some persons did not adhere to the utilitarian rules. The utilitarians were producing social values for social ends. Their social form was a shared intellectual and conceptual organization with specific classes within certain nations. The positivists attacked the useless "metaphysical" forms of knowledge successfully enough to render empirical knowledge a premium. Positivist reasoning was tied to the concept of the division of labor and based on achievement rather than on birth, which requires a canon of "pecuniary education," "conspicuous consumption," and similar corollary values.[20]

Positivism was the perfect fit for material production, why should positivism not work for social production and reproduction? Auguste Comte, an early sociologist of the positivist school, called for a *Positive Philosophy*. His philosophy was tied to the industrial revolution, which had caused disruption of the existing social institutions and class alignments. The positivist theorists of deviance were preoccupied with the themes of order, progress, integration, and cohesion as objective reactions to individual rationalism. The order the positivists encouraged seeks the eradication of deviance in much the same manner that the physician seeks to eradicate disease.[21]

The method of the physician is to classify, quantify (make the unofficial guess), and treat disease. The positivists proceeded to adopt accurate and calculable units of crime and deviance as the first order for study. Unable to distinguish crime and deviance in these terms, they relied heavily upon criminal statistics. The problems that the statistics raised were obvious: (1) statistics are based on crimes that the police report and thus reflect the crimes that police act on; (2) there are differential police reactions to crime (e.g., people in cities call the police more than people in rural areas); (3) crime statistics use legal categories that appear inappropriate for scientific analysis; (4) crime statistics define crime only in respect to the laws, which runs the risk of missing shared community morals.[22]

Since the 1960s the debates between the positivists and the group known as the phenomenologists have intensified. For most of the twentieth century the U.S. system itself became synonymous, at least in the eyes of those living in the United States, with affluence and unlimited social mobility. The consensus and order models of social rules, as provided in the positivists' paradigm, supported the adaptive technocratic, as well as the "American Dream," ideal. At that time, few in the business of studying U.S. deviance would have suggested a theory about conflict over authority in the U.S. institutional order. Even the Great Depression proved to be a serendipitous contribution to positivism's spirit of respect for the equilibrium of centripetal forces, since the emphasis on economic recovery was a constituent piece of adaptive behavior and the capacity of the system to regain equilibrium.

Nonetheless, Robert K. Merton's seminal paper, "Social Structure and Anomie," made the observation that not all the forces in the social system were functional.[23] Proponents of the social system were hard pressed to admit that there were classes, in the Marxist sense, in their society. In the social sciences generally, James Meisel's *The Myth of the Ruling Class* and David Reisman's *Lonely Crowd* represented the mainstream view.[24] In fact, at the time only C. Wright Mills suggested a *Power Elite*.[25] Mills confronted antagonism from some prominent sociologists. He earned the Left a more substantial platform from which to point out social inequities. Mills was before his time in the sense that the social turmoil of the 1960s that centered on the issue of civil rights and the Vietnam war, and the political and economic dislocations of the 1970s, including Watergate and the economic slump, were to dramatically challenge the rather romantic propositions about cohesion, order, and complacency. The positivists' conception of order gave way to the phenomenologists' liberal interpretations of deviance.

PHENOMENOLOGY AND DEVIANCE

Earl Rubington and Martin Weinberg, in a collection titled *Deviance: The Interactionist Perspective*, succinctly presented the problem:

There are at least two ways of studying deviance...objectively...and subjectively....Deviance as objectively given delineates the norms and values of the society under study and regards any deviation from these norms and values as "deviant"....Deviance as subjectively problematic...assumes that when people and groups interact and communicate...by means of shared symbols...people are able to type one another and formulate their actions accordingly...deviance can best be understood in terms of this process.[26]

In the objective perspective, deviance is treated as unproblematic. Everyone knows what is deviant. In search of a causal analysis, this perspective is mostly concerned with the elimination of deviance. The perspective is often referred to as the correctional view. The social scientist must assume the role of a moral entrepreneur if he adheres to the methods of such a perspective.

The phenomenologists are not strictly concerned with causal analysis because it assumes that deviance is predetermined. The "definitive" applications generally use the statistical concept of central tendency. According to statistical logic, the average cause (independent variable), if significant, is theoretically understood as preceding a result (dependent variable).[27] The subjectively problematic position, on the other hand, view groups as actively making choices and acting upon those decisions. The choices may be constrained by psychological or sociological factors, but the sine qua non of the subjectively problematic position is the activity of the subject.

Phenomenologists departed from the propositions that activity is dependent on personality structure alone, as in the metapsychological concept of ego, and the synapse responses that may be elicited or emitted as the sole cause of action, as in the theories of behavioral conditioning. The phenomenologists highlighted the fact that deviant persons are "normal" until they are socially constructed as deviant by agents or social situations. Under similar conditions anyone might be viewed as deviant. A concomitant concern of the phenomenologists was the process by which a person became set apart and pushed into the social role occupied by those called deviant. They were concerned with the definition of role behaviors for the actor, as well as for the audience. These concerns became a particular branch of the phenomenologists' movement called labeling theory. Howard Becker's *Outsiders* was a major statement on the propositions of the labeling theorists. Labeling theory views deviance as a matter of social definition. Deviance does not happen when a person commits a specific act, but is deviance when others define the act as deviant; deviance is relative. Deviance in one culture at a particular point of history may or may not be deviance at another time. Becker wrote, "Deviance is created by society."[28]

The concept of intention became important for the labeling theorists. Often, what is perceived is not what really exists. Also, the actions directed toward the things seen do not always result in what was intended. Because of these problems, the labeling theorists drew a distinction between the intended object and the intentional act.[29]

The phenomenological perspective was considered, above all, a pragmatic approach to the social sciences. Its influence entered U.S. mainstream scholarship through the works of George Herbert Mead, John Dewey, James Peirce, Chauncey Wright, and Oliver Wendell Holmes. In sociology the position was early termed "symbolic interactionist," a term introduced by Herbert Blumer.[30] The base for the development of the perspective was the American pragmatic movement, noted for its connection to the Chicago School of sociology at the turn of the century.

There have been several criticisms, both external and internal, of labeling theory. Becker has been criticized for a logical flaw in his analysis. He argued that an act is deviant when some audience reacts to the act as rule-breaking. He also developed the concept of "secret deviance" in reference to improper action that goes unnoticed. These two propositions appear to be contradictory; it is not possible to be secretly deviant if deviance requires a reaction. Here Becker's application of Mead's conceptualization of making an object of the self appears to require clarification. In Mead's symbolic interactionist vocabulary, the distinction between the "symbolic" and the "nonsymbolic" act is the ability of the subject to stand outside of and against the self. The subject makes an object of the self and reflects on the objectification. Becker's concept of the secret deviant might have been best formulated as the "self deviant."

Other internal problems, as Alvin Gouldner pointed out, are that (1) labeling theory offers an unacceptable characterization of deviance and (2) is guilty of an "underdog identification" with deviants. Gouldner suggests that labeling theory is biased, representing the deviant as "victim" of the agents of social reaction. This criticism addressed the labeling theorists' assumption that deviants are helpless persons, susceptible to the agents of social reaction. In this way of thinking the deviants are primarily determined by social consequences.[31]

The phenomenologists' posture is to view deviant subjects as rational in the classical sense of the term. However, the issue of power has never been refined in their theoretical position. For the phenomenologists, power is the classical Weberian probability of getting someone to do something in spite of the fact that they might not agree. This view of power creates an interpretation of subordinate groups, whom Georg Simmel called "strangers", as being primarily passive to top-down power relations. Ultimately, the Weberian definition of power grants privilege to legitimate bureaucratic status positions in a rational society. But, then, how are we to understand resistance?

The simple statement is that we have yet to develop a positive science, let alone a positive sociology, of deviance. The positivist philosophers painted a picture of deviance from a particular ideological perspective, resulting in the phenomenologists' reaction, which attempts to appreciate the subject. Paul Walton, Ian Taylor, and Jock Young indicated the danger with the naturalistic posture:

> Unless we are careful, therefore, the naturalistic perspective can lead (as it does with many ethnomethodologists) into a position where the only true account of how the deviant phenomena come into being, and what its [sic] real nature is, can be given by deviants themselves. This position is paradoxically (and Matza thrives on paradoxes) both true and untrue.[32]

In this paradoxical sense, the interpretive work of the naturalist requires a refined method of gathering knowledge and deriving meaning. The method becomes an object for careful scrutiny. The propensity of labeling theorists to side with the underdog is itself an ideological position. It says to positivism, "What is democracy?" It tells us little about what are to be the circumstances for the creation of deviance. It lacks epistemological clarity and it gives us no explanation of the power to will deviance, in the senses both of coercive force and of applying influence.

Because the labeling theorists qualify deviance in terms of perception, they give rise to classifying certain phenomena like "physical disabilities" as deviance when no rule-breaking would have been considered in the traditional sense. They have reorganized the definition rather than risking an analysis where physical disability is excluded from the domain of labeling theory. Alfred Schutz raised the issue of how clear the notion of "rules" was in the labeling theorists' usage. Is there enough room in their usage to describe deviation?[33] Edwin Schur suggested that some distinction must be maintained between "rules" and "expectations"; however, little is said about the distinction.[34]

Milton Mankoff formulated a distinction between ascribed and achieved rule-breaking. Ascribed rule-breaking is a particular physical or visible impairment. Therefore, "the very beautiful and the very ugly can be considered ascriptive rule breakers." On the other hand, achieved rule-breaking involves "activity on the part of the rule-breaker regardless of his positive attachment to a deviant way of life." The homosexual who attempts to hide his rule-breaking behavior, and the regular marijuana user who freely admits his actions and flaunts them for status, both achieve their deviance. Mankoff applied this reasoning to point to the "severe limitations of labeling theory as a general theory of career deviance."[35]

Mankoff concluded that social reaction or labeling theories were insufficient because, while social reaction is a *necessary* condition for deviant careers, it is not a *sufficient* condition, especially in the case of ascriptive rule-breaking. Then, from labeling theory's perspective, it can be argued that social reactions can be successful in preventing ascribed rule-breakers from taking up normal roles, and thereby forcing them into deviant careers. But ascribed deviance is exclusive of the intentions of the actor; it reflects the deviant situation. Of course, the fields of anthropology and sociology have commonly agreed that a person's self emerges from social reaction. There really are no strangers in the city, in the sense that if a person is known as a stranger, there is a role position assigned for the person to play. Mankoff's rigorously employed rhetoric is attractive; it is paradoxical as well. The question may be better posed: "Why would a man hide his homosexuality, but flaunt his marijuana smoking in particular communities at particular times?" Only social reaction will sufficiently label one act negatively and another positively at any given time. Sadly, but surely, social reaction is largely ephemeral; any model of human action must address its transitory nature.

It is unclear what rules the physically disabled break. On the other hand, it is clear that they have organized national political action groups to fight in their interest. Therefore, the conception of power is problematic in the sense in which it is employed in labeling theory. The reasons for inclusion of the handicapped in labeling theory's framework of deviance seem unclear. The only way to have included them is for the sociologist, having the power to include them, to do so. The accomplishment of the inclusion of the physically disabled among labeling theory's deviants points to its liberal assumption that the physically disabled are as they are; that the achieved deviant may be normal only if she/he would choose to be normal. But the choice argument may represent an ad hominem that overlooks social constraints in the free marketplace of choice.

On the other hand, the physically disabled and the effeminate type of male must achieve their deviation too. The point does not refute the contention that the subject knows the rule and the expectation, and that he intends to, makes a choice to, break the rule.[36] A person who appears at a social gathering "dressed to kill" knows the rule as well as a moviegoer who "fires up a joint" at the local showing of the film *Gandhi*. It may be "normal" for both characters to appear in their ways. It may be just as normal for a man to arrive in a wheelchair at a disco to ask someone to open a door for him or prop him against the wall to facilitate his dancing. The broken rule may always be looked at in an ethical frame of reference, just as the ethic may be looked at in a political frame.

Notwithstanding, this brief theoretical discussion of phenomenology suggests that "social reaction" and "the imputation of deviance" are problematic—in need of critical questioning in terms of sociologists defining the morality of agency. These issues can be highlighted only because common sense does not tell us what is or is not deviant. A society will have to make its own rules, realizing their propensity toward ideology, and stick by them and argue them effectively until in the end someone beats the social agents over their heads and changes the rules. But the more a society knows about rules and rule-breakers, the greater the chances are that the society can effectively understand and advise on rule-breaking for sociopolitical ends.

The central problem with the perspectives being traced is that they all share the assumption that authority is organized in the context of roles. Those authoritative roles which are effectively executed are considered to provide social control. All of these theories lack a sense of political economy. It is exactly on the point of the political economy where race becomes salient, where the question of the central organizing theme of the international class order presents itself as race.

TOWARD A POLITICAL ECONOMY OF DEVIANCE

In this section I am conceptualizing the deviant social system and a general system of political-economic action. It is, first, important to systematically organize the distinctions I will be applying in suggesting a theory. One of the most significant factors in looking scientifically at any social action in these times is to draw a line of distinction between a "behavioral organism" and a "behavioral system." In fact, psychology has become understood as the study of "behavior of organisms." However, following Durkheim, Weber, Simmel, Parsons, Freud, Mead, and others, I am emphasizing the symbolic processes that could simply be called human behavior. Freud's demand for the distinction between "organic" (that is, behavioral organism or psychology) and "psychic" is an extremely significant one for understanding a social perspective on deviance. The distinction means that while the psychological may be understood in individual terms, the psychic must be understood in social terms.

Of course, it is important for any social theory to make sense in terms of what is generally known by science. The relationships between the psychological and the biological are important, but the psychological and biological dimensions must not be confused with the sociological dimension. One aspect of postmodernity is the tendency to embrace interdisciplinary studies. What is known, or accepted as knowledge, in the various fields related to the human subject should be acknowledged by related fields. A sound theory should include biological and psychological disagreements by considering them as an integral part of the explanation. I have set the organic references to one side.[37]

A second line to be drawn for the interpretation of black male deviance is between the empirical and the nonempirical. If it were not for such a distinction, Weber's "ideal type" would make little sense. Weber's "problems of meaning" stressed the diversity of "orientations" in religious systems to accommodate the vagaries related to such problems. He treated Calvinism and early Buddhism as polar opposites in the range of variations of possible meaningful religious orientations.[38] I feel justified in considering both the problems of meaning and the diversity of orientations in my analysis of deviance. These nonempirical social facts would result in purely political arguments if they were left out of consideration.

Weber, like Immanuel Kant, was skeptical of "metaphysics." In the *Critique of Pure Reason*, Kant avoided treating the categories of understanding of space and time as empirical things in the usual sense. He claimed they held a "transcendental" organization in terms of which empirical knowledge is made possible. He repeatedly stressed the framework of "assumptions" that allowed valid judgments to be made. Kant did not share David Hume's epistemological skepticism; he did not ask if valid empirical knowledge was possible, but asserted that we have it. He clearly drew the line between the sense data of empirical knowledge and the categories of understanding.[39]

Talcott Parsons, in "A Paradigm of the Human Condition," stressed the connection between Kant's nonempirical assumptions and judgments that complement the kind of binary thinking used in fields: "The linguist's 'deep structures' and 'surface structures,' the biologist's 'genotypes' and 'phenotypes,' the...sociologist's 'values', or 'institutional patterns' and 'interest.'"[40] In U.S. society, there are four categories that assist in understanding social domination: (1) the empirical-symbolic, (2) the nonempirical-symbolic, (3) the empirical-organic, and (4) the nonempirical-organic. Category (1) is controlled by institutions; category (2) by ideal culture; category (3) by biology; and category (4) by psychology.

The nonempirical-symbolic category requires clarification in terms of its appearance as distinctive and as differentiated from its essence. It appears that deviance is a matter of choice and that deviants reject the social a priori of personal identity. The result is that they associate freedom with chaos. But, according to the deviance theorists, the order-and-rule dimension does not disintegrate because of the deviant's relation to it. Every order has its own rules. But the deviant can break through only by personal grace; order is assaulted by the dogma of spontaneity, of which deviance represents a large measure.

The powerful have an interest in defining a rule as an instrument of measurement, an index with which we may measure something or somebody. For them, a rule indicates regularity; it allows a person to anticipate and therefore act. A rule tells us where and who we are in relationship to a social universe. The rule tells what is proper: property in nature and proprieties in social relations. Following the logic of the powerful, a property tells us what belongs to what in nature, and propriety tells us what belongs to whom in society. It is the basis for appropriate action in a given situation. What belongs to whom also tells us how to give a person his due; his due is our duty. For the powerful, duty is based on the idea of rule.

These assumptions made by the deviance theorists embrace the status quo because there is no site in their construction of reality for legitimate disagreement over the moral order. But in fact, historically speaking, there have been disagreements. The purpose of the order and rule of a society comes under scrutiny by those who recognize the political implications of such claims. Some schools of thought in the social sciences argue that the organization of social life is tending toward an end and/or purpose. Sociologists use the concept "telic" to express the idea of a purpose for the organization of society. The functionalist group of deviance theorists conceptualized a cybernetic analogy to explain how the interrelationship of institutional functions resulted in the nonempirical telic goal. By "cybernetic" they meant human control functions present in the group of institutions in a society.

Parsons's reliance on the cybernetic idea of the telic in his action theory is his explanation of rule and order. The telic system is, in the first place, associated with religion. It is in the religious systems in cultural histories that some connection is first found between belief and some nonempirical reality that was embraced by a community. But the definitions of "community" themselves are teleology.

"WHITE" THEORETICAL COMMUNITY

The classical approaches to community of Frederic LePlay, Ferdinand Tonnies, and Durkheim reason that communities are characterized by (1) a high degree of interpersonal intimacy in which relationships grow stronger through propinquity; (2) social order that is based upon consensus of wills and is buttressed by folkways, mores, and religion; (3) high moral commitments and dependency on reciprocity norms, familistic ties, kinship organizations, neighborhood ties, and a high degree of communalism; (4) existence as organic wholes and not as sums of all the characteristics of individual members, and larger size and difference from these aggregate wholes; and (5) ongoing associations between the natural and the supernatural, which are reflected in every reality that is socially observed.[41]

Tonnies's studies dichotomously differentiate between rural and urban communities. His dichotomy has influenced community social studies over the modern period. He argued that certain patterns of social relations tend to predominate in underdeveloped societies, while others originate in highly technological societies. He designated as gemeinschaft "the social order which, being based upon consensus of wills—rests on harmony and is developed and enabled by folkways, mores, and religion." He called gesellschaft "order which, being based upon a union of rational wills—rests on convention and agreement, is safeguarded by political legislation, and finds its ideological justification in public opinion."[42]

Durkheim's analysis of communities depicts another dichotomy. He classifies communities into those which have mechanical solidarity and those which have organic solidarity. The classification is fundamentally the same as Tonnies's gemeinschaft and gesellschaft.

Parsons consolidates these approaches, conceptualizing five patterned variables which demonstrate that undeveloped communities are characterized by particularistic values, affective norms, functional diffuseness in terms of goals, ascriptive norms, traditional beliefs, familiaristic norms, and shared beliefs. Developed communities, on the other hand, are characterized by universalistic values, affective neutrality, functional specificity, achievement-oriented evaluation, rational value norms, contractual relationships, and secular beliefs.[43]

The traditional abstract classificatory concepts about communities serve to argue that undeveloped communities are homogeneous while developed systems are diverse. The symbol of two significant Western legends, "all niggers look alike" and "the melting pot," come close to the dichotomous dimensions, which have not been substantiated by observation of community life in the United States.

For instance, the arguments about higher and lower cultures remained in W. Lloyd Warner's studies of "Yankee City." For Warner, "America...assimilates and fails to assimilate large numbers of immigrants from different European cultures..." His worldview is a Eurocentric one in which high and low cultures form a whole. The undeveloped people of color are not permitted consideration. Warner selected the city of Newburyport, Massachusetts, as the site for his study. One wonders why he did not study Chicago, beyond the stated reason that he "did not want a community where the ordinary daily relations of the inhabitants were in confusion and conflict."[44]

Along these lines of commentary, Colin Bell and Howard Newby cite questions Ruth Kornhauser asks of Warner's major studies:

[W]hy does Warner describe a large number of classes when only the upper strata recognize that many? Why are six divisions more "real" than the three or four that are recognized by the local strata? Why has Warner adopted the view of class held by the upper-middle class when members of the lower middle, upper lower, and lower lower classes (the vast majority of the population) are said to base their rankings solely on money?[45]

The point here is that the conception of community and the explanation of community stratification in sociology leave several questions about the definition unanswered. For example, they assume that the basis of social interaction in communities is roles and values. They ignore the definition of the social situation, which is perhaps the most important motivating factor for social action. They ignore the fact that deviation from certain role expectations is an extremely common phenomenon. But more important, they ignore the fact that changing social contexts make it possible for any sociologist to observe the extreme dichotomous patterns of behavior occurring within the same social context; in a word, they are politically value-laden concepts. The traditional views of community fail to explain uneven development; nor do they properly consider conflict over value orientations and authority.

If the national consciousness is that of gesellschaft, organic, and universalistic, it is hard to explain why the rates of stereotyped beliefs held by whites about blacks remain so high. The Harris Polls that measure rates of stereotyped beliefs held by whites report that such attitudes have remained high, especially on the items probing beliefs about black ambition, crime, and violence. It is commonly understood that postindustrial communities are distinguishable by moral density and universalistic perspectives, yet racism remains as a brutal feature of modern society. Some will point to the suburbs to explain particularistic values. But the suburbs largely developed as a result of white flight from urban areas, as the latter became increasingly occupied by people of color.

DECONSTRUCTING DEVIANCE LOGICS OF DOMINANCE

The consideration of the logics of white supremacy is linked with the Kantian idea of metareality, or symbolic reality, which I have identified as controlled by ideal culture. If the Kantian epistemology failed to give content to the categories, had Kant insisted that nothing more could be said of them beyond designating their nominal form, they would have become weak. I am therefore assuming that this ideal culture has meaning in respect to sacred social life. I rely on Freud and Durkheim for an explanation of its process: it arises first in the restrictions related to the totem (primal group); second, in restrictions related to religion; and finally, restrictions related to science. I will argue the significance of the metareality for my interpretation of African-American culture in the next chapter.

The first division is between the physical world and the nonempirical world. I have formulated four categories of concern for an interpretation of African-American male deviance: the ideal culture cell; the biological cell; the psychological cell; and the institutional cell. I have also suggested that they all work together.

The institutional constraints on action are particularly interesting in terms of their dramatic nature. I have said that a widespread disapproval of conflict descriptions arose in sociology, particularly during periods when the nation was at war. In fact, according to the "human relations" perspective, conflict, aggression, hostility, and the like were popular heresy and stood in opposition to a rational and universalistic understanding of sociology. Often, the word "conflict" was associated with pictures of destruction.

THEORIES OF CONFLICT OVER VALUES

Conflict became an increasingly important sociological concept with the domestic social turmoil following World War II. Lewis Coser's *The Functions of Social Conflict* and Ralf Dahrendorf's *Class and Class Conflict in Industrial Society* are two important works developing the theme. In their works, however, conflict is treated as strains, tensions, or stresses of social structures, and is regarded as pathological.[46]

Nonetheless, some of the earlier sociologists used social conflict as a central element of their conceptual systems. In theoretical analysis, conflict was pictured as a process. It was viewed both as natural and as contributing to the integration of society. Ludwig Gumplowicz and Gustav Ratzenhofer used conflict as the basis of social process; Lester Ward and Albion Small used it as one of the basic social processes. William Graham Sumner, Edward A. Ross, and Charles Horton Cooley saw conflict as one of the major processes that laced society together. Robert Park and Ernest Burgess treated conflict as one of the processual pillars of their sociological systems.[47]

Some works have stressed a synthesis between the consensus and conflict modes of understanding social organization. Dahrendorf argued that the consensus structure and the conflict process are "the two faces of society."[48] Therefore, he held, social integration results from both consensus of values and the coercion to compliance. Up to this point, I have written as if these two elements are complementary, but I have also stressed the role of power in the process of dominating subjugated groups.

In the work of the German sociologist Georg Simmel, we find a considerable contribution to the social conflict theme. Simmel's seminal essay "Group Expansion and the Development of Individuality" stressed that "basic relation as a dualistic drive":

One could speak of a particular quantum of the tendency toward individualization and of the tendency toward non-differentiation. The quantum is determined by personal, historical, and social circumstances; and it remains constant, whether it applies to purely psychological configurations or to the social community to which the personality belongs....We lead, as it were, a doubled, or if one will, a halfed existence. We live as an individual within a social circle, with tangible separation from its other members, but also as a member of this circle, with separation from everything that does not belong to it.[49]

Simmel stressed the conflict between the psychological and the ideal-cultural dimensions of human agency. But conflict is present in dynamic ways between any of the dimensions as well as within the dimensions. If style of life is treated as an element of the ideal-cultural dimension, it must be understood that various racial and ethnic styles of life will be in conflict with other styles of life. Of course, there are the hegemonic form and the deviant form. Of the historically prominent deviant forms, which are historically persistent conflict positions? I have isolated the black culture form as a central position of opposition in which the members of the black group share a sense of group position. The effect of the focus on conflict led many sociologists to become sensitive to conflict as a perspective to investigate deviance. It also became central to race relations. Herbert Blumer's thesis that race prejudice is "a sense of group position" and that empirical study involves "a concern with the relationship of racial groups" is representative of U.S. sociology's turn toward conflict.[50]

ORGANIZATION OF THE MODEL

I shall draw the conflict theme more precisely in this section. In this way, I can demonstrate the social uses of conflict and how conflict may help in the affirmative understanding of African-American male deviance.

The four-cell model offers a method of considering the gestalt of social deviance and social control. My organization of the model does not pretend to be an exercise in formal logic. It is important to organize the meaning of a method of analysis in an intelligent way to promote its clarity. The vertical axis is treated as representing internal-external influences on the actor. This has been common practice since Descartes, in order to organize our consideration in reference to the Cartesian subject-object distinction. The internal usually is represented as the "low" row. But it should be kept in mind that the entire system, so far as agency is concerned, is internal. In this way there is a recognized connection to the relation between the cultural meaning and the actor. I am not suggesting a deterministic or mechanistic understanding of culture and institutions. In fact, I am attempting to grasp African-American agency as both institutionalized and spontaneous forms.

Organization of Model

	(Structure) *empirical*	(Function) *nonempirical*	
Symbolic	Institutions	Ideal Culture	*External*
Organic	Biology *(sign)*	Psychology *(symbol)*	*Internal*

First, the consciousness is primarily determined by the relationship between the structure of institutions and culture. Under capitalist organization, institutions are in the first instance economic structures. The group's position in the social order is administered by the relationship between the group and the hegemonic rule. This set of relationships primarily determines group consciousness.

Second, the distinction between structure and function seems to be justified. In Parsonian action theory these categories might be labeled "instrumental-consummatory." Prior to Parsons's labels, the prototype usually had been referred to as the means-ends relationship. Naturally, the means had to precede the ends. However, the means-ends vocabulary had developed to account for rational as well as irrational action. The polar concepts "rational-irrational" are, of course, admitted by those using them to be political positions. Hence, I have chosen to unveil them not as rational/irrational constructs but in terms of the practical interests of various groups. Much of what can be identified as black culture is viewed as irrational by instrumentalist standards of the status quo.

Third, symbolic meaning is the dividing line between the internal and the external; but the external systems themselves have meanings, are representations. Beyond the meaningful strivings there are strivings in the individual organic or psychological subject. These may often be said to be "subcultural" when they appear as group strivings; however, even if the term "subcultural" is used, the orientation of the action is primarily related to the acquisition of privilege in the structural sense of the term. (I have not accepted the subculture concept, for the reasons I wrote about in Chapter 4.)

Finally, I placed the institutional, empirical, symbolic structures on the "given" side of the model. Some will wonder why they have been placed there, since the social goals are usually thought to be inscribed in social institutions. However, I consider the telic organization inherent in the social construction of institutions to be clearly value-laden and filled with illusion. I claim the instrumentality of deviance as a constituent part of the telic. Thereby, even oppressed groups are considered to have institutional agency at specific sites of resistance. Furthermore, I recognize the analytical distinction between purposeful goals and actions. Telic systems do not act; humans act on telic systems. Physical systems do not act either, and they should not be considered telic, although their value may take on telic means. So, while I have created various distinctions, I have not divided the world from its finite conception as a totality. Nor have I created two conceptual standards to be applied to different groups based on their status, privilege, or interests.

It is important to indicate the specific structuralism I am suggesting in this study of black male deviance. Some of the structuralists have denied history, and others have denied that there is a real object that can be called history. I have understood that the structures which influence African-American male behavior are not real and universally given facts. Rather, I see specific phenomena resulting from the historical genesis and transformations in the society. The African-American element functions as a revolutionary force with diminished privileges.

Generally speaking, sociologists understand privilege as a guaranteed advantage for a person or group that is withheld from other persons or groups. Privileges are not only material phenomena but can also be symbolic. Symbolic and economic objectives that would be beneficial to a particular group or segment of society are interests. Of course, an interest can also be a favorable disposition toward an object (material or symbolic) or an activity, and a consistent preference for the object or activity over others.

METHOD OF INTERPRETING SYMBOLS OF MEANING

In this section I shall account for the functioning of secular moral culture. I am committed to examining the moral reasons that account for African-American cultural deviance from norms through a neutral process of observing competing norms. Since I have adopted the conflicting action point of view, I shall discuss the structural as if it is logically prior to the dynamic. However, I must add that it is not my project to determine the original dialectic between structure and dynamism.

I have suggested that human orientation takes the form of treating the world, including deviance itself, as a combination of parts that have symbolically apprehendable meaning to the actors. It has generally been agreed to call these parts "objects" and to speak of the relationship as a subject-object relationship. In psychology we call the relationship cognitive, a relationship of a knowing subject to a known object. Descartes made the classical statement in the seventeenth century. His epistemology addressed what contributes to knowing the external world and how it is known. The empiricists, generally using such concepts as "sense impressions," have stressed the contribution from outside the knowing object. Hume represents a rare and exemplary case of this perspective. He denied the existence of any other component. Kant refuted Hume's lack of faith with his insistence on the contribution from the "categories of understanding," which have been seen in combination with sense data. The Kantian epistemology relies upon symbiosis between the mind and things on the symbolic level or the mind and material things.

It seems appropriate to accept the Kantian view in our concern with deviance. In my view, African-American deviants are conceived as actors and as outside of the action system as well as in it. The start of social experience for all human actors is human language. But language, in my sense of usage, is not itself a form of knowledge; it is a medium through which knowing any object may be communicated. The object is conceived as an aspect of *relational organization* about which cognitively meaningful communication between human actors may occur. Thus, in order to be known, the object must have been "indicated" or, more commonly, "observed." At any rate, this implies that the object may be communicated about by an observer to another without the latter having actually observed the object.

My reason for defining knowledge as a social relationship that functions through the tool of language is that I would like to emphasize that it is both possible to picture an object with a word, to represent it, and possibly to misrepresent it with a word. Groups will very often create words to define an object for which there is no specific word. Think of recently coined words like "stagflation" or "postmodern." There is a famous quote by Karl Marx: "The concrete is the outcome of multiple determinations"; and words are tools in an ensemble of social relations where meanings are contested in situations of conflict. In fact, the reason for the communication in the first place is to tell another person about an object that is presumed by the teller to be unobserved by the person told, and to gain hegemony for that interpretation (reading) of the object.

Cognition, in the human sense, first acquired status as the cultural entity that developed into science. The move toward the empirical was probably buttressed by the fact that physical objects do not react to their human knowers in the same way as living objects do. Clearly, other tendencies of orientation exist above the cognitive mechanisms. Here, again, it would be an error to conceive of the "other" human object as a physical object simply because a power group defines the other in those terms. What is important is the struggle and resistance of the other; definitions of deviance emerge from struggle.

THE IMPORTANCE OF EMOTIONS

But the tendency to privilege the empirical raises another concern for students of deviance. It asks what is the place for the emotional (what empiricists label "irrational") part of action. The best modern discussion of emotions of which I am aware probably comes from Freud. He formulated the concept "cathexis," which is the investment of emotional significance in activities, objects, and ideas.[51] Freud increasingly used the word "object" in this context. The context dealt with the emotional, or affective, association of a subject to an object. The distinction was clearly raised between this level and the cognitive. Freud's thesis was concerned with human individuals, but he never excluded human collectivities or nonhuman objects.[52] Moreover, on the cathexis side of human action I also believe there is a sharing; by this I mean a subject-object relationship. Even if that relationship is one of struggle, the deviant subject (or the group as a collective subject) has something to give, as well as receive, from a dominating object. So, just as in the cognitive sense, in the emotional case a dialectic exists.

Freud contended that there exists an "energy" which is central to establishing and sustaining cathexes. He called this energy "libido," which has its point of departure in the human organism. He pointed out that certain aspects of the human organism, particularly the erogenous zones, collect symbolic meanings in the construction of objects for cathexis.[53] Of course, organisms are not the only objects that acquire strong emotional attachments by human actors. All classes of objects and ideas are open to strong emotional attachments; Freud, however, gave priority to the organic cathexis. The connection of the relation of the actors to the ideal symbolic system is a complex one, especially when we draw connections to the other categories that I have outlined.

However, I am suggesting that the most conspicuous feature takes the form of constructing meanings at the symbolic level, which are communicated in linguistic terms. The meta-objects are often talked about by actors as being themselves actors (as in a fetish), like deified heroes, but there is no truth to these deifications. These deifications are in the mind of the indicators or, as I indicated earlier, the linguistic terms only act as a medium through which an object may be known in the order of things. Meta-objects are formed, reproduced, and changed in struggle; it would be an error to regard the meta-object abstractions as real phenomena.

SOCIAL SYMBOLISM

Let us turn for the moment to an examination of this symbolism, its meaning and effect.[54] A simple reflection on the different epochs of civilization reveals variation in their attitudes toward symbolism. For example, the age of Romanticism in England, France, Germany, and the United States was marked with, aside from sadness, terror, and rebellion, a high regard for the symbolic. Gothic architecture was highly symbolic, the sentimental ceremonies were symbolic, the philosophers were symbolic. Men like Georg Hegel and Victor Hugo, who viewed their missions as approximating those of the angels, represented the symbols that dominated the culture's imagination. With the revolutions, the reassertion by Marx and Engels of the "material," Henry David Thoreau's *Civil Disobedience*, and the discovery of gold in California, men put away symbols in the sky for direct apprehension of the bottom line, the facts of matter.

This description of symbolism will not suffice for my purposes. The very fact that it can be pointed to at one time and not another proves that it is superficial. There is more meaningful symbolism, which is impossible to do without, in our lives. Language is one such symbolism. Again, it is not the sound of the word or its arrangement on paper that is substantive. Rather, the ideas, images, and emotions that the symbol raises in the mind of the listener or reader are central to scientific understanding of the symbol.

Mathematics is another kind of symbolism. Algebraic symbols, for example, are different from language symbols because the former do our reasoning for us. This is not true of ordinary language. We do not forget the meaning of language and seek mere syntax to bail us out. At any rate, there are major distinctions to be made in my definition of symbolism.

Another aspect of symbolism centers on perception. We look and see a particular object before us; we may say, "There is a chair." Suppose an Australian aborigine glanced at the chair also. He or she might see firewood. An artist, on the other hand, might see color and shape combined to create beauty. Most are not so cold as to burn chairs for firewood or artistic enough to be highly aroused in emotion and thought to see the art value of a chair. Most will see the chair as an object upon which to sit. It does not, however, require any abundance of intelligence to realize that a chair is a thing for sitting. In fact, I am suggesting just the opposite; the well-trained person will refrain from the use value of the chair that is an art object. He or she will neither burn it nor sit on it, but will appreciate it aesthetically. To know the combination of patterns, to sense a shape of material or light, does not require training, however. Imagine that if a dog came into the room where the chair was placed, it might jump onto it, using it for the purpose of support. Of course, if the dog were well trained, it would refrain from jumping onto the chair. Therefore, the development from a color shape or object to its various uses appears to be an ordinary one.

We may suppose that the combinations of patterns, or colored shapes, are symbols for some other aspect of human experience. When we see particular patterns, we adjust ourselves to those colored shapes. It is not simply an automatic response, because men and dogs often disregard chairs when they see them. Sense perception, then, appears to be characteristic of responses to environmental conditions. We need only reflect on a rose turning toward the sunshine to realize that all organisms have experience of stimulus response.

Symbolism is primarily related to the use of innocent sense perceptions in the form of more elementary experiences that groups have had. I am chiefly concerned with the influence of symbolism on social life. During the late nineteenth century there was a tendency toward studying the environmental influence of elementary experiences through the examination of plant and animal life. At that same time we find an increase in emphasis on the historical method. Freud's method of studying "savages" to ascertain the elementary patterns in the development of morons is an example of an heir of this focus.

Over and again we find, as I pointed out earlier, a strain between direct knowledge and symbolism. The empiricists say that what has been experienced is testable. On the other hand, symbolism is amorphous; it may elicit actions, feelings, and positions without a pattern existing in the universe from which we have extracted the symbolic. So we may suppose that symbolism is a basic element in the way we act, given our direct knowledge. Humanity can exist only on the basis of justified symbolic representations. But error comes from symbolism, too. The arena of politics determines what will be focused upon by "science," or collective reason, at a particular period. Moreover, it is the responsibility of social groups to form reasonable positions in conflict situations in order to resolve the contested meanings attached to various symbols.

In a peculiar way, the political aspect of the problem is generally filed under the rubric of epistemology: How do we know; how is error created; how do we know that our definitions for acting rightly and wrongly are correct? I am first drawing attention to the political sociology of domination and its symbolism. It might properly be called "direct recognition," because the experience of domination must be symbolically rationalized, accommodated, or resisted.

The Marxists have given considerable attention to consciousness, insisting on conscious political acts as the only real political action. Therefore, political action without established intent is inconceivable for them. Furthermore, the practice of this logic must be in the form of the established dogma of party organization in order to attract the people's interests. However, because of unintended consequences, individual and group intentionality and rationality are suspect. It is far more prudent to question resistance.

Therefore, my definition of the symbolic is that it is a function of the human mind in which some parts of experience elicit awareness, belief, emotion, and form with regard to other parts of experience. We may distinguish the symbol from the meaning. It is justifiable to refer to the organic transition from symbolic to meaningful as the symbolic reference. The symbolic world is the part of life that pulls together the world of the actor. Its base is the relationship between symbol and meaning. From this arrangement it is not necessary for an actor to create a symbolic reference; nor does the symbolic world determine which is symbol and which is the meaning; nor does it guarantee right action. But perception is the central tool of self-production. There are so many things in the social universe that the actor is limited to selecting those things to be acted on within the outlines of the available subject positions. Self-production is only partially a moral category. An opportunity to self-produce develops out of the congealed context of dissimilar self-producing activities, including feelings, perceptions, and purposes. For example, the actor may produce agitation or compliance.

Earlier, I suggested that the symbolic, or telic, structures and meanings are a cultural process. However, in a sense, they are more to us than that. Action is not only the choice of the actor, *given the constraints of structure*. The actor is the only qualified source for meaning of his action. It can be summed up in Herbert Blumer's well-known words:

> On the methodological or research side of the study of action, it would have to be made from the position of the actor. Since action is forged by the actor out of what he perceives, interprets, and judges, one would have to see the operating situation as the actor sees it, perceive objects as the actor perceives them, ascertain their meaning in terms of the meaning they have for the actor, and follow the actor's line of conduct as the actor organizes it—in short, one would have to take the role of the actor and see his world from his standpoint.[55]

We should not be left with a picture that the symbolic reference will always be the same for a person under similar conditions. It is not prudent to draw such a conclusion. For this very reason, I have been speaking in terms of themes throughout the book. Language is not a set of concrete rules with determined responses. Rather, language stories of life are being communicated by actors for a reason. The stories and the reasons are constantly in flux. While the individual transaction of a language story occurs only once, the themes are more enduring. My argument is that myth structures remain and are reproduced, transformed, or eliminated in historical blocs. One of the important parts of cultural analysis is to elaborate how certain myth themes endure, change, or become extinct among specific groups. For example, how is the dominant myth, assuming black male deviation, reproduced among social scientists? How is it transformed? How do aspects of its logic disappear? My bias is clearly that the process of deviation is irreversible. It is the work of analysis to find and trace the historical development of specific forms of deviance.

MATERIAL AND SYMBOLIC SCARCITY

Nicholas Georgescu-Roegen, in *The Entropy Law and the Economic Process*, points to the way that irreversibility of particular social processes acts upon our world.[56] The second law of thermodynamics states that if we burn a lump of coal, that act can occur only once. There is, of course, the same amount of energy in the heat, smoke, and ashes as there was in the original coal, but the energy bound up in the combustion products is so dissipated that it is unavailable for use, unlike the "free" energy in the coal.

Entropy is a measure of the energy bound up in the used products that is so dissipated that it is unavailable for use. The entropy law requires that the entropy of a closed system increase, the change being from free energy to bound energy, and not the other way around. Entropy, then, is a measure of disorderliness. The coal is more orderly than is the burned coal. The natural state of things is to always pass from order to disorder. The symbol for entropy is time's arrow.

The idea of entropy as an index of disorder includes two categories of description: low and high entropy. An ingot of copper has low entropy because its atoms are arranged in a more orderly state than they were in the original copper ore. The refiner is not responsible for the creation of low entropy in the creation of the ingot. But the smelting process has spent far more high entropy by converting free energy to bound energy. All of humankind's activities, according to the entropy law, end in deficit. We cannot produce anything except at a far greater cost in low entropy.

There is one other aspect of this law that might be of interest to students of deviance. Humans depend on low entropy for life: they absorb low entropy in the form of feeding, directly or indirectly, on sunlight, and they give out high entropy in the form of waste and heat. Life feeds on low entropy, and so do systems of privilege. Objects of economic value, such as fruit, cloth, china, lumber, and copper, are highly ordered low-entropy objects. Low entropy is truly the root of economic scarcity.

In large measure, social action is conflict in the struggle of self-production for the acquisition of low entropy. In the language of white patriarchy, the subject has two conflicting desires: to "hoard the women" and to direct the sharing of outcomes, at times given to one desire and at times given to the other. The life of the subject may be compared to a dream state in which she or he is "called" to the threshold with a poor awareness of reality. The waking state (by which I mean the rational part of the individual) is, in a particular sort of way, out of the subject's control, but it structures the order of morality. She or he is constrained to act as she or he is—to be what she or he is; but her or his consciousness is falsely determined by the structure.

It is only with this realization on the part of the subject that a person may develop atonement with the father symbol. In my view, the empiricists omit the process of this internal negotiation, at the symbolic level, between the individual and tradition. Yet, the empiricists want to treat the symbol as a thing. I want to treat the thing as a symbol. I am suggesting that the empirical should be treated as a symbol that is involved in a power relationship with other symbols in the social order. The task becomes to uncover the meaning of different representations of various symbols at different points in time.

SUMMARY

This chapter has traced the theme of liberal freedom and situated it as the guiding ideology in the articulation of African-American male deviance. The liberal perspectives were permeated by a tradition of racial supremacy. Thus, they ignored the social fact of black maleness. The liberals' promulgation of the a priori assumption of black male deviance was challenged at the site of social values. The challenge was essential from the inception of race superiority through the various historical periods of U.S. racial formations. The manifestations of the underlying conflict over social values were presented most prominently in popular culture. Nonetheless, the language of the social science community implicated the scientific intelligentsia in the cultural reproduction of African-American social suppression.

The utilitarian, positivist, phenomenological, and labeling approaches were all ultimately interested in pointing to the containment and control of African Americans, whether their agendas were stated or masked in obfuscating philosophical or statistical language. For them, *only their language represented knowledge*. On the other side of the struggle was a popular and persistent critique of social science arrogance.

In the course of this book I have arranged the presentation from the symbolic, employing Richard Wright's *Native Son* as an example, to the concrete, where I presented empirical examples of African-American male struggle, to the abstract, where I explored the theoretical and philosophical conflicts associated with African-American maleness. In the next chapter, I shall present a linkage for configuring these themes in a general Marxist framework.

CHAPTER 6

Fundamental Forms of Consciousness

The relations of production [correspond] to a given stage in the development of the material forces of production. The totality of these relations of production constitutes the economic structure of society, the real foundation, in which arises a legal consciousness.

Karl Marx

The peculiar aspect of the social history presented in this book reveals that black institutions developed separately from white institutions as colonial organizations. In the key institutional areas of family, schooling, religion, and state, blacks have historically been excluded and discriminated against. The general trend in sociological research has been to deny the race factor, and when a minority of social scientists have reminded its practitioners of their white supremacist history and their work within a racist society, the general leadership of the field has chosen to ignore those significant contributions.[1] Scholars of color who have worked outside of the mainstream conceptual frameworks within the field are invisible to the majority of U.S. sociologists; white scholars are legitimately allowed to address these concerns, in spite of the fact that, for the most part, their work is marginalized.

In the Preface, I suggested that the bourgeois ideology dominated the conceptual framework of sociology that depicted African-American males as deviant. In this chapter I will trace three bourgeois themes that had import for my research: Karl Mannheim's structure of thinking; Emile Durkheim's ritual solidarity; and Sigmund Freud's sociology of history. Naturally, I am interested in configuring these themes in a general Marxist framework in order to illuminate the forms of consciousness that have failed, due to a lack of a real humanist tradition (in the sense of the emancipating science that I stressed in earlier chapters) in U.S. social science study of marginalized, disreputed, excluded, and ignored groups.

KNOWLEDGE AND STRUCTURE OF THINKING

On the methodological side of the question, I insisted on not assessing the validity of any truth claim. Mannheim often referred to the "existential conditions of thought," which are concerned with cognition at the sociological level of study. He classified the existential conditions of thought as "pure sociology."[2] Pure sociology is a cultural analysis of specific communities. Mannheim wrote:

> In the case of pure sociology, to the extent that the pure structures of the social are worked out by grasping their essence, the character of necessity in assertions about them will be immediately evident. What is distinguished in community as essential for its characterization will be evident in the individual case, which is only to be taken as an exemplification. The essence of community cannot be inferred from a system. It must be exemplified by illustrative cases. Its presence cannot be "deduced" a priori, without any experience of communities. Once one has grasped the phenomenon of community, however, one will be able to grasp directly what is essential in it by stripping away the features which are merely factual.[3]

On the other hand, Mannheim also pointed to "general sociology," which he defined as a concern with "essence-generalities," proceeding inductively as it gathers facts. The generalizations are designed to remain on the surface, abstracted from cultural contexts and their historical stages. The only thing intended by the identification of patterns that recur in this realm is to establish in the most general terms the forms that are repeated in the world of appearance. This represents the function of the mythic form as I have used it in this book.[4]

The theme retained from Mannheim's sociology of knowledge (science) is the worldview that individuals are all members of groups; all groups have an interested position toward the existing order of things; and the organization of human thought in individuals is best understood by discriminating the relationship between groups and their interested position toward the existing order of things.[5]

A clear example of the validity of these generalizations in the early chapters of this book is the statement that the order of things is a racist order. Naturally, if this statement is placed before most white male officials of the U.S. institutions, they will vehemently disagree. On the other hand, most self-identified victims of racism will have a different orientation to the symbolic arrangement (manipulation) of knowledge that denies racism. The power relationship between blacks and whites in the United States means that white men may willy-nilly proclaim relationships, structures, institutions, and the general order of things not to be racist. Standing against the great power of white proclamation is fruitless. White power is impervious to argument or sentiment. So, it bears repeating: the sociology of knowledge does not address the truth claim.

It seems appropriate to remind the reader that in the Preface I pointed out that Marx distinguished between surface relations and essential patterns:

The *final pattern* of economic relations *as seen on the surface*, in their real existence and consequently in the conceptions by which the bearers and agents of these relations *seek to understand them*, is very different from, and indeed quite the reverse of, their *inner but concealed essential pattern and the conception corresponding to it.*[6]

The point here is a subtle issue raised in the social sciences that economic relations have not always held the determinate sites in social relations, particularly where politico-religious institutions are most salient.[7] I follow Marx's hypothesis that different social relations have unequal values in the production and reproduction of society that are determined by the functions they assume in the process. Social relations serve as the framework for the accumulation of wealth and control over all nature at the disposal of the society, and of all production. In short, social relations are determined in the first instance by economic organization, and social relations in the last instance determine the formation of society.

The base and superstructure metaphor suggests that under capitalist logic, the economic base conditions are distinguishable from the forms of state and social consciousness. Maurice Godelier should be credited with clarifying the base-superstructure distinction:

the distinction between infrastructure (base) and superstructures is neither a distinction between levels or instances, nor a distinction between institutions—although it may present itself as such in certain cases. In its underlying principle, it is a distinction between *functions.*[8]

A society is an organization of relations between human beings, relations that have more or less prominence based on the nature of their functions. These functions determine the effect of each of their activities on the society's reproduction. Godelier explained that the activities must fulfill the function of a relation of production:

For a social activity—and with it the ideas and institutions that correspond to and organize it—to play a dominant role in a society's functioning and evolution (and hence in the thought and actions of the individuals and groups who compose this society), it is not enough for it to fulfill several functions; in addition to its explicit ends and functions, it must of necessity directly fulfill the function of a relation of production.[9]

Usually, production is thought of only in terms of producing material goods (like tools and homes), and not in terms of mental representations, such as the production of rules for using tools or rules for living as families. However, there is a mental component in all social reality, and it is found in all its functions in all human activities which exist only in society.[10] All production of representations has developed in mankind to organize activities of production; they have all been illusory, according to those who do not believe in them. That is to say that disbelief in representation is the process of producing myth. As Godelier wrote:

> By definition, a myth is only a myth for those who do not believe in it, and the first to believe in myths are those who invent them, in other words who think them as fundamental "truths" which they imagine to have been inspired in them by supernatural beings such as gods, ancestors and so on.[11]

African-American men are produced and reproduced in society. This means that society is the context for the social relation of dominance. These uses of the terms "society" and "social relation" should be distinguished from relations that actually occur in a civil environment. In fact, as I will develop shortly, the relations are socially perverse, lacking civility, in the U.S. case. But the subject position of black maleness is an interested position in the social organization. Therefore, black men will assist in the reproduction of their subjection because the roles they are required to play in society are structured to reproduce all social production.

RITUAL SOLIDARITY

All societies have institutions the individual (i.e., socially constructed self) either believes in or does not believe in. Belief is produced by social relationships, generally based on indoctrination during the socialization process. The most graphic example in the United States is the reciting of the pledge of allegiance to the flag; the moment is perhaps the most sacred ritual period in the national experience.[12] Durkheim argued that the key to the sacred element is not the belief or the content of a "religious" experience, but the ritual performed in relationship to the experience. In his study of religions, Durkheim found that the solidarity produced during ritual had its source in group symbols.[13] This, in fact, is the nonrational part of both religious and civil-religious behavior. This finding helps us to understand not only religious and political behaviors and commitments but also other secular behaviors and commitments.[14]

Through symbols, individuals are able to construct a self, which sociologist Charles Horton Cooley termed "the looking glass self": the idea is that individual consciousness is a social construction. In earlier chapters I discussed this tendency and its application to deviance and social control. Here, I wish to remind the reader of the general idea that individual consciousness is socially produced and reproduced through social communication, which entails symbolic references.

These references are communicated through ritual action, where respect for the ritual is right and a violation of it is an error.[15]

There are, of course, monumental differences between the worldviews of Emile Durkheim and Karl Marx. However, that is not the concern here. The most salient similarity is the social construction of consciousness; or more specifically, the connection between the concepts of collective conscience and ideology. For Marx, the process of reproduction of society requires an ideology that is above the individuals in the society. This view was shared by Durkheim in his concept of the "collective conscience." As Marx wrote:

> In most Asiatic fundamental forms...the all-embracing *unity* which stands above all these small communities may appear as the higher or sole proprietor, the real communities may only as heredity possessors. Since the *unity* is the real owner, and the real pre-condition of common ownership, it is perfectly possible for it to appear as a particular being above the numerous real, particular communities. The individual is then in fact propertyless, or property...appears to be mediated by means of a grant from the total unity—which is realized in the despot as the father of the many communities—to the individual through the mediation of the particular community. It therefore follows that the surplus-product (which, incidentally, is legally determined as a consequence of the real appropriation through labour) *belongs of itself to this higher unity.*[16]

The theoretical recognition of the natural tendency to make a fetish of community morality through the mechanism of the symbolic and the mythic is critical to understanding the construction of African-American response to a social formation structured in dominance. The fetish conceals the real functioning of the principal structure of a social formation (society). An example is the aphorism "Work hard and you will get ahead." This particular statement will impact different groups according to their experience with other practices in the society. It would have been nearly impossible to convince any conscious slave under the organization of plantation slavery in the United States that the society really worked in a way to reward merit. It is far easier to convince a current-day African American that the reason most blacks do not get ahead is because they are lazy: *the fetish conceals the real functioning of the principal structure of the U.S. social formation.* On the other hand, an African American who has had the general experiences of most blacks in the United States will find the ideology linking merit and work impossible to argue against or replace.

METAPSYCHOLOGY

The final theme is of a sociology of history that was retained in my scientific analysis of African-American males in their specific social formation based on dominance. The bourgeois scholar Sigmund Freud revealed aspects of the unconscious and, in an earlier chapter, I used his concept of cathexis. The implication of the unconscious aspects of social life became of great significance, particularly for the Frankfurt School, which influenced the New Left and much of the leadership of the Black Power movement. The importance of this tendency has to do with the unseen mechanisms of consciousness and the effects of the unconscious on history.

We should not confuse the issues, since Freud was guilty of phallocentrism, heterosexism, misogyny, sexism, and homophobia. Avoiding the danger of presenting an apology (the apparent problems with translation, the historical misrepresentations, the various schools and nuances of the psychoanalytic movement), the salient aspect of the Freudian position is bourgeois. Freud reified bourgeois culture, failing to explicate the social structures for its moribund status. While the Frankfurt School (particularly Russell Jacoby, Herbert Marcuse, and Theodore Adorno) did not reach an identical conclusion, they recognized the inability of Freud to explain Hitler, Stalin, and other contradictions of the bourgeois period:

> The greatness of Freud consists in that, like all great bourgeois thinkers, he left standing undissolved such contradictions and disdained the assertion of pretended harmony where the thing itself is contradictory. He revealed the antagonistic character of the social reality.[17]

What Freud contributed to sociology was the connection between the conscious and unconscious dimensions of social life. When we say that black males are controlled by institutions, it should not be forgotten that these institutional relations include a dimension of the unconscious. Richard Lichtman wrote:

> Freud made an absolutely vital discovery in noting a connection between conscious and unconscious processes, the mode of mental organization and the nature of the defense mechanisms....It is...a crucial dimension of social life, because the ensemble of public-private relations that constitute the structure of the social world is also constituted out of diverse levels of mental organization. There has been almost no recognition of this fact in Marxist theory....Institutions are maintained, however, not only through (a) the formal and explicit rules that define their practice; (b) the implicit and informal procedures that both bind and interpret the meaning of these codified principles; (c) the structural mandates one aspect of the system imposes upon other sectors of the totality; but also (d) through the powerfully adhesive forces of the repressed, unconscious meanings and processes that bind each social agent to the preceding dimensions of the public realm.[18]

The unconscious dimension arises from experience. In earlier chapters I have attempted to graphically describe the kinds of experiences to which black males are typically exposed. It should be clear that the categories which were constructed are abstractions much like Simmel's ideal forms or Weber's ideal types. In fact, the Marxist categories are theoretical abstractions as well. Of course, Simmel's and Weber's processes of abstraction (or theoretical abstraction, if you will) differed from the Marxist process. I arrived at my abstractions by moving from the analysis of the concrete to the abstract.

Some learned persons will question the appropriateness of constructing a general black cultural experience and viewing the experience across the board, disregarding issues of region and religious background, and disregarding socioeconomic groups at points in the analysis. My point is to highlight the structural as it interfaces with consciousness/unconsciousness by revealing the essential in the black U.S. experience: *the level of reality that exists beyond the visible relations.*

Lichtman pointed to Freud's discussion of "topographic regression, the tendency of material at the level of the P[re]c[onsciou]s to be recognized according to the principle of the U[n]c[onsciou]s, Freud emphasizes the transformation of thoughts into images."[19] Freud wrote:

When regression has been completed, a number of cathexes are left over in the system *Ucs.*—cathexes of memories of *things.* The primary psychical process is brought to bear on these memories, till by condensation of them and displacement between their respective cathexes, it has shaped the manifest dream content.[20]

The problems that exist in Freud's account of the unconscious are not the concern here, since it would require another book to address the subject. I am calling attention to the analogy in the theoretical formulation of the hidden (repressed). And I am suggesting that a group's *memories of things* are both consciously and unconsciously passed from one generation to the next. It is exactly this memory that the bourgeoisie require to be forgotten; their ideological task becomes to revise history and reinscribe white supremacy. On the other side of the social relation, the white revision of history, is the black memory whose only escape into social being is to become a "white person"; otherwise, the blacks remain mere animals. As Frantz Fanon indicated:

We understand now why the black man cannot take pleasure in his insularity. For him there is only one way out, and it leads into the white world. Whence his constant preoccupation with attracting the attention of the white man, his concern with being powerful like the white man, his determined effort to acquire protective qualities—that is, the proportion of being or having what enters into the composition of an ego.[21]

The account of the social construction of consciousness in Freud is even implied in Marx. The task of the scientist becomes the demystification of the *"hidden"* and a reminder of what has been forgotten. In practice, and thus theoretically, the bourgeois revision of history is doomed to failure. The bourgeois fetishized consciousness has lost the awareness of history, of its brutality and oppression, which the oppressed experience as their circumstance. As Marx wrote in *The Eighteenth Brumaire of Louis Bonaparte*:

> Men make their own history, but they do not make it just as they please; they do not make it under circumstances chosen by themselves, but under circumstances directly encountered, given and transmitted from the past. The tradition of all dead generations weighs like a nightmare on the brain of the living. And just when they seem engaged in revolutionizing themselves and things, in creating something that has never yet existed, precisely in such periods of revolutionary crisis they anxiously conjure up the spirits of the past to their service and borrow from them names, battle cries and costumes in order to present the new scene of world history in this time-honored disguise and this borrowed language.[22]

Marx is describing what is analogous to Freud's return of the repressed, which is, after all, the function of psychoanalysis. But what is the relationship between the consciousness of the individual and the superego of the culture? This question is the crux of my understanding of the relationship between the black male individual and the mythic constructions of the community. Marx, in his *Economic and Philosophic Manuscripts of 1844*, wrote:

> My general consciousness is only the theoretical shape of that of which the living shape is the real community, the social fabric, although at the present day *general* consciousness is an abstraction from real life and as such antagonistically confronts it. Consequently, too, the *activity* of my general consciousness, as an activity, is my theoretical existence as a social being....Man, much as he may therefore be a *particular* individual (and it is precisely his particularity which makes him an *individual*, and a real individual social being), is just as much the *totality*—the ideal totality—the subjective existence of thought and experienced society present for itself; just as he exists also in the real world as the awareness and the real enjoyment of social existence, and as a totality of human life-activity.[23]

I stressed earlier that the consciousness of the individual derives not from ideas present in the person's mind but from the real experiences of social existence. *In the case of black males, that social existence produces a specific fundamental consciousness, given the structural location of black maleness as it develops to maturity in the context of its essential historical nature.*

Freud encouraged this scientific reading when, in *Civilization and Its Discontents*, he stressed the relationship between the community consciousness and the consciousness of the individual:

> The analogy between the process of civilization and the path of individual development may be extended in an important respect. It can be asserted that the community, too, evolves a super-ego under whose influence cultural development proceeds....In many instances the analogy goes still further, in that during their lifetime these figures [culture makers] were—often enough, even if not always—mocked and maltreated by others and even dispatched in a cruel fashion. In the same way, indeed, the primal father did not attain divinity until long after he had met his death by violence.[24]

Freud went on to describe the processes of individual and group cultural development as constituting an interlocked relationship, which is analogous to Marx's interpretation:

> At this point the two processes, that of the cultural development of the group and that of the cultural development of the individual, are, as it were, always interlocked. For that reason some of the manifestations and properties of the super-ego can be more easily detected in its behavior in the cultural community than in the separate individual.[25]

SUMMARY

In this chapter I discussed the importance of the mental in understanding African-American deviance. I stressed that social relations represent an element of the economic relations. Because my unit of analysis is society, I avoided privileging either the economic or some other aspect of the society. Rather, I stressed the fact that the mental involves both conscious and unconscious aspects and both individual and collective aspects of society.

Under the rule of white social organization, the only redemption for African-American men is to become "white," while simultaneously it is structurally impossible for them to be socially produced as white men. Examining the construction of African-American myths provided an understanding of both conscious and unconscious black collective memories perpetuated through ritualized social action. African-American ritualized action is conspicuous for its struggle and resistance.

CHAPTER 7

Conclusion: African-American Criminality and Emancipatory Democracy

In this book I have argued that African Americans essentially represent a cultural force in a struggle for real democracy, which does not yet exist in the United States. Social scientists, particularly leftist social scientists, have been unable to understand the revolutionary importance of African Americans because of their conceptions of race. Nonetheless, it is important to make clear what is meant by emancipatory democracy and revolutionary force in order to understand the social policy issues related to black communities in the United States.

EMANCIPATORY DEMOCRACY

Civil society is the association of persons who exist for each other while achieving their individual needs and expanding their individual gains. In one sense, civil society is detached from the reality of being human because it does not allow individuals to exist as fully natural human beings. From this view, humans are thought to be essentially social, and they may become full human beings only in community. There are philosophical and scientific, specifically anthropological, reasons for this view.[1]

Civil society exists in the political state that Marx distinguished from the real state. The political state is a formal organization in which not everyone has the opportunity to participate in deliberating and deciding on political matters. Currently, in matters of state, citizens are told that the state is the rational democratic organization that organizes society. In a real democracy the members of society would confer rationality on the state through constant participation in deliberations and decision-making activities. Under the rule of formal democracy, citizens lead a merely legal rather than a fully human existence. By organizing life under the rule of formal democracy, the citizen is separated from his or her human essence.[2]

When humans are separated from their essences, they are merely existing;

existence is different from reality. The reality is hidden under the conditions of the political state because citizens are subjected to the tyranny of the powerful in the state. But the hidden element of reality is also present in civil society as a potential force that is the true expression of human rationality. It is much like the difference between a caterpillar and a butterfly/moth. The caterpillar is essentially a butterfly/moth, but the element of the butterfly/moth is hidden in the reality. The essence of a thing is what it will be in its full, adult development; unrealized reality is in existence itself.

The nature of an essential form leads me to the conclusion that a thing will mature into its essence under conditions of normal development. However, there is the probability that an accident will result in the reality being aborted. For example, the caterpillar might be smashed accidentally by children exploring nature. At any rate, barring an accident, things develop into their essences. So humans may assist in the production, as well as the termination, of the essence of a thing; humans must participate in the emancipation of humanity through real democracy.

Humans create their own existence, but they do not do so under conditions they select.[3] There are restraints placed on what may be produced, depending on the stage of development of a society.[4] In fact, retrogressive turmoil will be produced in a society in which a material or ideal thing is introduced that the society has not been developed to accept.[5]

Humans will achieve real democracy when a social formation is achieved that presents opportunities for individual freedom. This individual freedom may be achieved *only* in community; humans are, after all, "an ensemble of social relations." For this reason, when true democracy is achieved the naturally sensuous and social individual will emerge. The previous institutional forms of oppression in human necessity will collapse, and real human history will arise with social collectives as its author. Human consciousness will become unshackled because, as Marx indicated, "It is not the consciousness of men that determines their being, but on the contrary, their social being that determines their consciousness."[6]

The worldview presented thus far suggests a theory of revolution. At a certain moment in the development of a society the workers, in both the legitimate and the illegitimate labor markets, come in conflict with the managers who organize the socialization, education, and management of labor in the society. At this point begins "an epoch of social revolution."[7] As Marx and Engels wrote:

> The ruling ideas of each age have ever been the ideas of its ruling class. When people speak of ideas that revolutionize society, they do but express the fact, that within the old society, the elements of a new one have been created, and that the dissolution of the old ideas keeps even pace with the dissolution of the old conditions of existence....But whatever form they may have taken, one fact is common to all past ages, viz., the exploitation of one part of society by the other. No wonder,

then, that the social consciousness of past ages, despite all the multiplicity and variety it displays, moves within certain common forms, or general ideas, which cannot completely vanish except with the total disappearance of class antagonisms.[8]

REVOLUTION

"Revolution" was used by Marx in a variety of ways to refer to a variety of social situations. Generally, it referred to the English, French, and American revolutions, which were revolutions by city dwellers, the earliest bourgeoisie, who created a new order led by ambitious sections of the middle classes in those nations. But Marx also referred to the disruption of the Indian village by British pressure as the first social revolution in Asia's history.[9]

The slightest social disruption that points to antagonisms between class relations and the forces of production is an indicator that revolution has developed as a social project. However, some social theorists have used the concept "passive revolution" to refer to a "revolution without a revolution."[10] Passive revolutions are characterized by two features: "(1) that no social formation disappears as long as the productive forces which have developed within it still find room for further forward movement; (2) that a society does not set itself tasks for whose solution the necessary conditions have not already been incubated."[11]

THE LEFT AND RACE

I argue that race theorists on the Left have primarily presented five ways of approaching the race problem in the United States. This does not mean that all of the theories will fit into my classification, but that most of the theories may be classified under one of the following categories.[12]

Some Marxists, though not a majority, argue that the position that race occupies is solely a class problem. This position was promoted by the U.S. Socialist Party and particularly its theoretical leader, Eugene V. Debs. This theme is on the rise again, particularly among those who argue that the concept of racism has been "inflated."[13]

The second minority position argued by the Left sees race as primarily an economic problem. The theorists working from this view argue that African Americans face general working-class exploitation and specific racial exploitation. This was primarily the position of the Progressive Labor Party, and they dubbed this concept "superexploitation."

The black nation thesis is the majoritarian position of the Left. This position was accepted by a large number of groups, including academics, black activists, the Socialist Workers Party, and the Sixth Congress of the Third International. The argument is that African Americans represent a nation within a nation that merits the right of self-determination. Some argue that the experiences of blacks in the United States parallel the colonial experiences of colonized nations; this experience in the United States is termed "internal colonialism," which is characterized by the geography of the ghetto, cultural domination and resistance, superexploitation, and externally based political control.[14]

The fourth conception of African-American oppression in the Marxist tradition claims that there has been a general working-class oppression and a specific African-American oppression. This position has been motivated primarily by opposition against the Black Nation thesis by smaller groups, such as the Spartacist League and, after 1959, the Communist Party of the United States of America.[15]

The final group of leftist conceptions treating African-American oppression is primarily represented by scholars who are concerned with the inscription of various oppressions in social formations. They have concerned themselves with linkages between all sorts of things in a society, which they refer to as "articulation." Sexism, heterosexism, anal sadism, ageism, anti-Semitism, and racism are viewed as a complex of oppressions that are the product of an articulation of contradictions incapable of being reduced to one another, and thus overdetermined.[16]

Each of the conceptions of race has made a contribution to the discussion of African Americans and other oppressed groups; I certainly do not intend to disturb anyone who has such orientations, but it seems clear that the conceptions share a view of the world in which the voice of the black subordinate group is absent. In various ways leftists expressed the following ideas:

1. Blacks represent a group who experienced universal powerlessness. Power is viewed either as the probability of someone doing something even if he or she is opposed, or as phenomenal relations that appear between the oppressor and oppressed.

2. In the attempt to conflate race and ethnicity, the theorists generally introduce allegedly universal values, such as the concept of antiracism, without a rigorous assessment of privilege and private property. Therefore, they run the risk of privileging their acts and actings out (verbal, intellectual, and physical) within the racist complex. Those supremacist acts are violence that denies the black voice and acts with contempt against the very African Americans the ethnicity theorists claim to desire to aid, educate, and organize. As Etienne Balibar states, the ethnicity argument inscribes the biological theme by assuming biological communities. For Balibar, these communities are racist and fictive. There have been no national states with an ethnic basis. Balibar argues that states come into existence and produce nations. In his conception, the culture of the ethnic group is actually the grouping of rules that requires parents belonging to the ethnic organization to teach their children. The

national leaders write a fictive ethnicity instituting, in real time, an imaginary unity against other achievable unities. This fictive system emerges as "a historical system of complementary exclusions and dominations which are mutually interconnected."[17]

3. The Eurocentric world view implied in 1 and 2 is precisely what the young Frantz Fanon referred to when he wrote: "When a Negro talks of Marx, the reaction [is]...'We have brought you up to our level and now you turn against your benefactors. Ingrates! Obviously nothing can be expected of you.'"[18]

The "misrecognition" for the Left is the social character of labor in which a person's products are the "direct embodiment of his individuality," resulting in women and men assisting themselves and fellow persons in being socially productive. Insofar as there will be revolutionary movement, in Marx's view, "likewise, however, both the material of labour and man as the subject, are the point of departure as well as the result of the movement."[19]

For this reason it is imperative to include the voice of the black masses, which has been excluded from the Left's discourse. The reason for this necessity is that, in a larger sense, I see a structural condition resulting in the reproduction of black consciousness as a passive revolutionary force.

RACE, CLASS AND CULTURE

The social fabric that includes the four major macro institutions of economic, political, cultural, and ideological structures forms the overdetermination of class exploitation and political repression under the hegemony of white supremacist logics. For most African Americans, the experience of everyday life is played on the landscape of the ghetto or internal colony, which is the backdrop for the "microphysics of power."[20] The lifelong process of African-American socialization includes the reproduction of "getting around old master," which is present in the remote goals and ambivalent moral moods of African-American culture. African-American culture represents a value system and worldview that have been created by a social history, and it means acting on that social formation.[21]

As I have argued throughout the book, the system of oppression is both a race and a class issue. I agree with Robert Staples, Michael Omi and Howard Winant, and Manning Marable that race functions as the central organizing theme of the class order. The cultural dimension of the articulation of dominance is significant because of the ongoing struggle to exterminate the culture of the dominated by the dominators and their agents, some of whom come from the dominated group.

Not only is the distinction between the dominated and dominator culture

important but, more important, the exclusion of the black dominated from participation in the legitimate political apparatus has resulted in modifications in terms
of the dominated group's political discourse. The black dominated were forced to
redefine "political" not merely in the sense of dominating political institutions
but also in cultural forms like language, music, religion, dance, and athletics.
Prior to World War II the racial order required that blacks wage a "war of
maneuver" to acquire some access to the political system. This feature of struggle did not disappear in the post-World War II period, but was absorbed in a "war
of position," where blacks achieved some representation in the political and ideological systems. Nonetheless, for most African Americans the "war of maneuver" remains a feature of the microphysics of domination in their everyday
existence in civil society.[22]

AFRICAN AMERICANS AS ESSENTIALLY REVOLUTIONARY

The black intellectual W. E. B. DuBois pointed out in the 1920s that the true
test of a democracy was always found in an examination of a nation's criminal
justice and penal systems.[23] I argue that the history of blacks in the United States
reveals that their inclusion in civil society has been essentially constructed as
criminal. This sociohistorical argument requires a distinction between the preconditions and precipitants socially constructing African Americans. Crudely
speaking, precipitants are the agents that actually give rise to the empirical occur-
rence of the African-American condition. The preconditions are responsible for
the effect, for the precise nature of the African-American condition.[24] I am referring to the preconditions of the dominant African-American condition.

Second, the condition of African-American criminality is associated with
resistance, where a culture of passive revolution represents a constant force
against forced criminality and simultaneously toward true democracy. The resistance and "criminality" of the slave developed as the legitimate revolutionary
force in the United States. As such, black culture became an essential feature of
U.S. culture. Slaves were forced to steal food and clothing to survive, forced to
lie to cultivate reading and writing skills, and forced to deceive in order to associate with the master class. The intention of the slave system was essentially economic in the sense of generating unfree labor, but the cultural repercussion was
protest and revolt enveloped in the social and moral universe.

Dogmatic Marxists view economic revolution as primary; in so doing, their
use of the method of Marxism fails by not understanding all the unity in social
relations of a capitalist society. Marcuse developed an understanding of this by
stressing an emancipatory theory of self-identity.[25] However, Marcuse locates the
emancipated, autonomous individual within the objective social institutions,
where he gives privilege to the subject; but subjects are as much of the historical
world of objective social institutions and are, in fact, largely constructed by those
structures. It is not enough to conceive of freedom as simple independence,

autonomy, self-ownership, or nonalienation. To do so would be to marginalize the process of emancipation whereby multiple institutional or social structural liberations are necessary prior to the subject's becoming sufficiently free. Even more important, it would mean embracing the bourgeois view of society as autonomous individuals coming together in self-interest; this view opposes the Marxist view of emancipatory democracy.[26]

CHALLENGE FOR THE LEFT

Frantz Fanon coined the concept "internalization of oppression," but the Left generally ignored his significant contributions. The dominant position of the Left has been peace, non-violence, social democracy, and the attendant agenda, which can be demystified as an unstated agenda of oppression. The position is tantamount to what Erich Fromm called "mass neurosis" and Wilhelm Reich called "emotional plague." However, black historical experience has been what Fanon asserts: "The colonized man finds his freedom in and through violence."[27]

The character of Bigger Thomas represents an enduring reflection of the black male role development in U.S. society. It is not as simple as bell hooks has suggested in her brilliant book, *Black Looks: Race and Representation*: that these issues can be reduced to phallocentric orientations. Rather, it is a question of how phallocentric orientations are produced and reproduced in culture.[28] Recall that Richard Wright's observational composite is based on five patterned types of black men: the black brute, the constant complainer, the subverter, the dreamer, and the resister.

Bigger may have bonded with the white male phallic order, but he did so *differently* than a white male would have. That is part of Bigger's *tragedy*; he is the tragic hero who represents all black men in the U.S. experience who refuse to be oppressed and must act out resistance through violence. Wright clearly suggests that Bigger is similar to other black men when he depicts Gus telling Bigger that he is just one additional out-of-control nigger.

Fanon correctly pointed out that the notion of a common humanity, which was so deeply embedded in the approaches to race in the Left's conceptual framework, was counter-revolutionary and would primarily function to legitimate values of the oppressors: "The essential qualities remain," Fanon wrote, "eternal—in spite of the blunders that men may make—the essential qualities of the West, of course."[29]

The challenge of Marxism, insofar as race is concerned, is to consider that the aim of U.S. race relations is not the moral reform of the oppressor. In my view, the dominant element in black culture has been and remains the passive revolutionary factor. Those Marxists who attempt to diminish the issue of race through the privileging of individualism and the reformist vision of autonomy might reflect on Fanon's position in the struggle for emancipatory democracy: "Bourgeois ideology, which is the proclamation of an essential equality of all men, manages to appear logical in its own eyes by inviting the sub-men to become human, and to take as their proto-type Western humanity as incarnated in the Western Bourgeoisie."[30]

Finally, in this book I have asked the question, How are black males produced as deviant? I have stressed their different and unique social circumstances. My question is different from such questions as Who is involved in crime? Who gets caught? Why don't all black men engage in crime? What happens to criminals when they are caught? My analysis is specifically an analysis of the African-American male place and voice in society. I have rejected the viewpoint of a black male subculture while attempting to elaborate the contracultural and passive revolutionary functions of the African-American male role.

Notes

PREFACE

1. Marx argued that the real basis of the state is "independent of the will of individuals...[it rests on the] material life of individuals...their mode of production and forms of intercourse." He argued that the state is formed by the bourgeoisie and exists as an apparatus delegated with its class power. "In general the relationship between the political...representatives of a class and the class they represent [is that] in their minds [the former] do not get beyond the limits which the latter do not get beyond in life, that they are consequently driven, theoretically, to the same problems and solutions to which the material interests and social position drive the latter practically." Karl Marx and Frederick Engels, *Selected Works in Three Volumes*, vol. 1 (Moscow: Progress Publishers, 1969), pp. 78-79, 424.

2. This view is generally accepted by both labeling and conflict theory. Howard S. Becker, *Outsiders* (New York: Free Press, 1973); Richard Quinney, *Class, State, and Crime: On the Theory and Practice of Criminal Justice* (New York: Longman, 1977).

3. Ben Agger, *Fast Capitalism* (Urbana: University of Illinois Press, 1989).

4. Jewelle Taylor Gibbs, *Young, Black, and Male in America* (New York: Auburn House, 1988).

5. Benjamin P. Bowser, ed., *Black Male Adolescents: Parenting and Education in Community Context* (Lanham, Md.: University Press of America, 1991.)

6. Haki Madhubuti, *Black Men: Obsolete, Single, Dangerous?* (Chicago: Third World Press, 1990).

7. Robert Staples, *Black Masculinity: The Black Male's Role in American Society* (San Francisco: Black Scholar Press, 1982).

8. Jawanza Kunjufu, *Countering the Conspiracy to Destroy Black Boys* (Chicago: Afro-American Publishing Company, 1984); Nathan Hare and Julia

Hare, *The Endangered Black Family: Coping with the Unisexualization and Coming Extinction of the Black Race* (San Francisco: Black Think Tank, 1984); Richard Majors and Janet Mancini Billson, *Cool Pose* (New York: Macmillan, 1991); Lawrence Gray, *Black Men* (Newbury Park, Calif.: Sage, 1981).

9. Michael S. Kimmel, *Changing Men* (Newbury Park, Calif.: Sage, 1987); Clyde W. Franklin, *Men and Society* (Chicago: Nelson-Hall, 1988); Amos Wilson, *Black on Black Violence* (New York: Afrikan Word Infosystems, 1990); Peter Edelman and Joyce Ladner, eds., *Adolescence and Poverty: Challenge for the 1990s* (Washington, D.C.: Center for National Policy Press, 1991); Delores Aldridge, *Focusing: Black Male-Female Relationships* (Chicago: Third World Press, 1991); Na'im Akbar, *Visions for Black Men* (Nashville: Winston-Derek Publishers, 1991); Nathan Hare and Julia Hare, *Crisis in Black Sexual Politics* (San Francisco: Black Think Tank Press, 1989); Brenda Evans and James Whitfield, *Black Males in the United States: An Annotated Bibliography from 1967-1987* (Washington, D.C.: American Psychological Association, 1988); Nathan Hare and Julia Hare, *Bringing the Black Boy to Manhood: The Passage* (San Francisco: Black Think Tank Press, 1985); Robert L. Factor, *The Black Response to America* (Reading, Mass.: Addison-Wesley Publishing, 1970); Harry Bailey and Ellis Katz, eds., *Ethnic Group Politics* (Columbus, Ohio: Merrill, 1969); Elijah Anderson, *Street Wise* (Chicago: University of Chicago Press, 1990).

10. Frederick Engels, *Anti-Duhring* (Moscow: Progress Publishers, 1969), p. 38.

11. William Z. Foster, *The Negro People in American History* (New York: International Publishers, 1954).

12. Engels, op. cit., pp. 233-261.

13. Ibid., p. 51.

14. Ibid.

15. I am using the fundamental sociological meaning for the term "ideology," which is a set of beliefs, values, and ideas that promote the *interest* of the *dominant group.*

16. Maurice Godelier, *Perspectives in Marxist Anthropology* (London: Cambridge University Press, 1977), pp. 44, 63. I am following the methods Godelier explicated.

17. Ibid., p. 53.

18. "Vulgar economy actually does no more than interpret, systematize and defend in doctrinaire fashion the conceptions of the agents of bourgeois production who are entrapped in bourgeois production relations. It should not astonish us, then, that vulgar economy feels particularly at home in the estranged outward appearances of economic relations in which these prima facie absurd and perfect contradictions appear and that these relations seem the more self-evident the more their internal relationships are concealed from it, although they are understandable to the popular mind. *But all science would be superfluous if the outward appearance and the essence of things directly coincided*" [emphasis

added]. Karl Marx, *Capital*, vol. 3 (Moscow: Foreign Languages Publishing House, 1956), p. 797. The form of Marxist structuralism being proposed is a morphological analysis that attempts to uncover the essential connection between form, function, mode of articulation, and perimeter for the development of African-American males.

CHAPTER 1

1. For an excellent overview see Ian Taylor, Paul Walton, and Jock Young, *The New Criminology* (New York: Harper and Row, 1973). For a discussion of the black male question see Robert Staples, *Black Masculinity* (San Francisco: Black Scholar Press, 1982).

2. Of particular concern is Hegel's dialectic, directed at "staking one's life" for freedom to be won. "The individual who has not risked his life may well be recognized as a person, but he has not attained to the truth of this recognition as an independent self-consciousness." See George W. F. Hegel, *The Philosophy of Right*, E. S. Haldane, trans. (Oxford: Clarendon Press, 1942) and *Phenomenology of Spirit*, A. V. Miller, trans. (Oxford: Oxford University Press, 1977).

3. Antonio Gramsci, *Selections from Prison Notebooks*, Quintin Hoare and Geoffrey N. Smith, trans. (New York: International Publishers, 1987); Walker Adamson, *Hegemony and Revolution* (Berkeley: University of California Press, 1980); Robert Bocock, *Hegemony* (London: Tavistock, 1986).

4. An excellent overview of structuralist development is found in Richard Harland, *Superstructuralism* (London: Methuen, 1987). See also Anthony P. Cohen, *The Symbolic Construction of Community* (London: Tavistock, 1985).

5. For a perspective on the positive social science issue, consult Ernesto Laclau and Chantal Mouffe, *Hegemony and Socialist Strategy: Towards a Radical Democratic Politics* (New York: Verso, 1985), pp. 93-148. Also see Anthony Giddens, *Central Problems in Social Theory* (Berkeley: University of California Press, 1979); Cedric Robinson, *Black Marxism the Making of the Black Radical Tradition* (London: Zed Press, 1983), pp. 416-440.

6. I am using "human" in the same sense as does Herbert Marcuse—as a liberated, polymorphous, undifferentiated self free to choose the Golden Rule. See Marcuse's *One-Dimensional Man* (Boston: Beacon Press, 1964).

7. The collection of *Critical Essays on Richard Wright*, Yoshinobu Hakutani, ed., (Boston: G. K. Hall, 1982), represents a selection of the most important commentaries on Wright. Also see Robert Felger, *Richard Wright* (Boston: Twayne, 1980; Keneth Kinnamon, *The Emergence of Richard Wright* (Urbana: University of Illinois Press, 1972); Katherine Fishburn, *Richard Wright's Hero: The Faces of a Rebel-Victim* (Metuchen, N.J.: Scarecrow Press, 1977). Perhaps the best extant contribution on Bigger Thomas is found in Joyce Ann Joyce, *Richard Wright's Art of Tragedy* (Iowa City: University of Iowa Press, 1986). The reconsideration of Bigger Thomas in a deconstruction context

can be found in Houston A. Baker, Jr., *Blues, Ideology and Afro-American Literature* (Chicago: University of Chicago Press, 1984).

8. Bigger becomes a mythic character not because Wright created him in his role as a culture maker but because Wright reflected the mythic character existing in black culture. See Louis Irving Horowitz, *Radicalism and the Revolt Against Reason: The Social Theories of Georges Sorel* (Carbondale: Southern Illinois University Press, 1961).

9. Bronislaw Malinowski, *Magic, Science and Religion* (Glencoe, Ill.: Free Press, 1948), p. 79.

10. Richard Wright, *Native Son* (New York: Harper and Row, 1940). All quotations in the text are from this edition and are hereafter marked by page numbers in parentheses.

11. Cornel West, "Black Radicalism and the Marxist Tradition," *Monthly Review* (September 1988):55.

12. Michel Foucault, *Power/Knowledge*, Colin Gordon, trans. (New York: Pantheon Books, 1972), pp. 112-113. Also see John Rajchman, *Michel Foucault The Freedom of Philosophy* (New York: Columbia University Press, 1985), p. 25.

13. Richard Wright, *Black Boy* (New York: Harper and Row, 1966), p. 272.

14. Manning Marable, *How Capitalism Underdeveloped Black America* (Boston: South End Press, 1983).

15. C. L. R. James, *Mariners, Renegades and Castaways* (New York: Allison and Busby, 1985), p. 21.

16. Rene Girard, "Freud and the Oedipus," in his *Violence and the Sacred* (Baltimore: Johns Hopkins University Press, 1972), pp. 169-192. Also see Patrick H. Hutton, "Foucault, Freud, and the Technologies of the Self," in *Technologies of the Self: A Seminar with Michel Foucault*, H. Martin, Huck Gutman, and Patrick H. Hutton, eds. (Amherst: University of Massachusetts Press, 1988), pp. 121-144.

17. Ralph Ellison, "Richard Wright's Blues," *Antioch Review* 5 (June 1945):198-211.

18. Charles Fillmore, *The Metaphysical Bible Dictionary* (Unity Village, Mo.: Unity School of Christianity Press, 1931), pp. 354-355.

19. Lloyd Graham, *Deceptions and Myths of the Bible*, Secaucus, N.J.: University Books, 1975), pp. 269-278.

20. Michel Foucault, "Technologies of the Self," in *Technologies of the Self: A Seminar with Michel Foucault*, H. Martin, Huck Gutman, and Patrick H. Hutton, eds. (Amherst: University of Massachusetts Press, 1988), pp. 16-49.

21. Ibid., p. 19.

22. Ibid., p. 33.

23. Hannah Arendt, *On Revolution* (London: Penguin Books, 1963), p. 83. Arendt wrote, "Billy Budd's violent act is the goodness in nature."

24. Foucault, "Technologies of the Self," pp. 42-43.

25. Gramsci, op. cit., pp. 5-43.

26. Arendt, op. cit., pp. 18-20, 100.

27. This logic is found in the anthropological aspects of Freud's model. It appears to be widely accepted even among the critics of Freud. See Sigmund Freud, *Civilization and Its Discontents*, James Strachey, trans. (New York: W.W. Norton, 1962).

28. David Martin, "Order and Rule," in his *Two Critiques of Spontaneity* (London: Broad Water Press, 1973), pp. 1-31.

29. Rodney Needham, "Polythetic Classification," in his *Against the Tranquility of Axioms* (Berkeley: University of California Press, 1983), pp. 36-66. I am extending Professor Needham's polythetic argument to a race group (i.e., status group) in postmodern society.

30. Girard, op. cit., pp. 143-168.

31. Rene Girard, "The Founding Murder in the Philosophy of Nietzsche," in Paul Dumouchel, ed., *Violence and Truth* (Stanford: Stanford University Press, 1988), pp. 227-246.

32. Frantz Fanon, *The Wretched of the Earth*, Constance Farrington, trans. (New York: Grove Press, 1963), p. 43.

33. Eldridge Cleaver, *Soul on Ice* (New York: McGraw-Hill, 1968). "I became a rapist...I started practicing on black girls in the ghetto...when I considered myself smooth enough, I...sought out white prey" (p. 14).

34. Arendt, op. cit., pp. 99-100.

35. See the collection of essays edited by Elizabeth Burns and Tom Burns, *Sociology of Literature and Drama* (Baltimore: Penguin, 1973). Also see Raymond Williams, *The Sociology of Culture* (New York: Schocken Books, 1981).

36. Wright, Richard, *How 'Bigger' Was Born* (New York: Harper and Brothers, 1940).

37. Perry Anderson, "The Antinomies of Antonio Gramsci," *New Left Review* 100 (1976-1977):5-78. Also see Bocock, op. cit., pp. 28-32.

38. Stuart Hall, "Gramsci's Relevance for the Study of Race and Ethnicity," *Journal of Communication Inquiry* 10 (Summer 1986):5-27; Raymond Williams, *Marxism and Literature* (New York: Oxford University Press, 1977).

39. Michel Foucault, *The History of Sexuality* (New York: Vintage Books, 1980), p. 93.

CHAPTER 2

1. Edward Banfield, *The Unheavenly City Revisited* (Boston: Little, Brown, 1968); Daniel Patrick Moynihan, *The Negro Family: The Case for National Action* (Washington, D.C.: U.S. Department of Labor, Office of Policy Planning and Research, 1965); William Sheldon, *Varieties of Delinquent Youth: An Introduction to Constitutional Psychiatry* (New York: Harper, 1949); James Q. Wilson and Richard Herrnstein, *Crime and Human Nature* (New York: Simon

and Schuster, 1985).

2. Robert Staples, *Black Masculinity: The Black Male's Role in American Society* (San Francisco: Black Scholar Press, 1982), pp. 135-146.

3. Ibid., p. 22.

4. Daniel Bell, *The Coming of Post-Industrial Society* (New York: Basic Books, 1973); Michael Young, *The Rise of Meritocracy* (Baltimore: Penguin, 1961).

5. G. W. F. Hegel, *Lectures on the History of Philosophy*, vol. 1 (New York: Humanities Press, 1955), p. 24.

6. David Matza, *Becoming Deviant* (Englewood Cliffs, N.J.: Prentice-Hall, 1969).

7. Alphonso Pinkney, *The Myth of Black Progress* (London: Cambridge University Press, 1984), pp. 46-57.

8. Ibid., p. 103; U.S. Bureau of the Census, Current Population Reports, series P-20, no. 448, *The Black Population in the United States: March 1990 and 1989* (Washington D.C.: U.S. Government Printing Office, 1991).

9. James E. Blackwell, *The Black Community* (New York: Harper and Row, 1985), p. 17.

10. *USA Today*, January 11, 1988, pp. 1A, 6A.

11. *Statistical Abstract of the United States* (Washington, D.C.: U.S. Government Printing Office, 1985), p. 422; Bureau of National Affairs, "Economic Statistics," *Daily Report for Executives*, March 9, 1992, p. n1.

12. David H. Swinton, "The Economic Status of the Black Population," in David H. Swinton, ed., *The State of Black America* (New York: National Urban League, 1983), pp. 45-114.

13. Robert Nisbet, *The Social Bond* (New York: Knopf, 1970).

14. Irving Louis Horowitz, *Radicalism and the Revolt Against Reason: The Social Theories of Georges Sorel* (Carbondale: Southern Illinois University Press, 1961). I am using "overdetermination" in the sense of Nicos Poulantzas's political usage, where the "ensemble of structures" in a society where the state's economic and ideological functions are performed by its political function. The state creates and reproduces the orientation of the professional managers through its "educational" function. *Political Power and Social Classes* (New York: Verso, 1968), p. 55.

15. Bronislaw Malinowski, *Magic, Science and Religion* (Glencoe, Ill.: Free Press, 1948), p. 79.

16. Jurgen Habermas, *Legitimation Crisis* (Boston: Beacon Press, 1975), pp. 1-5; Nathan Hare and Julia Hare, *The Endangered Black Family* (San Francisco: Black Think Tank, 1984), pp. 7-30.

17. Manning Marable, "Groundings with My Sisters," in his *How Capitalism Underdeveloped Black America* (Boston: South End Press, 1983), pp. 69-104.

18. Edna Bonacich, "Advanced Capitalism and Black/White Race Relations in the United States: A Split Labor Market Interpretation," *American*

Sociological Review, 41 (February, 1976):34-51; Nicos Poulantzas, *Classes in Contemporary Capitalism* (London: NLB, 1975).

19. Carter G. Woodson, *The Mis-Education of the Negro* (Philadelphia: Hakim's Publications, 1933); Manning Marable, *Black American Politics* (London: Verso, 1985).

20. Kenneth M. Jones, "The Black Male in Jeopardy," *The Crisis* 93, no. 3 (March 1986):16-29.

21. Daniel Bell, *The Cultural Contradictions of Capitalism* (New York: Basic Books, 1976), pp. 54-80; Robert K. Merton, *Social Theory and Social Structure* (Glencoe, Ill.: Free Press, 1949), pp. 125-133.

22. James P. Pitts, "The Afro-American Experience," in Anthony Dworkin and Rosalind Dworkin, eds., *The Minority Report* (New York: Holt, Rinehart and Winston, 1982), pp. 141-167; James McGhee, "Running the Gauntlet: Black Men in America," (New York: National Urban League, 1984); Staples, op. cit., p. 101; U.S. Bureau of the Census, Current Population Reports, series P-20, no. 448, *The Black Population in the United States, March 1990 and 1989* (Washington D.C.: U.S. Government Printing Office), p. 41.

23. Nancy Chodorow, *The Reproduction of Mothering: Psycho-Analysis and the Sociology of Gender* (Berkeley: University of California Press, 1978).

24. Gayle Rubin, "The Traffic in Women: Notes on the Political Economy of Sex," in Rayna Reiter, ed., *Towards an Anthropology of Women* (New York: Monthly Review Press, 1976); Zillah Eisenstein, ed., *Capitalist Patriarchy and the Case for Socialist Feminism* (New York: Monthly Review Press, 1979).

25. *Statistical Abstract of the United States* Washington, D.C.: U.S. Government Printing Office, 1982-1983), p. 142.

26. Blackwell, op. cit., pp. 150-193.

27. Samuel Bowles, and Herbert Gintis, "IQ in the United States Class Structure," *Social Policy*, 3, nos. 4 and 5 (November-December, 1972 and January-February, 1973):65-96; Christopher Jencks, et al., eds., *Inequality* (New York: Basic Books, 1972).

28. McGhee, op. cit.; Paula Rothenberg, ed., *Racism and Sexism* (New York: St. Martin's Press, 1988), pp. 82-98; U.S. Bureau of the Census, Current Population Reports, Series P-23, *Population Profile of the United States, 1991* (Washington, D.C.: U.S. Government Printing Office, 1991), p. 14; Federal Bureau of Investigation, *Crime in the United States: Uniform Crime Reports 1990* (Washington, D.C.: U.S. Government Printing Office, 1991).

29. Robert Staples, "American Racism and High Crime Rates: The Inextricable Connection," *The Western Journal of Black Studies* 8, no. 2 (1984):62-72. Also see Marable, *How Capitalism Underdeveloped Black America*, pp. 105-130.

30. McGhee, op. cit., pp. 5-9; U.S. Bureau of the Census, *Statistical Abstract of the United States: 1992* (Washington, D.C.: U.S. Government Printing Office, 1992), p. 90.

31. Frederick Douglass, *The Narrative of the Life of Frederick Douglass, An*

American Slave: Written by Himself (New York: New American Library, 1968), p. 43.

32. H. Bruce Franklin, *Prison Literature in America* (Westport, Conn.: Lawrence Hill, 1982).

33. Raymond Bauer and Alice Bauer, "Day to Day Resistance to Slavery," *Journal of Negro History* 27 (1942):388-419.

34. Jack M. Bloom, *Class, Race and the Civil Rights Movement* (Bloomington: Indiana University Press, 1987), pp. 26-29.

35. Allen Trelease, *White Terror* (New York: Harper and Row, 1971), p. 28.

36. Mississippi John Hurt, *Today* (recording) (New York: Vanguard Recording Society, 1966). Also see Howard W. Odum and Guy B. Johnson, *Negro Workday Songs* (New York: Negro Universities Press, 1926); Guy B. Johnson, *John Henry: Tracking Down a Negro Legend* (Chapel Hill: University of North Carolina Press, 1929).

37. Paul Boyer, *Urban Masses and Moral Order in America, 1820-1920* (Cambridge, Mass.: Harvard University Press, 1978); Jane Addams, *Democracy and Social Ethics* (New York: Macmillan, 1902).

38. Chester Himes, *The Quality of Hurt: The Autobiography of Chester Himes*, vol. 1 (Garden City, N.Y.: Doubleday, 1972), p. 60.

39. Tricia Rose, *Black Noise: Rap Music and Black Culture in Contemporary America* (Hanover, N.H.: Wesleyan University Press, 1994), pp. 54-56.

40. For a historical overview of appropriation, see Walter Rodney, *How Europe Underdeveloped Africa* (Washington, D.C.: Howard University Press, 1974). For a case study of appropriation and black music, see Frank Kofsky, *Black Nationalism and the Revolution in Music* (New York: Pathfinder Press, 1970). For African-American applications, see Robert Blauner, *Racial Oppression in America* (New York: Harper and Row, 1972).

41. Leroi Jones, *Blues People* (New York: Morrow Quill, 1963); Charles Keil, *Urban Blues* (Chicago: University of Chicago Press, 1966), pp. 50-68.

42. Janheinz Jahn, *Muntu* (London: Faber and Faber, 1961), pp. 217-239.

43. David Toop, *The Rap Attack* (London: Pluto Press, 1984), p. 19; Janice C. Simpson, "Yo! Rap Gets on the Map," *Time*, February 5, 1990, pp. 60-62. Also see Yvonne Olson, "As Rap Goes Pop, Some Say Black Radio is Missing Out," *Billboard*, June 18, 1988, pp. 1, 68; Kevin Zimmerman, "Rap Music: Pop for the '90s?," *Variety*, November 12, 1990, pp. 73-74. The best statement on the cultural politics of rap is Houston A. Baker, Jr., *Black Studies, Rap, and the Academy* (Chicago: University of Chicago Press, 1993).

44. David Gates and David Medina, "Play That Packaged Music," *Newsweek*, December 3, 1990, p. 68.

45. Peter Watrous, "Public Enemy's Politics," *New York Times*, January 3, 1990, p. A14.

46. Jon Pareles, "Rap and Violence: Perception vs Reality," *New York Times*, September 13, 1988, p. Y17.

47. Richard Cook, "Caught Rapping," *Punch*, September 28, 1990; Terry Teachout, "Rap and Racism," *Commentary*, March 1990, pp. 60-62; David Samuels, "Rap on Rap," *New Republic*, November 11, 1991, pp. 24-29. The misogynist theme also has been highlighted: see Kim France, "Women with Attitude," *Working Women*, January 1992, pp. 60-64; Dominique DiPrima, "Beat the Rap," *Mother Jones*, September 1990, pp. 32-36; David Thigpen, "Not for Men Only," *Time*, May 27, 1991, pp. 71-72; Jack E. White, "Sister Souljah: Capitalist Tool," *Time*, June 29, 1992, p. 88; Jimmy Mass, "Queen Latifah Raps the World's Petty People," *Indianapolis Star*, January 9, 1992, p. B5.

48. The blues phrase cited was often understood to be a reference to the U.S. government and not to a woman. The phrase may be understood as political rather than as sexist. For an account of the historical development of the hidden messages in black culture, see Lawrence Levine, *Black Culture and Black Consciousness* (New York: Oxford University Press, 1977).

49. Greg Kit, "Rap is all the Rage," *Chicago Times*, June 14, 1990, pp. 1, 3; Jan Pareles, "Distributor Withdraws a Rap Album Over Explicit Lyrics," *New York Times*, August 28, 1990, pp. B1-B2; Steve Dougherty and J. D. Podolsky, "Charges of Anti-Semitism Give Public Enemy a Rep That's Tough to Rap Away," *People*, March 5, 1990, 2 pages.

50. John Leland, "Rap and Race," *Newsweek*, June 29, 1992, pp. 46-52. Manning Marable, "At the End of The Rainbow," *Race and Class* 34, no. 2 (October-December 1992):75-81.

51. Frantz Fanon, *The Wretched of the Earth*, Constance Farrington, trans. (New York: Grove Press, 1963), p. 61.

52. Ken Auletta, *The Underclass* (New York: Random House, 1982), pp. xiii-xviii. Also see William J. Wilson, "The Urban Underclass," in Leslie W. Dunbar, ed., *Minority Report* (New York: Pantheon Books, 1984), pp. 75-117.

CHAPTER 3

1. Manford Kuhn, "Major Trends in Symbolic Interaction Theory in the Past Twenty-five Years," *The Sociological Quarterly* no. 5 (1964):61-84; Herbert Blumer, *Symbolic Interaction: Perspective and Method* (Garden City, N.Y.: Prentice-Hall, 1969).

2. Reinhard Bendix, *Max Weber: An Intellectual Portrait* (New York: Doubleday, 1962), p. 464.

3. Claude Brown, *Manchild in the Promised Land* (New York: Signet, 1965), p. 171.

4. The quotes that follow are taken from research accumulated over five years in central Pacific cities. Interviews of both focus groups and one-on-one in-depth interviews were taped and transcribed.

5. Huey P. Newton, "The Black Panther, January 17, 1969," in Norman Hill, ed., *The Black Panther Menace* (New York: Webster's Red Seal Publications,

1971), pp. 247-248.

6. Paulo Freire, *Pedagogy of the Oppressed*, Myra Bergman, trans. (New York: Continuum, 1970), p. 457.

7. Ralph Ellison, *Invisible Man* (New York: Vintage Books, 1972), pp. 19-20.

8. Charles Silberman, *Criminal Violence, Criminal Justice* (New York: Vintage Books, 1980), pp. 159-224.

9. Harry Edwards, "The Draft: No Equality for Blacks," *San Francisco Examiner*, April 15, 1979, p. 13.

10. Robert Staples, "American Racism and High Crime Rates: The Inextricable Connection," *Western Journal of Black Studies* 8, no.2 (1984):62-72.

11. Harold Garfinkel, "Conditions of Successful Degradation Ceremonies," *American Journal of Sociology* 61 (1956):420-424; David Matza, "Poverty and Disrepute," in Robert K. Merton and Robert Nisbet, eds., *Contemporary Social Problems* (New York: Harcourt, Brace and World, 1971), pp. 601-656.

12. Richard Wright, *Native Son* (New York: Harper and Row, 1940), p. 260.

13. Delos Kelly, *Creating School Failure: Youth Crime and Deviance* (Los Angeles: Trident Shop, 1982).

14. Robert Staples, *Black Masculinity: The Black Male's Role in American Society* (San Francisco: Black Scholar Press, 1982).

CHAPTER 4

1. Stokely Carmichael and Charles V. Hamilton, *Black Power* (New York: Vintage Books, 1967), pp. 4-6.

2. Allison Davis, Burleigh Gardner, and Mary Gardner, *Deep South* (Chicago: University of Chicago Press, 1941).

3. John Dollard, *Caste and Class in a Southern Town* (Garden City, N.Y.: Doubleday Anchor, 1957); Gerald Berreman, "Caste in India and the United States," in Jack Roach, Llewellyn Gross, and Orville Gursslin, eds., *Social Stratification in the United States* (Englewood Cliffs, N.J.: Prentice Hall, 1960).

4. George Eaton Simpson and J. Milton Yinger, *Racial and Cultural Minorities: An Analysis of Prejudice and Discrimination* (New York: Harper and Row, 1953).

5. Oliver Cox, *Caste, Class and Race* (New York: Modern Reader, 1948).

6. Kwame Nkrumah, *Class Struggle in Africa* (New York: International Publishers, 1970).

7. Frantz Fanon, *The Wretched of the Earth*, Constance Farrington, trans. (New York: Grove Press, 1963).

8. Albert Memmi, *The Colonizer and the Colonized* (Boston: Beacon Press, 1965).

9. Carmichael and Hamilton, op. cit.; Tom Hayden, "Colonialism and

Liberation in America," *Viet-Report*, Summer 1968, pp. 32-39.

10. Robert Blauner, *Racial Oppression in America* (New York: Harper and Row, 1972).

11. Robert Allen, *Black Awakening in Capitalist America* (New York: Doubleday, 1969).

12. Mario Barrera, *Race and Class in the Southwest: A Theory of Racial Inequality* (London: University of Notre Dame Press, 1979).

13. Gunnar Myrdal, *An American Dilemma: The Negro Problem and Modern Democracy* (New York: Pantheon, 1962).

14. Robert Merton, "Social Structure and Anomie," *American Sociological Review* 3 (1938):672-682; Albert Cohen, *Delinquent Boys: The Culture of the Gang* (Glencoe, Ill.: Free Press, 1955); Richard Cloward and Lloyd Ohlin, *Delinquency and Opportunity: A Theory of Delinquent Gangs* (Glencoe, Ill.: Free Press, 1960).

15. Cohen, op. cit., p. 133.

16. Dennis H. Wrong, "The Oversocialized Conceptions of Man in Modern Societies," *American Sociological Review* 26 (April 1971):183-193; Richard Quinney, "A Conception of Man and Society for Criminology," *Sociological Quarterly*, Spring 1965, pp. 119-127.

17. Clifford R. Shaw and Henry D. McKay, "Social Factors in Juvenile Delinquency," in *Report on the Causes of Crime, The National Commission of Law Observance and Enforcement*, vol. 2 (Washington, D.C.: U.S. Government Printing Office, 1931).

18. Edwin Sutherland and Donald Cressey, *Criminology* (New York: J.P. Lippincott, 1970).

19. Walter Miller, "Lower Class Culture as a Generating Milieu of Gang Delinquency," *Journal of Social Issues* 14 (April 1958):5-19.

20. Ralf Dahrendorf, *Class and Class Conflict in Industrial Society* (Stanford: Stanford University Press, 1959), p. 76.

21. William Ryan, *Blaming the Victim* (New York: Vintage Books, 1971); Sidney Willhelm, *Who Needs the Negro?* (New York: Anchor Books), 1971.

22. Karl Marx and Frederick Engels, *The Communist Manifesto*, authorized trans. (New York: International Publishers, 1976), p. 9.

23. Ibid., p. 11.

24. Erik Olin Wright, "Class Boundaries in Advanced Capitalist Societies," *New Left Review*, July-August 1976, pp. 3-41.

25. Barbara Ehrenreich and John Ehrenreich, "The Professional-Managerial Class," *Radical America*, April-May 1977, pp. 17-22.

26. This is not to suggest that Trotskyism was a majoritarian position or that Lenin was insensitive or lacking clear analytical thought on imperialist and racist economism. See Leon Trotsky, *On Black Nationalism and Self Determination* (New York: Pathfinder Press, 1978); Marxist Studies no. 5, *What Strategy for Black Liberation: Trotskyism vs. Black Nationalism* (New York: Spartacist League, 1977).

27. V. I. Lenin, *The Nascent Trend of Imperialist Economism* (Moscow: Progress Publishers, 1982).

28. Cedric J. Robinson, *Black Marxism: The Making of the Black Radical Tradition* (London: Zed Press, 1983).

29. Eugene D. Genovese, "Class and Nationality in Black America," in his *Red and Black* (New York: Vintage Books, 1968).

30. Paul Baren and Paul Sweezy, *Monopoly Capital* (New York: Monthly Review Press, 1966).

31. Michael Reich, "The Economics of Racism," in Richard Edwards, Michael Reich, and Thomas Weisskopf, eds., *The Capitalist System* (Englewood Cliffs, N.J.: Prentice-Hall, 1972), pp. 313-321.

32. Cox, op. cit.

33. Barrera, op. cit., pp. 206-212; Peter Doeringer and Michael Piore, *Internal Labor Markets and Manpower Analysis* (Lexington Mass.: D.C. Heath, 1971).

34. Nicos Poulantzas, "On Social Classes," *New Left Review*, March-April 1973, pp. 27-54.

35. Michael Omi and Howard Winant, *Racial Formation in the United States from the 1960s to the 1980s* (New York: Routledge and Kegan Paul, 1986).

36. Robert Staples, "What Is Black Sociology? Toward a Sociology of Black Liberation," in Joyce Ladner, ed., *The Death of White Sociology* (New York: Vintage Books, 1973), pp. 161-172.

37. Alvin Gouldner, cited in ibid., p. 163.

38. Sheldon Wolin and John Schaar, "The Battle of Berkeley," in Norman S. Cohen, ed., *Civil Strife in America* (Hinsdale, Ill.: Dryden Press, 1972), pp. 210-255.

39. Ibid., p. 238.

40. Charles A. Valentine, *Black Studies and Anthropology: Scholarly and Political Interest in Afro-American Culture* (Indianapolis: Addison-Wesley Modular Publications, 1972).

41. Nathan Glazer and Daniel Patrick Moynihan, *Beyond the Melting Pot* (Cambridge, Mass.: MIT Press, 1963), p. 53.

42. Ibid., p. xx.

43. Myrdal, op. cit.

44. Ibid., p. 928.

45. E. Franklin Frazier, *The Negro Family in the United States* (Chicago: University of Chicago Press, 1939).

46. Ibid., pp. 89-107.

47. Ibid., p. 368.

48. I do not intend to suggest that Frazier did not face racism or that he did not struggle against the racism he confronted. See, e.g., Anthony Platt, "Racism in Academia: Lessons from the Life of E. Franklin Frazier," *Monthly Review* 42 (September 1990):29-45.

49. Here I draw a distinction between race and ethnicity. Race is a discourse on power relations that is always in the process of coming-to-be. Ethnicity is a romance with the national origin of subjects.

50. Frances Fox Piven and Richard A. Cloward, *Regulating the Poor: The Functions of Public Welfare* (New York: Vintage Books, 1971).

51. Melville J. Herskovits, *The Myth of the Negro Past* (New York: Harper and Brothers, 1941).

52. St. Clair Drake and Horace Cayton, *Black Metropolis* (New York: Harper and Row, 1962).

53. Ryan, op. cit., p. 134.

54. Charles Keil, *Urban Blues* (Chicago: University of Chicago Press, 1966).

55. Elliot Leibow, *Tally's Corner: A Study of Negro Street Corner Men* (Boston: Little, Brown, 1967).

56. Ibid., p. 222.

57. Ulf Hannerz, *Soulside: Inquiries into Ghetto Culture and Community* (New York: Columbia University Press, 1969).

58. I also have in mind those theories which blame black culture for the production of criminality and delinquency, including the value stretch theories. See Hyman Rodman, "Lower Class Value Structure,"*Social Forces* 42 (1963):205-215; Walter Miller, "Lower Class Culture as a Generating Milieu of Gang Delinquency," *Journal of Social Issues* 14 (April 1958):5-19; Oscar Lewis, *La Vida* (New York: Random House, 1966).

59. Hannerz, op. cit., p. 203.

60. John Horton, "Time and Cool People," in Russell Endo and William Strawbridge, eds., *Perspectives on Black America* (Englewood Cliffs, N.J.: Prentice-Hall, 1970), pp. 365-375.

61. R. Brown and U. Bellugi, "Three Processes of a Child's Acquisition of Syntax," *Harvard Educational Review* 34 (1964):133-151; M. D. Braine, "The Ontogeny of English Phrase Structure: The First Phase," *Language* 39 (1963):1-13; L. Bloom, *Language Development: Form and Function in Emerging Grammars* (Cambridge, Mass.: M.I.T. Press, 1970); William Labov, *The Study of Nonstandard English* (Urbana, Ill.: National Council of Teachers of English, 1970).

62. Roger Abrahams, *Deep Down in the Jungle: Negro Narrative Folklore from the Streets of Philadelphia* (Chicago: Aldine, 1970); and *Positively Black* (Englewood Cliffs, N.J.: Prentice-Hall, 1970).

63. Thomas Kochman, *Black and White Styles in Conflict* (Chicago: University of Chicago Press, 1981).

64. Joan Baratz and Stephen Baratz, "Black Culture on Black Terms: A Rejection of the Social Pathology Model," in Thomas Kochman, *Rappin' and Stylin' Out* (Chicago: University of Chicago Press, 1972); J. L. Dillard, *Black English* (New York: Random House, 1972); Edith A. Folb, *Running Down Some Lines: The Language and Culture of Black Teenagers* (Cambridge: Harvard

University Press, 1980); Geneva Smitherman, *Talkin and Testifying: The Language of Black America* (Boston: Houghton Mifflin, 1977).

65. Paul Takagi and Tony Platt, "Behind the Gilded Ghetto: An Analysis of Race, Class, and Crime in China Town," *Crime and Social Justice*, Spring-Summer 1978, pp. 2-25.

66. Angela Y. Davis, *Women, Race and Class* (New York: Vintage Books, 1983).

67. Omi and Winant, op. cit.

68. As I pointed out earlier, the term "myth" is used in Sorel's sense, which designates a composition of remote goals, ambivalent moral moods, and expectations of the divine good being manifested. It is a value system and worldview. Even more, I am assuming a functional role for the myth, stressing Bronislaw Malinowski's indispensable function of the myth as being taken literally in a society to enhance, express, and codify belief; to safeguard and enforce morality. Irving Louis Horowitz, *Radicalism and the Revolt Against Reason: The Social Theories of Georges Sorel* (Carbondale: Southern Illinois University Press, 1961); Bronislaw Malinowski, *Magic, Science and Religion* (Glencoe, Ill.: Free Press, 1948), p. 79.

69. There were about 4,000 parliamentary acts of enclosure, most in the 1760s and 1770s and between 1793 and 1816. Eric Hobsbawm and George Rude, *Captain Swing* (New York: Pantheon, 1968), p. 27.

70. William A. Williams, "Empire as a Way of Life," *The Nation*, August 2-9, 1980, pp. 104-119; Steve Talbot, *Roots of Oppression* (New York: International Publishers, 1981).

71. Walter R. Agard, *The Greek Mind* (Princeton: Van Nostrand, 1957).

72. I am applying Marx's historical and economic observations, found in his essays "The So-called Primitive Accumulation" and "The Modern Theory of Colonisation" in *Capital* (New York: International Publishers, 1967), pp. 713-716, 765-774.

73. Paulo Freire, *Pedagogy of the Oppressed*, Myra Bergman, trans. (New York: Continuum, 1970).

74. Blauner, op. cit.; Nikolai Bukharin, *Imperialism and World Economy* (New York: Monthly Review Press, 1929).

75. Alice Walker describes the colonial project in succinct terms in her award-winning novel, *The Color Purple* (New York: Washington Square Press, 1982). A general treatment that focuses on historical variations is Georges Balandier, "The Colonial Situation: A Theoretical Approach," in Immanuel Wallerstein, ed., *Social Change: The Colonial Situation* (New York: Wiley, 1966), pp. 34-61. Studies focused on the structure of slavery and colonization are J. S. Furnivall, *Colonial Polity and Practice* (New York: New York University Press, 1948); Richard Rubenstein, *Rebels in Eden* (Boston: Little, Brown, 1970); Immanuel Wallerstein, *Africa, the Politics of Independence* (New York: Random House, 1961); Sidney W. Mintz, ed., *Slavery, Colonialism, and Racism* (New York: W.W. Norton, 1974); Also see Memmi, op. cit.; Fanon, op. cit.; Ronald

Takaki, *Iron Cages: Race and Culture in 19th Century America* (New York: Knopf, 1979); O. Mannuni, *Prospero and Caliban: The Psychology of Colonization* (London: Methuen, 1956). For postcolonial approaches, see Patrick Williams and Laura Chrisman, eds., *Colonial Discourse and Post-Colonial Theory: A Reader* (New York: Columbia University Press, 1994); Gayatari Charkravorty Spivak, *In Other Worlds: Essays in Cultural Politics* (New York: Methuen, 1987); and *The Post Colonial Critic: Interviews, Strategies, Dialogues* (New York: Routledge, 1990); Michael T. Taussig, *Shamanism, Colonialism, and the Wild Man: A Study in Terror and Healing* (Chicago: University of Chicago Press, 1987).

76. For an empirical demonstration of domestic colonialism, see H. P. Savitch, "Black Cities/White Suburbs: Domestic Colonialism as an Interpretive Idea," *The Annals of the American Academy* 439 (September 1978):118-134.

77. I am following the typology developed by J. Herman Blake; however, I am adding the moral phase to Blake's previous conception, "The Resurgence of Black Nationalism," in Joseph Boskin and Robert Rosenstone, eds., *Seasons of Rebellion* (New York: Holt, Rinehart and Winston, 1972), pp. 39-53.

78. Baldwin's most important essay, "Letter to My Nephew," renders his general disillusionment with white moral consciousness, wherein he concludes, "It is the innocence which constitutes the crime." *The Fire Next Time* (New York: Dial Press, 1962). Also see Harold Cruse, *The Crisis of the Negro Intellectual* (New York: William Morrow, 1967).

79. Robert Blauner, "The Question of Black Culture," in John F. Szwed, ed., *Black America* (New York: Basic Books, 1970).

80. Valentine, op. cit.

81. Lerone Bennett, Jr., *Before the Mayflower* (New York: Penguin Books, 1966), pp. 274-326.

82. Ibid., pp. 389-399. Also see Joseph Boskin, *Urban Racial Violence* (Beverly Hills, Calif.: Glencoe Press, 1969), pp. 21-37.

83. Amy Jacques-Garvey, ed., *Philosophy and Opinions of Marcus Garvey* (New York: Atheneum, 1974).

84. Bennett, op. cit., p. 296.

85. Blake, op. cit.

86. C. Eric Lincoln, *The Black Muslims in America* (Boston: Beacon Press, 1961), pp. 12-20.

87. Ibid.

88. Malcolm X, *The Autobiography of Malcolm X* (New York: Grove Press, 1966), pp. 1-22.

89. Malcolm X, *Two Speeches by Malcolm X* (New York: New American Library, 1963).

90. Lincoln, op. cit., pp. 208-216.

91. Martin Luther King, *Why We Can't Wait* (New York: New American Library, 1963).

92. Herbert Warren Richardson, "Martin Luther King—Unsung

Theologian," in Martin Marty and Dean G. Peerman, eds., *New Theology No. 6* (New York: Macmillan, 1969), pp. 178-184.

93. Martin Luther King, *Where Do We Go From Here: Chaos or Community* (Boston: Beacon Press, 1968).

94. Lawrence Kohlberg, "Stage and Sequence: The Cognitive-Developmental Approach to Socialization," in D. A. Goslin, ed., *Handbook of Socialization Theory and Research* (Chicago: Rand McNally, 1969).

95. Capital derives from the Latin *caput*, meaning "head," which was used in the phrase *pars capitalis debiti*, meaning the capital part, or principal, of a debt. As we have seen, capital requires the existence of class domination. Karl Marx, *Economic and Philosophic Manuscripts of 1844* (London: Lawrence and Wishart, 1959). Also see Dharendorf, op. cit.

96. Herbert Marcuse, *One-Dimensional Man* (Boston: Beacon Press, 1964); and *Eros and Civilization* (Boston: Beacon Press, 1955); Sigmund Freud, *Civilization and Its Discontents*, James Strachey, trans. (New York: W. W. Norton, 1953); Karl Marx and Frederick Engels, *The German Ideology* (New York: International Publishers, 1970).

97. Richard Wright, *Uncle Tom's Children* (New York: Harper and Row, 1965); and *White Man, Listen* (Garden City, N.Y.: Anchor Books, 1964).

98. Ralph Ellison, *Invisible Man* (New York: Vintage Books, 1972).

99. Baldwin, op. cit.

100. Walker, op. cit.

101. Isaiah Berlin, *Two Concepts of Liberty* (Oxford: Oxford University Press, 1958).

102. Anthony Lemelle, "Killing The Author of Life, or Decimating 'Bad Niggers'," *Journal of Black Studies* 19, no. 2 (December 1988):216-231.

103. Thomas Hobbes, "Of the Liberty of Subjects," in F. J. E. Woodbridge, ed., *Hobbes Selections* (New York: Charles Scribner's Sons, 1958), pp. 369-380.

104. Stephen J. Gould, *The Mismeasure of Man* (New York: W. W. Norton, 1981).

105. Ibid., pp. 146-334.

106. Frederick Douglass, *Narrative of the Life of Frederick Douglass An American Slave, Written by Himself* (New York: New American Library, 1968). Also see Angela Davis, "Unfinished Lecture on Liberation II," in Leonard Harris, ed., *Philosophy Born of Struggle: Anthology of Afro-American Philosophy from 1917* (Dubuque, Iowa: Kendall/Hunt, 1983), pp. 130-151.

107. George Dennis O'Brien, *Hegel on Reason and History* (Chicago: University of Chicago Press, 1975), pp. 148-149.

108. Dhoruba Bin Wahad, Mumia Abu-Jamal, and Assata Shakur, *Still Black, Still Strong*, Jim Fletcher, Tanaquil Jones, and Sylvere Lotringer, eds. (New York: Semiotext(e), 1993), pp. 126, 142.

109. Ibid., p. 93.

CHAPTER 5

1. Paul Walton, Ian Taylor, and Jock Young, *The New Criminology: For a Social Theory of Deviance* (New York: Harper, 1973), pp. 240-274.

2. Emile Durkheim, *The Divison of Labor in Society*, George Simpson, trans. (New York: Free Press, 1933), pp. 291-293.

3. Max Weber, *The Theory of Social and Economic Organization*, A. M. Henderson and Talcott Parsons, trans. (New York: Free Press, 1947), pp. 28-29.

4. Vilfredo Pareto, *Mind and Society*, Andrew Bongiorno and Arthur Livingston, trans. (New York: Harcourt, Brace, 1935), vol. 3, p. 2025.

5. Max Horkheimer, *Critical Theory*, Matthew J. O'Connell, trans. (New York: Continuum, 1982), pp. 47-128.

6. Erich Fromm, *Escape from Freedom* (New York: Farrar and Rinehart, 1941); Herbert Marcuse, *Eros and Civilization* (Boston: Beacon Press, 1955).

7. A. C. Johnson, "Our Schools Make Criminals," *Journal of Criminal Law and Criminology* 33 (1942):315-320; A. B. Clegg, "Delinquency and Discipline: The Role of the School," *Education* 19 (1962):1239-1240; Martin Gold, *Status Forces in Delinquent Boys* (Chicago: University of Michigan Institute of Social Research, 1963); Arthur Stinchcomb, *Rebellion in a High School* (Chicago: Quadrangle, 1964); J. Webb, "The Sociology of a School," *British Journal of Sociology* 13 (1962):264-272; David Downes, *The Delinquent Solution* (London: Routledge and Kegan Paul, 1966); David Hargreaves, *Social Relations in a Secondary School* (London: Routledge and Kegan Paul, 1967); Kenneth Polk and Walter Schafer, *Schools and Delinquency* (Englewood Cliffs, N.J.: Prentice Hall, 1967); L. McDonald, *Social Class and Delinquency* (London: Faber and Faber, 1969); Mary Haywood Metz, *Classrooms and Corridors: The Crisis of Authority in Desegregated Secondary Schools* (Berkeley: University of California Press, 1978); Delos Kelly, *Creating School Failure: Youth Crime and Deviance* (Los Angeles: Trident Shop, 1982).

8. Albert K. Cohen, *Delinquent Boys: The Culture of the Gang* (Glencoe, Ill.: Free Press, 1955); Richard Cloward and Lloyd Ohlin, *Delinquency and Opportunity: A Theory of Delinquent Gangs* (Glencoe, Ill.: Free Press, 1960).

9. David Matza, *Becoming Deviant* (New York: Prentice-Hall, 1969); Howard Becker, *Outsiders: Studies in the Sociology of Deviance* (New York: Free Press, 1973).

10. Edwin M. Lemert, *Social Pathology* (New York: McGraw Hill, 1951); and *Human Deviance: Social Problems and Social Control* (Englewood Cliffs, N.J.: Prentice-Hall, 1967).

11. Lemert, *Human Deviance*, p. 59.

12. Aaron V. Cicourel, *The Social Organization of Juvenile Justice* (New York: Wiley, 1968).

13. Carl Werthman, "Delinquent in School: A Test of the Legitimacy of Authority," *Berkeley Journal of Sociology* 8 (1963):39-60.

14. David Matza, *Delinquency and Drift* (New York: John Wiley, 1964).

15. Cicourel, op. cit., p. 169.

16. David Hargreaves, Stephen Hester, and Frank Mellor, *Deviance in the Classrooms* (London: Routledge and Kegan Paul, 1975).

17. Thomas Kuhn, *The Structure of Scientific Revolutions* (Chicago: University of Chicago Press, 1962), p. 162.

18. Douglass Hay, *Albion's Fatal Tree* (New York: Pantheon Books, 1975). Also see Michel Foucault, *Discipline and Punish*, Alan Sheridan, trans. (London: Allen Lane, 1977).

19. Walton, Taylor, and Young, op. cit.

20. Thorstein Veblen, *The Higher Learning in America* (New York: Huebsch, 1918).

21. Auguste Comte, *The Positive Philosophy*, Harriet Martineau, trans. (London: Bell, 1915).

22. Like the utilitarians, the positivists have a wide variety of theories, from theories about head size (cephalic index) to theories about "cultural goals" and "institutionalized means."

23. Robert K. Merton, "Social Structure and Anomie," *American Sociological Review* 3 (1938):672-682.

24. James Meisel, *The Myth of the Ruling Class* (Ann Arbor: University of Michigan Press, 1958); David Reisman, *The Lonely Crowd: A Study of Changing American Culture* (New Haven: Yale University Press, 1961).

25. C. Wright Mills, *The Power Elite* (New York: Oxford University Press, 1956).

26. Earl Rubington and Martin S. Weinberg, eds., *Deviance: An Interactionist Perspective* (New York: Macmillan, 1968), p. 34.

27. Herbert Blumer, "What Is Wrong with Social Theory?" *American Sociological Review* 19, no. 1 (1954):3-10.

28. Becker, op. cit.

29. Edmund Husserl, *Ideas: General Introduction to Pure Phenomenology* (New York: Collier Books, 1962). Labeling theory's philosophical basis is grounded in Husserl's "pure psychology." Pure psychology pointed to Rene Descartes's formulation of intentionality of consciousness as an incomplete concept. *Ego cogito* should be expanded to *ego cogito cogitatum*. Husserl's concern drew a distinction between the object as it is perceived, the noema, and the perception of the object, the noesis.

30. Herbert Blumer, "Sociological Implications of the Thought of George Herbert Mead," *American Journal of Sociology* 71 (1966):535-548.

31. Alvin Gouldner, "The Sociologist as Partisan: Sociology and the Welfare State," *American Sociologist* 3 (1968):103-116.

32. Walton, Taylor, and Young, op. cit., p. 173.

33. Alfred Schutz, "Common Sense and Scientific Interpretation of Human Action," *Philosophy and Phenomenological Research* 14, no. 1 (1953):1-37.

34. Edwin Schur, *Labeling Deviant Behavior* (New York: Harper and Row, 1971).

35. Milton Mankoff, "Societal Reaction and Career Deviance: A Critical Analysis," *The Sociological Quarterly* 12 (1971):205-206.

36. Hargreaves, Hester, and Mellor, op. cit.

37. Robert Edgerton, *Deviance: A Cross-cultural Perspective* (Menlo Park, Calif.: Cummings, 1976), discusses a range of behavioral and organic issues in authoritative detail.

38. Max Weber, *Sociology of Religion*, E. Fischoff, trans. (Boston: Beacon, 1963).

39. Immanuel Kant, *Critique of Pure Reason*, Norman Kemp Smith, trans. (New York: St. Martin's Press, 1929).

40. Talcott Parsons, *Action Theory and the Human Condition* (New York: Free Press, 1976), p. 356.

41. See the excellent discussion of Frederic Le Play's school in Pitirim Sorokin, *Contemporary Sociological Theories* (New York: Harper and Brothers, 1928), pp. 63-98.

42. Ferdinand Tonnies, *Community and Society*, C. P. Loomis, trans. (East Lansing: Michigan State University Press, 1956).

43. Talcott Parsons, *The Social System* (Glencoe, Ill.: Free Press, 1951).

44. W. Lloyd Warner and Paul S. Lunt, *The Social Life of a Modern Community* (New Haven: Yale University Press, 1941), pp. 34-38.

45. Colin Bell and Howard Newby, *Community Studies* (New York: Praeger Publishers, 1974), p. 198.

46. Lewis Coser, *The Functions of Social Conflict* (New York: Free Press, 1956), p. 20; Ralf Dahrendorf, *Class and Class Conflict in Industrial Society* (Stanford: Stanford University Press, 1959), ch. 5.

47. George Ritzer, *Sociological Theory* (New York: Knopf, 1983).

48. Dahrendorf, op. cit., pp. 157-165.

49. George Simmel, "Group Expansion and the Development of Individuality," in Donald Levine, ed., *George Simmel: Individuality and Social Forms* (Chicago: University of Chicago Press, 1971), p. 259.

50. Herbert Blumer, "Race Prejudice as a Sense of Group Position," *Pacific Sociological Review* 1 (1958):3-7.

51. Sigmund Freud, *The Ego and the Id*, James Strachey, trans. (New York: W.W. Norton, 1961), pp. 12-16.

52. Talcott Parsons and Edward A. Shils, *Toward a General Theory of Action* (New York: Harper and Row, 1962), pp. 243-247.

53. Sigmund Freud, *New Introductory Lectures on Psychoanalysis*, James Strachey, trans. (New York: W.W. Norton, 1965), pp. 182-185.

54. For this discussion I am relying on Alfred North Whitehead, *Symbolism: Its Meaning and Effect* (New York: Capricorn Books, 1927).

55. Blumer, "Sociological Implications of the Thought of George Herbert Mead," p. 542.

56. Nicholas Georgescu-Roegen, *The Entropy Law and the Economic Process* (Cambridge, Mass.: Harvard University Press, 1971).

CHAPTER 6

1. Vernon J. Williams, Jr., *From a Caste to a Minority: Changing Attitudes of American Sociologists Toward Afro-Americans, 1896-1945* (New York: Greenwood Press, 1989).
2. David Kettler, Volker Meja, and Nico Stehr, *Karl Mannheim* (London: Tavistock, 1984), pp. 33-79.
3. Karl Mannheim, *Structures of Thinking*, Jeremy S. Shapiro and Shierry Weber Nicholsen, trans. (London: Routledge and Kegan Paul, 1982), p. 110.
4. Ibid., pp. 111-112.
5. See, e.g., Troy Duster, *Backdoor to Eugenics* (New York: Routledge, 1990), pp. 19-36.
6. Karl Marx, *Contribution to a Criticism of Political Economy* (London: Lawrence and Wishart, 1971). Marx added: "The relations of production [correspond] to a given stage in the development of the material forces of production. The totality of these relations of production constitutes the economic structure of society, the real foundation, in which arises a legal and political superstructure and to which correspond definite forms of social consciousness" (p. 20).
7. Michael Polanyi, *The Study of Man* (Chicago: University of Chicago Press, 1959), pp. 71-99.
8. Maurice Godelier, *The Mental and the Material*, Martin Thom, trans. (London: Verso, 1986), p. 128.
9. Ibid., p. 147.
10. Ibid., pp. 149-156.
11. Ibid., p. 154.
12. Robert N. Bellah, "Civil Religion in America," *Daedalus* 96 (Winter 1967):1-21.
13. Emile Durkheim, *The Elementary Forms of Religious Life*, Joseph W. Swain, trans. (New York: Collier Macmillan, 1961).
14. Randall Collins, *Sociological Insight* (New York: Oxford University Press, 1992), p. 32.
15. Ibid., p. 39.
16. Karl Marx, *Pre-Capitalist Economic Formations*, trans. from the *Grundrisse* by Jack Cohen and Eric Hobsbawm (London: Lawrence and Wishart, 1964), p. 64; cited by Etienne Balibar in Louis Althusser and Etienne Balibar, *Reading Capital* (London: Verso, 1990), pp. 218-219.
17. Theodore W. Adorno cited in Russell Jocoby, *Social Amnesia* (Boston: Beacon Press, 1973), p. 120; and in Richard Lichtman, *The Social Production of Desire* (New York: Free Press, 1982), p. 103.
18. Lichtman, op. cit., p. 188.
19. Ibid., p. 189.
20. Sigmund Freud, cited in Lichtman, p. 189.
21. Frantz Fanon, *Black Skin, White Masks*, Charles L. Markmann, trans. (New York: Grove Press, 1967), p. 51; cited in Lichtman, op. cit., p. 204.

22. Karl Marx, *The Eighteen Brumaire of Louis Bonaparte* (New York: International Publishers, 1977), p. 15.

23. Karl Marx, "Economic and Philosophic Manuscripts of 1844," in Robert C. Tucker, ed., *The Marx-Engels Reader* (New York: W.W. Norton, 1978), p. 86.

24. Sigmund Freud, *Civilization and Its Discontents*, James Strachey, trans. (New York: W.W. Norton, 1962), pp. 88-89.

25. Ibid., p. 89.

CHAPTER 7

1. I am using Karl Marx's "Theses on Feuerbach" as the source of my distinction between civil and social society. See Karl Marx and Frederick Engels, *The Marx Engels Reader*, Robert Tucker, ed. (New York: W.W. Norton, 1978), pp. 143-145.

2. Karl Marx, *Early Writings*, Tom Bottomore, trans. (Harmondsworth, England: Penguin, 1975), pp. 87-89.

3. The actual quote from Marx reads, "Men make their own history, but they do not make it just as they please; they do not make it under circumstances chosen by themselves, but under circumstances directly found, given and transmitted from the past." Marx and Engels, op. cit., p. 595.

4. Ibid., p. 5. "mankind always sets itself only such tasks as it can solve; since, looking at the matter more closely, it will always be found that the task itself arises only when the material conditions for its solution already exist or are at least in the process of formation."

5. See, e.g., George James, *Stolen Legacy* (San Francisco: Julian Richardson Associates, 1976). Professor James demonstrated how when ideas were introduced into Greek culture that had not developed within that culture, there were violent reactions from the culture, most notably the death of Socrates.

6. Marx and Engels, op. cit., p. 4.

7. Ibid., p. 5.

8. Ibid., p. 489.

9. Karl Marx, "The British Rule in India," *New York Daily Tribune*, June 25, 1853, cited in Tom Bottomore, ed., *Dictionary of Marxist Thought* (Cambridge, Mass.: Harvard University Press, 1983), p. 425.

10. Antonio Gramsci, *Selections from the Prison Notebooks*, Quintin Hoare and Geoffrey Nowell Smith, trans. and eds. (New York: International Publishers, 1971), p. 59.

11. Ibid., p. 106. While Gramsci's definition specifically referred to the conservative Vincenzo Cuoco's attempt in Italy to stall the Risorgimento through the use of certain state powers, I am extending the usage in a slightly different sense, as Gramsci himself suggested. I am asking in what forms, and by what means, blacks in the United States succeeded in establishing the apparatus of their consciousness.

12. I am using the classification system developed by Cornel West, "Marxist Theory and the Specificity of Afro-American Oppression," in Cary Nelson and Lawrence Grossberg, eds., *Marxism and the Interpretation of Culture* (Chicago: University of Illinois Press, 1988), pp. 17-29. I am adding an additional category to account for the "inscription" and postmodern social formation theorists.

13. Eugene Debs, "The Negro in Class Struggle," *International Socialist Review* 4, no. 5 (November 1903):257-260. Also see more recent attempts to deflate racism: Floya Anthias, "Race and Class Revisited—Conceptualizing Race and Racisms," *The Sociological Review* 38 (February 1990):19-42; Robert Miles, *Racism* (London: Routledge, 1989).

14. Robert Blauner, *Racial Oppression in America* (New York: Harper and Row, 1972).

15. Oliver Cox, *Caste, Class and Race: A Study of Social Dynamics* (New York: Doubleday, 1948); Mario Barrera, *Race and Class in the Southwest: A Theory of Racial Inequality* (Notre Dame, England: University of Notre Dame Press, 1979).

16. Stuart Hall, "Race, Articulation and Societies Structured in Dominance," *Sociological Theories: Race and Colonialism* (Paris: UNESCO Press, 1980), pp. 305-345. Also see Michael Omi and Howard Winant, *Racial Formation in the United States from the 1960s to the 1980s* (London: Routledge and Kegan Pual, 1986); Cornel West, op. cit.

17. Etienne Balibar and Immanuel Wallerstein, *Race, Nation, Class: Ambiguous Identities* (London: Verso, 1991).

18. Frantz Fanon, *Black Skin, White Masks*, Charles L. Markmann, trans. (New York: Grove Press, 1967), p. 35.

19. Karl Marx, *Economic and Philosophic Manuscripts* (Moscow: International Publishers, 1967), p. 97.

20. I am using "microphysics of power," from Michel Foucault, to refer to the microinstitutional ways white supremacist logics are articulated. Although, I am not joining the ex-Marxist anarchist project of Foucault, I am involved in a similar project of the "insurrection of subjugated knowledge." See, e.g., "The Juridical Apparatus," Colin Gordon, ed., *Power/Knowledge* (New York: Pantheon Books, 1980), pp. 80-87, 92-108.

21. The idea of African-American culture is broad and complex. Two introductory pieces that might provide the reader with some insight are Lawrence Levine, *Black Culture and Black Consciousness* (New York: Oxford University Press, 1977); Roger Abrahams, ed., *Afro-American Folktales* (New York: Pantheon, 1985). The term "getting around old master" is taken from Abrahams; his epigraph from Zora Neale Hurston, "Now you are going to hear lies above suspicion," is the notion I refer to in the concept of "remote moral moods."

22. Gramsci, op. cit., pp. 108-110. There is a dialectical relationship between "war of maneuver" and "war of position." In fact, Gramsci relates the latter to the concept of passive revolution. For this reason these concepts should not be understood as static, nor should they be reified.

23. See, e.g., Manning Marable, *How Capitalism Underdeveloped Black America* (Boston: South End Press, 1983), p. 12.

24. J. M. Barbalet, *Marx's Construction of Social Theory* (London: Routledge and Kegan Paul, 1983), p. 85.

25. Herbert Marcuse, *An Essay on Liberation* (Boston: Beacon Press, 1969); and *One-Dimensional Man* (Boston: Beacon Press, 1964), see introduction.

26. Michael Ryan, *Marxism and Deconstruction* (Baltimore: John Hopkins University Press, 1982), pp. 71-72.

27. Fanon, op. cit., p. 198.

28. bell hooks, *Black Looks: Race and Representation* (Boston: South End Press, 1992).

29. Frantz Fanon, *The Wretched of the Earth*, Constance Farrington, trans. (New York: Grove Press, 1965), p. 42.

30. Ibid., p. 163.

Bibliography

Abrahams, Roger. *Deep Down in the Jungle: Negro Narrative Folklore from the Streets of Philadelphia*. Chicago: Aldine, 1970.

Abrahams, Roger. *Positively Black*. Englewood Cliffs, NJ: Prentice Hall, 1970.

Abrahams, Roger, ed. *Afro-American Folktales*. New York: Pantheon, 1985.

Adam, Heribert. *Modernizing Racial Domination: South Africa's Political Dynamics*. Berkeley: University of California Press, 1971.

Adamson, Walker. *Hegemony and Revolution*. Berkeley: University of California Press, 1980.

Addams, Jane. *Democracy and Social Ethics*. New York: Macmillan, 1902.

Adorno, T. W., et al. *The Authoritarian Personality*. New York: Harper and Row, 1950.

Agard, Walter R. *The Greek Mind*. Princeton: Van Nostrand Company, 1957.

Agger, Ben. *Fast Capitalism*. Urbana: University of Illinois Press, 1989.

Akbar, Na'im. *Visions for Black Men*. Nashville, Tenn.: Winston-Derek Publishers, 1991.

Aldridge, Delores. *Focusing: Black Male-Female Relationships*. Chicago: Third World Press, 1991.

Ali, Shahrazad. *The Blackman's Guide to Understanding the Blackwoman*. Philadelphia: Civilized Publications, 1990.

Allen, Robert. *Black Awakening in Capitalist America*. New York: Doubleday, 1969.

Allport, Gordon W. *The Nature of Prejudice*. Reading, Mass.: Addison-Wesley Publishing, 1954.

Althusser, Louis, and Etienne Balibar. *Reading Capital*. London: Verso, 1990.

Anderson, Elijah. *Street Wise*. Chicago: University of Chicago Press, 1990.

Anderson, Perry. "The Antinomies of Antonio Gramsci." *New Left Review* 100 (1976-1977): 5-78.

Angelou, Maya. *I Know Why the Caged Bird Sings*. New York: Random House, 1972.

Anthias, Floya. "Race and Class Revisited—Conceptualizing Race and Racisms." *The Sociological Review* 38 (February 1990):19-42.

Arendt, Hannah. *On Revolution.* London: Penguin Books, 1963.

Asante, Molefi. *Afrocentricity.* New York: Amulefi Publishers, 1980.

Auletta, Ken. *The Underclass.* New York: Random House, 1982.

Bahr, Howard M., Bruce A. Chadwick, and Robert C. Day, eds. *Native Americans Today: Sociological Perspectives.* New York: Harper and Row, 1972.

Bailey, Harry, and Ellis Katz, eds. *Ethnic Group Politics.* Columbus, Ohio: Merrill, 1969.

Baker, Houston A., Jr. *Blues, Ideology and Afro-American Literature.* Chicago: University of Chicago Press, 1984.

Baker, Houston A., Jr. *Black Studies, Rap, and the Academy.* Chicago: University of Chicago Press, 1993.

Baldwin, James. *Notes of a Native Son.* New York: Lorgi Books, 1949.

Baldwin, James. *The Fire Next Time.* New York: Dial Press, Inc., 1962.

Balibar, Etienne, and Immanuel Wallerstein. *Race, Nation, Class: Ambiguous Identities.* New York: Verso, 1991.

Banfield, Edward. *The Unheavenly City Revisited.* Boston: Little, Brown, 1968.

Banton, Michael. *Race Relations.* London: Tavistock, 1967.

Barbalet, J. M. *Marx's Construction of Social Theory.* London: Routledge and Kegan Paul, 1983.

Baren, Paul, and Paul Sweezy. *Monopoly Capital.* New York: Monthly Review Press, 1966.

Barrera, Mario. *Race and Class in the Southwest: A Theory of Racial Inequality.* Notre Dame, England: University of Notre Dame Press, 1979.

Barth, Fredrik. *Ethnic Groups and Boundaries.* Boston: Little, Brown, 1969.

Bauer, Raymond, and Alice Bauer. "Day to Day Resistance to Slavery." *Journal of Negro History* 27 (1942):388-419.

Becker, Howard S. *Outsiders: Studies in the Sociology of Deviance.* New York: Free Press, 1973.

Bell, Colin and Howard Newby. *Community Studies.* New York: Praeger, 1974.

Bell, Daniel. *The Coming of Post-Industrial Society.* New York: Basic Books, 1973.

Bell, Daniel. *The Cultural Contradictions of Capitalism.* New York: Basic Books, 1976.

Bellah, Robert N. "Civil Religion in America." *Daedalus* 96 (Winter 1967):1-21.

Bendix, Reinhard. *Max Weber: An Intellectual Portrait.* Garden City, N.Y.: Doubleday, 1962.

Bennett, Lerone, Jr. *Before the Mayflower.* New York: Penguin Books, 1966.

Berlin, Isaiah. *Two Concepts of Liberty.* Oxford: Oxford University Press, 1958.

Bernard, Jessie. *Marriage and Family Among Negroes.* Englewood Cliffs, N.J.: Prentice-Hall, 1966.

Biko, Steve. *I Write What I Like.* San Francisco: Harper and Row, 1978.

Billingsley, Andrew. *Black Families in White America.* Englewood Cliffs, N.J.: Prentice-Hall, 1968.

Blackwell, James E. *The Black Community.* New York: Harper and Row, 1985.

Blalock, Hubert M. *Toward a Theory of Minority-Group Relations.* New York: Wiley, 1967.

Blassingame, John. *The Slave Community.* New York: Oxford University Press, 1972.

Blauner, Robert. *Racial Oppression in America.* New York: Harper and Row, 1972.

Bloom, Jack M. *Class, Race and the Civil Rights Movement.* Bloomington: Indiana University Press, 1987.

Blumer, Herbert. "What Is Wrong with Social Theory?" *American Sociological Review* 19, no. 1 (1954):3-10.

Blumer, Herbert. "Race Prejudice as a Sense of Group Position." *Pacific Sociological Review* 1 (1958):3-7.

Blumer, Herbert. "Sociological Implications of the Thought of George Herbert Mead." *American Journal of Sociology* 71 (1966):535-538.

Blumer, Herbert. *Symbolic Interaction: Perspective and Method.* Englewood Cliffs, N.J.: Prentice-Hall, 1969.

Bocock, Robert. *Hegemony.* London: Tavistock Publications, 1986.

Bonacich, Edna. "Advanced Capitalism and Black/White Race Relations in the United States: A Split Labor Market Interpretation." *American Sociological Review* 41 (February 1976):34-51.

Bonacich, Edna, and John Modell. *The Economic Basis of Ethnic Solidarity: Small Business in the Japanese American Community.* Berkeley: University of California Press, 1980.

Boskin, Joseph. *Urban Racial Violence.* Beverly Hills, Calif.: Glencoe Press, 1969.

Boskin, Joseph, and Robert Rosenstone, eds. *Seasons of Rebellion.* New York: Holt, Rinehart and Winston, 1972.

Bottomore, Tom, ed. *Dictionary of Marxist Thought.* Cambridge, Mass.: Harvard University Press, 1983.

Bowles, Samuel, and Herbert Gintis. "I.Q. in the United States Class Structure." *Social Policy* 3, nos. 4 and 5 (November-December 1972, January-February 1973):65-96.

Bowser, Benjamin P., ed. *Black Male Adolescents: Parenting and Education in Community Context.* Lanham, Md.: University Press of America, 1991.

Bowser, Benjamin P., and Raymond G. Hunt, eds. *Impacts of Racism on White Americans.* Beverly Hills, Calif.: Sage, 1981.

Boxer, Charles R. *Race Relations in the Portuguese Colonial Empire, 1415-1825.* Oxford: Clarendon Press, 1963.

Boyer, Paul. *Urban Masses and Moral Order in America, 1820-1920.* Cambridge, Mass.: Harvard University Press, 1978.

Boyle, Kevin, and Tom Hadden. *Ireland: A Positive Proposal.* Harmondsworth,

England: Penguin, 1985.

Brown, Claude. *Manchild in the Promised Land*. New York: Signet Books, 1965.

Brown, Cynthia Stokes, ed. *Ready from Within: Septima Clark and the Civil Rights Movement*. Navarro, Calif.: Wild Tree Press, 1986.

Brown, Dee A. *Bury My Heart at Wounded Knee*. New York: Holt, Rinehart, Winston, 1970.

Bukharin, Nikolai. *Imperialism and World Economy*. New York: Monthly Review Press, 1973.

Burns, Elizabeth, and Tom Burns. *Sociology of Literature and Drama*. Baltimore: Penguin, 1973.

Cade, Toni, ed. *The Black Woman: An Anthology*. New York: New American Library, 1970.

Carmichael, Stokely, and Charles V. Hamilton. *Black Power*. New York: Vintage Books, 1967.

Carson, Clayborne. *In Struggle: SNCC and the Black Awakening of the 1960s*. Cambridge, Mass.: Harvard University Press, 1981.

Chisholm, Shirley. *Unbought and Unbossed*. New York: Avon, 1970.

Chodorow, Nancy. *The Reproduction of Mothering: Psychoanalysis and the Sociology of Gender*. Berkeley: University of California Press, 1978.

Christian, Barbara. *Black Feminist Criticism: Perspectives on Black Women Writers*. New York: Pergamon, 1985.

Cicourel, Aaron V. *The Social Organization of Juvenile Justice*. New York: Wiley, 1968.

Clark, Kenneth B. *Dark Ghetto: Dilemmas of Social Power*. New York: Harper and Row, 1965.

Cleaver, Eldridge. *Soul on Ice*. New York: McGraw-Hill, 1968.

Clegg, A. B. "Delinquency and Discipline: The Role of the School." *Education* 19 (1962):1239-1240.

Cloward, Richard, and Lloyd Ohlin. *Delinquency and Opportunity: A Theory of Delinquent Gangs*. Glencoe, Ill.: Free Press, 1960.

Cohen, Albert K. *Delinquent Boys: The Culture of the Gang*. Glencoe, Ill.: Free Press, 1955.

Cohen, Anthony P. *The Symbolic Construction of Community*. London: Tavistock, 1985.

Cohen, Norman S., ed. *Civil Strife in America*. Hinsdale, Ill.: The Dryden Press, 1972.

Collins, Patricia Hill. *Black Feminist Thought: Knowledge, Consciousness, and the Politics of Empowerment*. New York: Routledge, 1991.

Collins, Randall. *Sociological Insight*. New York: Oxford University Press, 1992.

Comer, James P. *Beyond Black and White*. New York: Quadrangle Books, 1972.

Comte, Auguste. *The Positive Philosophy*. Harriet Martineau, trans. London: Bell, 1915.

Cone, James H. *God of the Oppressed.* New York: Seabury Press, 1978.

Cone, James H. *A Black Theology of Liberation.* New York: Orbis, 1990.

Conyers, James E., and Walter L. Wallace. *Black Elected Officials.* New York: Russell Sage Foundation, 1976.

Coser, Lewis. *The Functions of Social Conflict.* Glencoe, Ill.: Free Press, 1956.

Cox, Oliver. *Caste, Class and Race: A Study of Social Dynamics.* New York: Modern Reader, 1970.

Crouch, Stanley. *Notes of a Hanging Judge.* New York: Oxford University Press, 1990.

Cruse, Harold. *The Crisis of the Negro Intellectual.* New York: William Morrow, 1967.

Dahrendorf, Ralf. *Class and Class Conflict in Industrial Society.* Stanford: Stanford University Press, 1959.

Davis, Allison, Burleigh Gardner, and Mary Gardner. *Deep South.* Chicago: University of Chicago Press, 1941.

Davis, Angela Y. *If They Come in the Morning.* New York: Signet, 1971.

Davis, Angela Y. *With My Mind on Freedom.* New York: Bantam Books, 1974.

Davis, Angela Y. *Women, Race and Class.* New York: Vintage Books, 1983.

Davis, George and Glegg Watson. *Black Life in Corporate America.* New York: Anchor, 1985.

Debs, Eugene. "The Negro in Class Struggle." *International Socialist Review* 4, no. 5 (November 1903):257-260.

Delaney, Martin. *The Condition, Elevation, Immigration and Destiny of the Colored People of the United States, Politically Considered.* Salem, N.H.: Ayer, 1968.

Deloria, Vine, Jr. *Custer Died for Your Sins.* New York: Avon Books, 1970.

Diop, Cheikh. *The African Origin of Civilization: Myth or Reality.* New York: Lawrence Hill, 1974.

Doeringer, Peter, and Michael Piore. *Internal Labor Markets and Manpower Analysis.* Lexington, Mass.: D.C. Heath, 1971.

Dollard, John. *Caste and Class in a Southern Town.* Garden City, N.Y.: Doubleday Anchor Books, 1957.

Douglass, Frederick. *The Narrative of the Life of Frederick Douglass.* New York: New American Library, 1968.

Downes, David. *The Delinquent Solution.* London: Routledge and Kegan Paul, 1966.

Drake, St. Clair, and Horace R. Cayton. *Black Metropolis: A Study of Negro Life in a Northern City.* New York: Harper and Row, 1962.

DuBois, W. E. B. *Black Titan.* New York: Beacon Press, 1970.

Dunbar, Leslie W., ed. *Minority Report.* New York: Pantheon Books, 1984.

Dunn, Lynn P. *Asian-Americans: A Study Guide and Source Book.* San Francisco: R & E Publishers, 1975.

Durkheim, Emile. *The Division of Labor in Society.* George Simpson, trans. New York: Free Press, 1933.

Durkheim, Emile. *The Elementary Forms of Religious Life*. Joseph W. Swain, trans. New York: Free Press, 1965.

Duster, Alfreda M., ed. *Crusade for Justice: The Autobiography of Ida B. Wells*. Chicago: University of Chicago Press, 1970.

Duster, Troy. *Backdoor to Eugenics*. New York: Routledge, 1990.

Dworkin, Anthony, and Rosalind Dworkin, eds. *The Minority Report*. New York: Holt, Rinehart and Winston, 1982.

Edelman, Peter, and Joyce Ladner, eds. *Adolescence and Poverty: Challenge for the 1990s*. Washington, D.C.: Center for National Policy Press, 1991.

Edgerton, Robert. *Deviance: A Cross-cultural Perspective*. Menlo Park, Calif.: Cummings, 1976.

Edwards, Richard, Michael Reich, and Thomas Weisskopf, eds. *The Capitalist System*. Englewood Cliffs, N.J.: Prentice-Hall, 1972.

Ehrenreich, Barbara, and John Ehrenreich. "The Professional-Managerial Class." *Radical America*, April-May 1977, pp. 17-22.

Eisenstein, Zillah, ed. *Capitalist Patriarchy and the Case for Socialist Feminism*. New York: Monthly Review Press, 1979.

Elkins, Stanley. *Slavery*. Chicago: University of Chicago Press, 1959.

Ellison, Ralph. "Richard Wright's Blues." *Antioch Review* 5 (June 1945):198-211.

Ellison, Ralph. *Invisible Man*. New York: Vintage Books, 1972.

Endo, Russell, and William Strawbridge, eds. *Perspectives on Black America*. Englewood Cliffs, N.J.: Prentice-Hall, 1970.

Engels, Frederick. *Anti-Duhring*. Moscow: Progress Publishers, 1969.

Evans, Brenda, and James Whitfield. *Black Males in the United States: An Annotated Bibliography from 1967-1987*. Washington, D.C.: American Psychological Association, 1988.

Factor, Robert L. *The Black Response to America*. Reading, Mass.: Addison-Wesley, 1970.

Fanon, Frantz. *The Wretched of the Earth*. Constance Farrington, trans. New York: Grove Press, 1963.

Fanon, Frantz. *Black Skin, White Masks*. Charles L. Markmann, trans. New York: Grove Press, 1967.

Felger, Robert. *Richard Wright*. Boston: Twayne, 1980.

Fillmore, Charles. *The Metaphysical Bible Dictionary*. Unity Village, Mo.: Unity School of Christianity Press, 1931.

Fishburn, Katherine. *Richard Wright's Hero: The Faces of a Rebel-Victim*. Metuchen, N.J.: Scarecrow Press, 1977.

Folb, Edith A. *Running Down Some Lines: The Language and Culture of Black Teenagers*. Cambridge, Mass.: Harvard University Press, 1980.

Forbes, Jack. *Black Africans and Native Americans*. Cambridge, Mass.: Blackwell, 1980.

Foster, Herbert L. *Ribbin', Jivin' and Playin' the Dozens: Unrecognized Dilemma of Inner City Schools*. Cambridge, Mass.: Ballinger, 1974.

Foster, William Z. *The Negro People in American History.* New York: International Publishers, 1954.

Foucault, Michel. *Power/Knowledge.* Colin Gordon, trans. New York: Pantheon Books, 1972.

Foucault, Michel. *Discipline and Punish.* Alan Sheridan, trans. London: Allen Lane, 1977.

Foucault, Michel. *The History of Sexuality.* Robert Hurley, trans. New York: Vintage Books, 1980.

Franklin, H. Bruce. *The Victim as Criminal and Artist.* New York: Oxford University Press, 1978.

Franklin, Clyde W. *Men and Society.* Chicago: Nelson-Hall, 1988.

Franklin, John Hope. *From Slavery to Freedom.* New York: Knopf, 1980.

Franklin, Raymond S., and Solomon Resnik. *The Political Economy of Racism.* New York: Holt, Rinehart and Winston, 1973.

Frazier, E. Franklin. *The Negro Family in the United States.* Chicago: University of Chicago Press, 1939.

Frazier, E. Franklin. *Black Bourgeoisie.* New York: Free Press, 1957.

Fredrickson, George M. *The Black Image in the White Mind.* New York: Harper and Row, 1971.

Freire, Paulo. *Pedagogy of the Oppressed.* Myra Bergman, trans. New York: Continuum, 1970.

Freud, Sigmund. *The Ego and the Id.* James Strachey, trans. New York: W.W. Norton, 1961.

Freud, Sigmund. *Civilization and Its Discontents.* James Strachey, trans. New York: W.W. Norton, 1962.

Freud, Sigmund. *New Introductory Lectures on Psychoanalysis.* James Strachey, trans. New York: W.W. Norton, 1965.

Fromm, Erich. *Escape from Freedom.* New York: Farrar and Rinehart, 1941.

Furnivall, J. S. *Colonial Policy and Practice, A Comparative Study of Burma and Netherlands India.* New York: New York University Press, 1956.

Garfinkel, Harold. "Conditions of Successful Degradation Ceremonies." *American Journal of Sociology* 61 (1956):420-424.

Garon, Paul. *Blues and the Poetic Spirit.* New York: Da Capo, 1978.

Genovese, Eugene D. *Red and Black.* New York: Vintage Books, 1968.

Genovese, Eugene D. *Roll, Jordan, Roll: The World the Slaves Made.* New York: Vintage Books, 1976.

Georgescu-Roegen, Nicholas. *The Entropy Law and the Economic Process.* Cambridge, Mass.: Harvard University Press, 1971.

Gibbs, Jewelle Taylor. *Young, Black, and Male in America.* New York: Auburn House, 1988.

Giddens, Anthony. *Central Problems in Social Theory.* Berkeley: University of California Press, 1979.

Giddings, Paula. *When and Where I Enter...The Impact of Black Women on Race and Sex in America.* New York: William Morrow, 1984.

Gilroy, Paul. *"There Ain't No Black in the Union Jack": The Cultural Politics of Race and Nation*. Chicago: University of Chicago Press, 1991.

Girard, Rene. *Violence and the Sacred*. Baltimore: Johns Hopkins University Press, 1972.

Glazer, Nathan. *Affirmative Discrimination: Ethnic Identity and Public Policy*. New York: Basic Books, 1975.

Godelier, Maurice. *Perspectives in Marxist Anthropology*. Robert Brain, trans. London: Cambridge University Press, 1977.

Godelier, Maurice. *The Mental and the Material*. Martin Thom, trans. London: Verso, 1986.

Gold, Martin. *Status Forces in Delinquent Boys*. Chicago: University of Michigan Institute of Social Research, 1963.

Gordon, Milton. *Assimilation in American Life*. New York: W.W. Norton, 1981.

Goslin, D. A., ed. *Handbook of Socialization Theory and Research*. Chicago: Rand McNally, 1969.

Gould, Stephen Jay. *The Mismeasure of Man*. New York: W.W. Norton, 1981.

Gouldner, Alvin. "The Sociologist as Partisan: Sociology and the Welfare State." *American Sociologist* 3 (1968):103-116.

Graham, Lloyd. *Deceptions and Myths of the Bible*. Secaucus, N.J.: University Books, 1975.

Gramsci, Antonio. *Selections from the Prison Notebooks of Antonio Gramsci*. Quintin Hoare and Geoffrey Nowell Smith, trans. London: Lawrence and Wishart, 1971.

Gray, Lawrence E. *Black Men*. Newbury Park, Calif.: Sage, 1981.

Gregory, Dick. *No More Lies*. New York: Harper and Row, 1971.

Grier, William H., and Price M. Cobbs. *Black Rage*. New York: Basic Books, 1980.

Griggs, Sutton. *Imperium in Imperio*. Miami: Mnemosyne, 1969.

Gutman, Herbert. *The Black Family in Slavery and Freedom: 1750-1925*. New York: Pantheon, 1976.

Habermas, Jurgen. *Legitimation Crisis*. Boston: Beacon Press, 1975.

Hakutani, Yoshinobu, ed. *Critical Essays on Richard Wright*. Boston: G.K. Hall, 1982.

Haley, Alex. *Roots*. New York: Doubleday, 1976.

Hall, Stuart. "Gramsci's Relevance for the Study of Race and Ethnicity." *Journal of Communication Inquiry* 10 (Summer 1967):5-27.

Hall, Stuart. "Race, Articulation and Societies Structured in Dominance." *Sociological Theories: Race and Colonialism*. Paris: UNESCO Press, 1980.

Hall, Stuart. "Deviance, Politics and the Media." In Henry Abelove, Michele Aina Barale, and David M. Halperin, eds., *The Lesbian and Gay Studies Reader*. New York: Routledge, 1993.

Hall, Stuart, and Tony Jefferson, eds. *Resistance Through Rituals*. London: Harper Collins, 1976.

Halsell, Grace. *Soul Sister*. Greenwich, Conn.: Fawcett, 1969.

Handlin, Oscar. *Race and Nationality in American Life.* Boston: Little, Brown, 1957.

Hannerz, Ulf. *Soulside: Inquiries into Ghetto Culture and Community.* New York: Columbia University Press, 1969.

Hansberry, Lorraine. *Les Blancs: The Collected Last Plays of Lorraine Hansberry.* Robert Nemiroff, ed. New York: Random House, 1972.

Hare, Nathan, and Julia Hare. *The Endangered Black Family: Coping with the Unisexualization and Coming Extinction of the Black Race.* San Francisco: Black Think Tank Press, 1984.

Hare, Nathan, and Julia Hare. *Bringing the Black Boy to Manhood: The Passage.* San Francisco: Black Think Tank Press, 1985.

Hare, Nathan, and Julia Hare. *Crisis in Black Sexual Politics.* San Francisco: Black Think Tank Press, 1989.

Hargreaves, David. *Social Relations in a Secondary School.* London: Routledge and Kegan Paul, 1967.

Hargreaves, David, Stephen Hester, and Frank Mellor. *Deviance in the Classrooms.* London: Routledge and Kegan Paul, 1975.

Harland, Richard. *Superstructuralism.* London: Methuen, 1987.

Harris, Leonard, ed. *Philosophy Born of Struggle: Anthology of Afro-American Philosophy from 1917.* Dubuque, Iowa: Kendall/Hunt Publishing Co., 1983.

Harris, Sheldon. *Blues Who's Who.* New Rochelle, N.Y.: Arlington House, 1979.

Hay, Douglass. *Albion's Fatal Tree.* New York: Pantheon Books, 1975.

Hegel, George W. F. *The Philosophy of Right.* T. M. Knox, trans. Oxford: Clarendon Press, 1952.

Hegel, George W. F. *Lectures on the History of Philosophy.* Vol. 1. E. S. Haldane, trans. New York: Humanities Press, 1955.

Hegel, Geroge W. F. *Phenomenology of Spirit.* A. V. Miller, trans. Oxford: Clarendon Press, 1977.

Henry, Charles P. *Culture and African American Politics.* Bloomington: Indiana University Press, 1992.

Hernton, Calvin. *Sex and Racism in America.* Garden City, N.Y.: Doubleday, 1965.

Herskovits, Melville J. *The Myth of the Negro Past.* New York: Harper and Brothers, 1941.

Hill, Norman, ed. *The Black Panther Menance.* New York: Webster's Red Seal Publications, 1971.

Hill, Robert B. *The Strengths of Black Families.* New York: Emerson Hall, 1971.

Himes, Chester. *The Quality of Hurt: The Autobiography of Chester Himes.* Garden City, N.Y.: Doubleday, 1972.

Hobsbawm, Eric, and George Rude. *Captain Swing.* New York: Pantheon, 1968.

Hoch, Paul. *White Hero, Black Beast: Racism, Sexism, and the Mask of Masculinity.* London: Pluto Press, 1979.

Hogan, Lloyd. *Principles of Black Political Economy.* Boston: Routledge and Kegan Paul, 1984.

hooks, bell. *Yearning: Race, Gender, and Cultural Politics*. Boston: South End Press, 1990.

hooks, bell. *Black Looks: Race and Representation*. Boston: South End Press, 1992.

hooks, bell, and Cornel West. *Breaking Bread: Insurgent Black Intellectual Life*. Boston: South End Press, 1991.

Horkheimer, Max. *Critical Theroy*. Matthew J. O'Connell, trans. New York: Continuum, 1982.

Horowitz, Louis Irving. *Radicalism and the Revolt Against Reason: The Social Theories of Georges Sorel*. Carbondale: Southern Illinois University Press, 1961.

Huggins, Nathan. *Black Odyssey*. New York: Vintage Books, 1963.

Hurston, Zora Neale. *Their Eyes Are Watching God*. Greenwich, Conn.: Fawcett, 1969.

Husserl, Edmund. *Ideas: General Introduction to Pure Phenomenology*. W. R. Boyce Gibson, trans. New York: Collier Books, 1962.

Jackson, George. *Soledad Brother: The Prison Letters of George Jackson*. New York: Bantam Books, 1970.

Jacques-Garvey, Amy, ed. *Philosophy and Opinions of Marcus Garvey*. New York: Atheneum, 1974.

Jahn, Janheinz. *Muntu: An Outline of Neo-African Culture*. London: Faber and Faber, 1961.

James, C. L. R. *The Black Jacobins*. New York: Vintage Books, 1989.

James, C. L. R. *Mariners, Renegades and Castaways*. New York: Allison and Busby, 1985.

James, George. *Stolen Legacy*. San Francisco: Julian Richardson Associates, 1976.

Jencks, Christopher, et al., eds. *Inequality: A Reassessment of the Effect of Family and Schooling in America*. New York: Basic Books, 1972.

Jocoby, Russell. *Social Amnesia*. Boston: Beacon Press, 1973.

Johnson, A. C. "Our Schools Make Criminals." *Journal of Criminal Law and Criminology* 33 (1942):315-320.

Johnson, Guy B. *John Henry: Tracking Down a Negro Legend*. Chapel Hill: University of North Carolina Press, 1929.

Jones, Kenneth M. "The Black Male in Jeopardy." *Crisis* 93, no. 3 (March 1986):16-29.

Jones, LeRoi. *Blues People*. New York: Morrow Quill, 1963.

Jones, Reginald L. *Mainstreaming Minority Youth*. Reston, Va.: Council of Exceptional Children, 1976.

Jordan, June. *On Call*. Boston: South End Press, 1985.

Jordan, Winthrop. *White over Black*. Baltimore: Penguin, 1969.

Joyce, Joyce Ann. *Richard Wright's Art of Tragedy*. Iowa City: University of Iowa Press, 1986.

Kant, Immanuel. *Critique of Pure Reason*. Norman Kemp Smith, trans. New

York: St. Martin's Press, 1929.

Kardiner, Abram, and Lionel Ovesey. *The Mark of Oppression*. New York: World, 1951.

Katz, William. *Black Indians*. New York: Macmillan, 1986.

Keil, Charles. *Urban Blues*. Chicago: The University of Chicago Press, 1966.

Kelly, Delos. *Creating School Failure: Youth Crime and Deviance*. Los Angeles: Trident Shop, 1982.

Kettler, David, Volker Meja, and Nico Stehr. *Karl Mannheim*. London: Tavistock, 1984.

Kimmel, Michael S. *Changing Men*. Newbury Park, Calif.: Sage, 1987.

King, Martin Luther. *Stride Toward Freedom*. New York: Harper and Row, 1958.

King, Martin Luther. *Why We Can't Wait*. New York: New American Library, 1963.

King, Martin Luther. *Where Do We Go from Here: Chaos or Community*. Boston: Beacon Press, 1968.

King, Martin Luther. *Strength to Love*. Philadelphia: Fortress Press, 1981.

Kinnamon, Kenneth. *The Emergence of Richard Wright*. Urbana: University of Illinois Press, 1972.

Kitano, Harry. *Japanese Americans: The Evolution of a Subculture*. Englewood Cliffs, N.J.: Prentice-Hall, 1976.

Knowles, Louis L., and Kenneth Prewitt, eds. *Institutional Racism in America*. Englewood Cliffs, N.J.: Prentice-Hall, 1969.

Kochman, Thomas. *Black and White Styles in Conflict*. Chicago: University of Chicago Press, 1981.

Kochman, Thomas, ed. *Rappin' and Stylin' Out*. Urbana: University of Illinois Press, 1972.

Kozol, Jonathan. *Death at an Early Age: The Destruction of the Hearts and Minds of Negro Children in the Boston Public Schools*. Boston: Houghton Mifflin, 1967.

Kuhn, Manford. "Major Trends in Symbolic Interaction Theory in the Past Twenty-five Years." *The Sociological Quarterly* no. 5 (1964):61-84.

Kuhn, Thomas. *The Structure of Scientific Revolutions*. Chicago: University of Chicago Press, 1962.

Kunjufu, Jawanza. *Countering the Conspiracy to Destroy Black Boys*. Chicago: Afro-American Publishing Company, 1984.

Labov, William. *The Study of Nonstandard English*. Urbana, Ill.: National Council of Teachers of English, 1970.

Laclau, Ernesto, and Chantal Mouffe. *Hegemony and Socialist Strategy: Towards a Radical Democratic Politics*. Winston Moore and Paul Cammack, trans. New York: Verso, 1985.

Ladner, Joyce. *Tomorrow's Tomorrow: The Black Woman*. New York: Doubleday, 1971.

Ladner, Joyce, ed. *The Death of White Sociology*. New York: Vintage Books,

1973.

Leibow, Elliot. *Tally's Corner: A Study of Negro Street Corner Men.* Boston: Little, Brown, 1967.

Lemert, Edwin M. *Social Pathology.* New York: McGraw-Hill, 1951.

Lemert, Edwin M. *Human Deviance, Social Problems, and Social Control.* Englewood Cliffs, N.J.: Prentice-Hall, 1967.

Lenin, V. I. *The Nascent Trend of Imperialist Economism.* Moscow: Progress Publishers, 1982.

Lerner, Gerda, ed. *Black Women in White America.* New York: Random House, 1973.

Levine, Donald, ed. *Georg Simmel: Individuality and Social Forms.* Chicago: University of Chicago Press, 1971.

Levine, Lawrence. *Black Culture and Black Consciousness.* New York: Oxford University Press, 1977.

Lewis, Oscar. *La Vida.* New York: Random House, 1966.

Lichtman, Richard. *The Social Production of Desire.* New York: Free Press, 1982.

Light, Ivan, and Edna Bonacich. *Immigrant Entrepreneurs: Koreans in Los Angeles 1965-1982.* Berkeley: University of California Press, 1988.

Lincoln, C. Eric. *The Black Muslims in America.* Boston: Beacon, 1961.

Little, Malcolm (El Hajj Malik El Shabazz). *Two Speeches by Malcolm X.* New York: Pathfinder Press, 1965.

Little, Malcolm (El Hajj Malik El Shabazz). *The Autobiography of Malcolm X.* New York: Grove Press, 1967.

Litwack, Leon. *North of Slavery.* Chicago: University of Chicago Press, 1961.

MacRobert, Iain. *The Black Roots and White Racism of Early Pentecostalism in the U.S.A.* New York: Macmillan, 1988.

Madhubuti, Haki R. *Black Men: Obsolete, Single, Dangerous?: Afrikan American Families in Transition.* Chicago: Third World Press, 1990.

Majors, Richard, and Janet Mancini Billson. *Cool Pose: The Dilemmas of Black Manhood in America.* New York: Macmillan, 1991.

Malinowski, Bronislaw. *Magic, Science and Religion.* Glencoe, Ill.: Free Press, 1948.

Mankoff, Milton. "Societal Reaction and Career Deviance: A Critical Analysis." *The Sociological Quarterly,* 12 (1971):205-206.

Mannheim, Karl. *Structures of Thinking.* Jeremy S. Shapiro and Shierry Weber Nicholsen, trans. London: Routledge and Kegan Paul, 1982.

Mannuni, O. *Prospero and Caliban: The Psychology of Colonization.* London: Methuen, 1956.

Marable, Manning. *How Capitalism Underdeveloped Black America.* Boston: South End Press, 1983.

Marable, Manning. *Black American Politics.* London: Verso, 1985.

Marcuse, Herbert. *Eros and Civilization.* Boston: Beacon Press, 1955.

Marcuse, Herbert. *One-Dimensional Man.* Boston: Beacon Press, 1964.

Marcuse, Herbert. *An Essay on Liberation*. Boston: Beacon Press, 1969.

Martin, David. *Two Critiques of Spontaneity*. London: Broad Water Press, 1973.

Marty, Martin, and Dean G. Peerman, eds. *New Theology No. 6*. New York: Macmillan, 1969.

Marx, Karl. *Capital*. Moscow: Foreign Languages Publishing House, 1956.

Marx, Karl. *Contribution to the Criticism of Political Economy*. London: Lawrence and Wishart, 1971.

Marx, Karl. *Early Writings*. Tom Bottomore, trans. Harmondsworth, England: Penguin, 1975.

Marx, Karl. *The Eighteenth Brumaire of Louis Bonaparte*. New York: International Publishers, 1977.

Marx, Karl, and Frederick Engels. *Selected Works in Three Volumes*. Moscow: Progress Publishers, 1969.

Marx, Karl, and Frederick Engels. *The Communist Manifesto*. New York: International Publishers, 1976.

Marx, Karl, and Frederick Engels. *The Marx-Engels Reader*. Robert C. Tucker, ed. New York: W.W. Norton, 1978.

Matza, David. *Delinquency and Drift*. New York: John Wiley, 1964.

Matza, David. *Becoming Deviant*. Englewood Cliffs, N.J.: Prentice-Hall, 1969.

Mazrui, Ali A. *A World Federation of Cultures: An African Perspective*. New York: Free Press, 1976.

Mbiti, John S. *African Religions and Philosophy*. London: Heinemann, 1969.

Meir, August, and Elliot Rudwick. *The Making of Black America*. New York: Atheneum, 1969.

Meisel, James. *The Myth of the Ruling Class*. Ann Arbor: University of Michigan Press, 1958.

Memmi, Albert. *The Colonizer and the Colonized*. Boston: Beacon Press, 1965.

Merton, Robert K. "Social Structure and Anomie." *American Sociological Review* 3 (1938):672-682.

Merton, Robert K. *Social Theory and Social Structure*. Glencoe, Ill.: Free Press, 1949.

Merton, Robert K., and Robert Nisbet, eds. *Contemporary Social Problems*. New York: Harcourt, Brace and World, 1971.

Metz, Mary Haywood. *Classrooms and Corridors: The Crisis of Authority in Desegregated Secondary Schools*. Berkeley: University of California Press, 1978.

Miles, Robert. *Racism*. London: Routledge, 1989.

Miller, Walter. "Lower Class Culture as a Generating Milieu of Gang Delinquency." *Journal of Social Issues* 14 (April 1958):5-19.

Mills, C. Wright. *The Power Elite*. New York: Oxford University Press, 1956.

Mintz, Sidney W., ed. *Slavery, Colonialism, and Racism*. New York: W.W. Norton, 1974.

Moore, Robert B. *Racism in the English Language*. New York: Council on Interracial Books for Children, 1976.

Moynihan, Daniel P. *The Negro Family: The Case for National Action.* Washington, D.C.: U.S. Government Printing Office, 1965.

Moynihan, Daniel P. *Maximum Feasible Misunderstanding.* New York: Free Press, 1969.

Myrdal, Gunnar. *An American Dilemma, The Negro Problem and Modern Democracy.* New York: Pantheon, 1962.

Needham, Rodney. *Against the Tranquility of Axioms.* Berkeley: University of California Press, 1983.

Nelson, Cary, and Lawrence Grossberg, eds. *Marxism and the Interpretation of Culture.* Urbana: University of Illinois Press, 1988.

Newton, Huey P. *Revolutionary Suicide.* New York: Harcourt Brace Jovanovich, 1973.

Nisbet, Robert. *The Social Bond.* New York: Knopf, 1970.

Nkrumah, Kwame. *Class Struggle in Africa.* New York: International Publishers, 1970.

Odum, Howard W., and Guy B. Johnson. *Negro Workday Songs.* New York: Negro Universities Press, 1926.

Omi, Michael, and Howard Winant. *Racial Formation in the United States from the 1960s to the 1980s.* New York: Routledge and Kegan Paul, 1986.

Pareto, Vilfredo. *Mind and Society.* Andrew Bongiorno and Arthur Livingston, trans. New York: Harcourt, Brace, 1935.

Parsons, Talcott. *The Social System.* Glencoe, Ill.: Free Press, 1951.

Parsons, Talcott. *Action Theory and the Human Condition.* New York: Free Press, 1976.

Parsons, Talcott, and Edward A. Shils. *Toward a General Theory of Action.* New York: Harper and Row, 1962.

Paterson, Orlando. *Slavery and Social Death.* Cambridge, Mass.: Harvard University Press, 1982.

Perlman, Janice. *The Myth of Marginality.* Berkeley: University of California Press, 1976.

Perlo, Victor. *Economics of Racism U.S.A.* New York: International Publishers, 1975.

Peters, Erskine. *William Faulkner: The Yoknapatawpha World and Black Being.* Darby, Pa.: Norwood Editions, 1984.

Pettigrew, Thomas F. *A Profile of the Negro American.* Princeton, N.J.: D. Van Nostrand, 1964.

Pinkney, Alphonso. *The Myth of Black Progress.* London: Cambridge University Press, 1984.

Pinkney, Alphonso. *Black Americans.* Englewood Cliffs, N.J.: Prentice Hall, Inc., 1993.

Piven, Frances Fox, and Richard A. Cloward. *Regulating the Poor: The Functions of Public Welfare.* New York: Vintage Books, 1971.

Platt, Anthony. "Racism in Academia: Lessons from the Life of E. Franklin Frazier." *Monthly Review* 42 September (1990):29-45.

Polk, Kenneth, and Walter Schafer. *Schools and Delinquency*. Englewood Cliffs, N.J.: Prentice-Hall, 1967.

Polanyi, Michael. *The Study of Man*. Chicago: University of Chicago Press, 1959.

Poulantzas, Nicos. *Political Power and Social Classes*. New York: Verso, 1968.

Poulantzas, Nicos. "On Social Classes." *New Left Review*, March-April, 1973, pp. 27-54.

Poulantzas, Nicos. *Classes in Contemporary Capitalism*. London: NLB, 1975.

Quinney, Richard. "A Conception of Man and Society for Criminology." *Sociological Quarterly*, Spring 1965, pp. 119-127.

Quinney, Richard. *Class, State, and Crime: On the Theory and Practice of Criminal Justice*. New York: Longman, 1977.

Raboteau, Albert J. *Slave Religion: The Invisible Institution in the Antebellum South*. London: Oxford University Press, 1978.

Rajchman, John. *Michel Foucault: The Freedom of Philosophy*. New York: Columbia University Press, 1985.

Reid, Inez Smith. *"Together" Black Women*. New York: Emerson Hall, 1972.

Reisman, David. *The Lonely Crowd: A Study of Changing American Culture*. New Haven: Yale University Press, 1961.

Reiter, Rayna, ed. *Towards an Anthropology of Women*. New York: Monthly Review Press, 1976.

Rex, John. *Race Relations in Sociological Theory*. New York: Schocken, 1970.

Ritzer, George. *Sociological Theory*. New York: Knopf, 1983.

Roach, Jack, Llewellyn Gross, and Orville Gursslin, eds. *Social Stratification in the United States*. Englewood Cliffs, N.J.: Prentice-Hall, 1960.

Robinson, Cedric J. *Black Marxism: The Making of the Black Radical Tradition*. London: Zed Press, 1983.

Rodman, Hyman. "Lower Class Value Structure." *Social Forces* 42 (1963): 205-215.

Rodriguez, Clara. *The Ethnic Queue in the United States: The Case of Puerto Ricans*. San Francisco: R and E Research Associates, 1974.

Rose, Peter I. *They and We: Racial and Ethnic Relations in the United States*. New York: Random House, 1974.

Rose, Tricia. *Black Noise: Rap Music and Black Culture in Contemporary America*. Hanover, N.H.: Wesleyan University Press, 1994.

Rothenberg, Paula, ed. *Racism and Sexism*. New York: St. Martin's Press, 1988.

Rubenstein, Richard. *Rebels in Eden*. Boston: Little, Brown, 1970.

Rubington, Earl, and Martin S. Weinberg, eds. *Deviance: An Interactionist Perspective*. New York: Macmillan, 1968.

Rudwick, Elliott, and August Meier, eds. *The Making of Black America: Essays in Negro Life and History*. New York: Atheneum, 1969.

Ryan, Michael. *Marxism and Deconstruction*. Baltimore: Johns Hopkins University Press, 1982.

Ryan, William. *Blaming the Victim*. New York: Vintage Books, 1971.

Savitch, H. V. "Black Cities/White Suburbs: Domestic Colonialism as an Interpretive Idea." *Annals of the American Academy* 439 (September 1978):118-134.

Scanzoni, John H. *The Black Family in Modern Society.* Boston: Allyn and Bacon, 1971.

Schutz, Alfred. "Common Sense and Scientific Interpretation of Human Action." *Philosophy and Phenomenological Research* 14, no. 1 (1953):1-37.

Schur, Edwin. *Labeling Deviant Behavior.* New York: Harper and Row, 1971.

Shange, Ntozanke. *For Colored Girls Who Have Considered Suicide When the Rainbow Is Enuf.* San Lorenzo, Calif.: Shameless Hussy Press, 1975.

Shaw, Clifford R., and Henry D. McKay. "Social Factors in Juvenile Delinquency." *Report on the Causes of Crime, The National Commission of Law Observance and Enforcement* Vol 2. Washington, D.C.: U.S. Government Printing Office, 1931.

Sheldon, William. *Varieties of Delinquent Youth: An Introduction to Constitutional Psychiatry.* New York: Harper, 1949.

Shibutani, Tamotsu, and Kian M. Kwan. *Ethnic Stratification: A Comparative Approach.* New York: Macmillan, 1965.

Silberman, Charles. *Criminal Violence, Criminal Justice.* New York: Vintage Books, 1980.

Simpson, George E., and J. Milton Yinger. *Racial and Cultural Minorities: An Analysis of Prejudice and Discrimination.* New York: Harper, 1953.

Smitherman, Geneva. *Talkin and Testifying: The Language of Black America.* Boston: Houghton Mifflin, 1977.

Sorokin, Pitirim. *Contemporary Sociological Theories.* New York: Harper and Row, 1928.

Sowell, Thomas. *Ethnic America.* New York: Basic Books, 1981.

Spivak, Gayatari Charkravorty. *In Other Worlds: Essays in Cultural Politics.* New York: Methuen, 1987.

Spivak, Gayatari Charkravorty. *The Post Colonial Critic: Interviews, Strategies, Dialogues.* New York: Routledge, 1990.

Stack, Carol B. *All Our Kin.* New York: Harper and Row, 1974.

Stampp, Kenneth. *The Peculiar Institution: Slavery in the Ante-Bellum South.* New York: Knopf, 1956.

Staples, Robert. *Black Masculinity: The Black Male's Role in American Society.* San Francisco: Black Scholar Press, 1982.

Staples, Robert. "American Racism and High Crime Rates: The Inextricable Connection." *The Western Journal of Black Studies* 8, no. 2 (1984):62-72.

Staples, Robert, ed. *The Black Family: Essays and Studies.* Belmont, Calif.: Wadsworth, 1971.

Stearns, William, and William Chaloupka, eds. *Jean Baudrillard.* New York: St. Martin's Press, 1992.

Steinberg, Stephen. *The Ethnic Myth: Race, Ethnicity and Class in America.* New York: Atheneum, 1981.

Steiner, Stan. *La Raza: The Mexican Americans.* New York: Harper and Row, 1970.

Steele, Shelby. *The Content of Our Character: A New Vision of Race in America.* New York: Harper Perennial, 1991.

Stinchcomb, Arthur. *Rebellion in High School.* Chicago: Quadangle, 1964.

Sullivan, Mercer L. *"Getting Paid": Youth Crime and Work in the Inner City.* Ithaca, N.Y.: Cornell University Press, 1989.

Sutherland, Edwin and Donald Cressey. *Criminology.* New York: J.P. Lippincott, 1970.

Swinton, David H. "The Economic Status of the Black Population." In *The State of Black America.* New York: National Urban League, 1983.

Szwed, John F., ed. *Black America.* New York: Basic Books, 1970.

Takagi, Paul, and Tony Platt. "Behind the Gilded Ghetto: An Analysis of Race, Class and Crime in China Town." *Crime and Social Justice*, Spring-Summer 1978, pp. 2-25.

Takaki, Ronald. *Iron Cages: Race and Culture in 19th Century America.* New York: Knopf, 1979.

Talbot, Steve. *Roots of Oppression.* New York: International Publishers, 1981.

Taussig, Michael T. *Shamanism, Colonialism, and the Wild Man: A Study in Terror and Healing.* Chicago: University of Chicago Press, 1987.

Taylor, Ian, Paul Walton, and Jock Young. *The New Criminology: For a Social Theory of Deviance.* New York: Harper and Row, 1974.

Thomas, W. I., and Florian Znaniecki. *The Polish Peasant in Europe and America.* New York: Knopf, 1918.

Thurow, Lester. *Poverty and Discrimination.* Washington, D.C.: Brookings Institution, 1969.

Tonnies, Ferdinand. *Community and Society.* C. P. Loomis, trans. East Lansing: Michigan State University Press, 1956.

Toop, David. *The Rap Attack.* London: Pluto Press, 1984.

Trelease, Allen. *White Terror.* New York: Harper and Row, 1971.

Trotsky, Leon. *On Black Nationalism and Self Determination.* New York: Pathfinder Press, 1978.

Valentine, Charles A. *Culture and Poverty.* Chicago: University of Chicago Press, 1968.

Valentine, Charles A. *Black Studies and Anthropology: Scholarly and Political Interest in Afro-American Culture.* Indianapolis: Addison-Wesley Modular Publications, 1972.

Van Sertima, Ivan. *They Came Before Columbus.* New York: Random House, 1976.

Veblen, Thorstein. *The Higher Learning in America.* New York: Huebsch, 1918.

Wahad, Dhoruba Bin, Mumia Abu-Jamal, and Assata Shakur. *Still Black, Still Strong.* Jim Fletcher, Tanaquil Jones, and Sylvere Lotringer, eds. New York: Semiotext(e), 1993.

Walker, Alice. *The Color Purple.* New York: Washington Square Press, 1982.

Walker, Alice. *The Temple of My Familiar.* San Diego: Harcourt Brace Jovanovich, 1989.

Walker, Margaret. *Jubilee.* New York: Bantam, 1966.

Wallace, Michele. *Black Macho and the Myth of the Superwoman.* New York: Dial Press, 1970.

Wallerstein, Immanuel. *Africa, the Politics of Independence.* New York: Random House, 1961.

Wallerstein, Immanuel, ed. *Social Change: The Colonial Situation.* New York: Wiley, 1966.

Warner, W. Lloyd, and Leo Srole. *The Social Systems of American Ethnic Groups.* New Haven: Yale University Press, 1945.

Warner, W. Lloyd, and Paul S. Lunt. *The Social Life of a Modern Community.* New Haven: Yale University Press, 1945.

Wax, Murray L. *Indian Americans: Unity and Diversity.* Englewood Cliffs, N.J.: Prentice-Hall, 1971.

Webb, J. "The Sociology of a School." *British Journal of Sociology* 13 (1962):264-272.

Weber, Max. *The Theory of Social and Economic Organization.* A. M. Henderson and Talcott Parsons, trans. Glencoe, Ill.: Free Press, 1947.

Weber, Max. *Sociology of Religion.* E. Fischoff, trans. Boston: Beacon, 1963.

Werthman, Carl. "Delinquent in School: A Test of the Legitimacy of Authority." *Berkeley Journal of Sociology* 8 (1963):39-60.

West, Cornel. *Prophesy Deliverance! An Afro-American Revolutionary Christianity.* Philadelphia: Westminster Press, 1982.

West, Cornel. "Black Radicalism and the Marxist Tradition." *Monthly Review,* September 1988, pp. 51-56.

Whitehead, Alfred North. *Symbolism: Its Meaning and Effect.* New York: Capricorn Books, 1927.

Willhelm, Sidney. *Who Needs the Negro?* New York: Anchor Books, 1971.

Williams, Patrick, and Laura Chrisman. *Colonial Discourse and Post-Colonial Theory: A Reader.* New York: Columbia University Press, 1994.

Williams, Raymond. *Marxism and Literature.* New York: Oxford University Press, 1977.

Williams, Raymond. *The Sociology of Culture.* New York: Schocken Books, 1981.

Williams, Vernon J., Jr. *From Caste to a Minority: Changing Attitudes of American Sociologists Toward Afro-Americans, 1896-1945.* New York: Greenwood, 1989.

Williams, William A. "Empire as a Way of Life." *The Nation,* August 2-9, 1980, pp. 104-119.

Willie, Charles V. *The Family Life of Black People.* Columbus, Ohio: Charles E. Merrill, 1970.

Willie, Charles V. *Caste and Class Controversy on Race and Poverty.* Dix Hills, N.Y.: General Hall, 1989.

Wilson, Amos. *Black on Black Violence.* New York: Afrikan Word Infosystems, 1990.

Wilson, James Q., and Richard Herrnstein. *Crime and Human Nature.* New York: Simon and Schuster, 1985.

Wilson, William J. *Power, Racism and Privilege.* New York: Macmillan Company, 1972.

Wilson, William J. *The Declining Significance of Race.* Chicago: University of Chicago Press, 1980.

Wilson, William J. *The Truly Disadvantaged: The Inner City, the Underclass and Public Policy.* Chicago: University of Chicago Press, 1987.

Woodbridge, F. J. E., ed. *Hobbes Selections.* New York: Charles Scribner's Sons, 1958.

Woodson, Carter G. *The Mis-Education of the Negro.* Philadelphia: Hakim's Publications, 1933.

Woodward, C. Vann. *The Strange Career of Jim Crow.* New York: Oxford University Press, 1974.

Wright, Erik Olin. "Class Boundaries in Advanced Capitalist Societies." *New Left Review,* July-August 1976, pp. 3-41.

Wright, Richard. *White Man, Listen.* Garden City, N.Y.: Anchor Books, 1964.

Wright, Richard. *Uncle Tom's Children.* New York: Harper and Row, 1965.

Wright, Richard. *Black Boy, A Record of Childhood and Youth.* New York: Harper and Row, 1966.

Wright, Richard. *Native Son.* New York: Harper and Row, 1940.

Wrong, Dennis H. "The Oversocialized Conceptions of Man in Modern Societies." *American Sociological Review* 26 (April 1971):183-193.

Yinger, Milton J. *Countercultures: The Promise and the Peril of a World Turned Upside Down.* New York: Free Press, 1982.

Young, Michael. *The Rise of Meritocracy.* Baltimore: Penguin, 1981.

Index

About the Author

ANTHONY J. LEMELLE, JR., is Associate Professor of Sociology at Purdue University. He has taught, researched, and published in the areas of race and ethnic relations, social theory, and deviance since 1977.

ISBN 0-275-95004-2

90000>

EAN

HARDCOVER BAR CODE